CW00498507

USURPER
ADAM LOFTHOUSE

For Martin,

Thanks for supporting Park
in the Past!

6/2/24

Also by Adam Lofthouse:

Path of Nemesis:
The Centurion's Son
War in the Wilderness
Shield of the Rising Sun

Ravensworn:
Oathbreaker
Ravensworn

Victorinus:
Valentia
Usurper

For my Mum
(who will never read this)

PROLOGUE
AFRICA. 373 AD

T he dust swirled around him, assaulting his eyes so he had to squint beneath his headscarf. His mount was skittish, tossing its head from side to side, as desperate as he to be out of the basking heat. He stroked the beast, whispering in its ear until it calmed. Before him, sand coloured walls rose ten feet to the air, dwarfed by the mountain peaks behind them.

Just another fort, he thought. No more or less remarkable than any of the others that had fallen to him over the previous months. He smiled to himself. This one would fall just like the others. 'Your orders, *dominus*?' came a voice from behind him. He turned his horse, coming face to face with Prefect Gaius Felicius, one of his more competent commanders.

'Have the men battle ready and in formation. All packs dropped to the rear. Tell the men to empty their water skins now. We'll be drinking theirs by sunset,' he said, throwing a thumb over his shoulder. The *comes rei militaris* Theodosius shared a smile with his officer, before turning back to the wall. An iron gate barred passage to within, but between the grates he could see men running from left to right, hear the orders being shouted over the dust covered wind. For a moment, the general closed his eyes and thought back to his time in Gaul and Britannia. He remembered complaining of the cold, tried to remember the howling wind and driving rain. God, what he would do for some of that now.

'State your name and rank!' a shrill voice called from atop the gate. Looking up, he saw a dark-skinned man, fat bellied and bald, small hands clasping the clay walls. The man was no warrior, no general to match him. Of that he was certain. He smiled once more.

'I am the *comes* of Valentinian, lord of the world, sent to destroy a murderous robber. Unless you give him to me at once as the invincible emperor has ordered, you will perish utterly with the race over which you rule.'

A silence then, spreading like the dust on the wind. 'Big words from a man at the head of such a small army! And still you have not spoken your name.'

'I am Theodosius, *comes rei militaris* of Rome. I am the man that won back Britannia, that vanquished the Alamanni on the banks of the Danube! I am the man that fought Firmus from the northern seas to the mountains! Now go and get him, bring him to me and let him face Roman justice!'

Firmus. The reason for him being there, on that dust covered plain, in front of those tired walls. Theodosius had been sent there the previous year by Valentinian, his emperor under God. Word had spread of uprisings in the African provinces, raids on cities going unanswered. Thrust from the never ending war on the Danube, Theodosius had crossed the sea with an army taken from Gaul.

They were auxiliaries all, good men, if undisciplined. But the core of his force was made up of the Fourth Cohort of Gauls, under the command of Gaius Felicius. The two had fought together five years previous, winning Britannia back for the empire after it had been all but cut off.

To say they had found the going tough would be an understatement. They landed with thick woollen cloaks, heavy tunics and trousers. They were men kitted out for Britannia and Gaul, not for the basking heat of the African plains. But, as always, they had so far prevailed. Theodosius had found the cause of the raids quickly enough. It seemed the local governor, Romanus, had made an agreement with the local barbarian tribes. They would raid the cities of North Africa, Romanus would do nothing to stop them and take his share of the proceeds.

Theodosius had despised the man as soon as he set eyes on him. He was young and impertinent, claiming his family could trace their lineage back to the Republic, like his blood counted for anything. A man's actions were what defined him, not the blood that flowed through his veins. Any man worth their salt knew that.

Realising the man could prove problematic to him, and knowing the close relationship he shared with Gratian, Valentinian's son, Theodosius said nothing of treachery when he met Romanus, instead ordering him to take command of a small force of men guarding an outpost. Those men, however, belonged to Theodosius. He smiled, even then as the dust whirled around him, to think of the horror Romanus must have felt when he realised the men he had been sent to command were actually his jailors. Packed off back to court with a letter from Theodosius, the general hoped Valentinian would be much sterner with him than he had. Friend of the Caesar or not.

With Romanus out the way, it had been simpler. War. War was what he knew. Firmus was the rebel leader. A good man by all accounts, and one that had been loyal to Rome. He, though, had suffered like most of the local populace under the raids the governor had done nothing to stop, and had decided to take things into his own hands. Raising a huge army of Moors, Firmus had spent months causing havoc for Rome, even going as far to call himself a king, claiming 'his' lands now stood outside the empire.

Theodosius felt some pity for the man, and those that followed him. Always he tried to put himself in his opponents shoes, think like them. Would he have acted any differently under the circumstances? He supposed not. But he could not allow a threat to the empire to go unchallenged.

Firmus had been retreating from him for weeks. Hiding in the mountainous terrain, striking where he was least expected. Theodosius had come to form a grudging respect for the man. He was competent. But now, finally, he had him cornered. The fat man had disappeared from atop the battlement. Theodosius cursed the dust. He couldn't see a thing. Hoofbeats on the dirt behind him. Turning, he saw Felicius galloping towards him. 'Enemy army coming from the west, sir! All on horseback by the look of things!'

Theodosius cursed again. He cast one more longing look at the walls. 'May God spite them!' he spat. 'I shall come for you later!' he shouted at the walls, knowing it was petulant and not caring. 'Have the men form up in one big square,' he said to Felicius.

'Sir? Is that wise against cavalry?'

'Just do it Gaius!'

With the prefect riding off, Theodosius steered his own mount away from the fort and cantered over to the waiting army. The men had improvised their kit where they could. Their trousers were long discarded, and now they wore tunics with the sleeves cut off, mail the same. Around half the men had been able to swap their leather boots for sandals, but even with every cobbler in Africa working around the clock, they hadn't been able to make enough for all two thousand men. Theodosius had thought his force tiny when his ship had docked and he'd had time to take stock of the task at hand. Now, though, he was almost grateful he had no more men to worry about.

They had lost over a hundred to the heat, men literally boiling in their armour. Another fifty or so were at a hospital by the coast recovering from extreme heat stroke. Every man had skin redder than sacrificial blood. Theodosius drunk deep from his waterskin, relishing the last drops slipping down his throat. 'No more water,' he said to the aide, waiting to give him his helmet. 'We'll have to take theirs, hey?' he said, smiling at the man with a confidence he did not feel. He'd taken a gamble, marching here without properly supplying first, banking on a quick victory and pillaging his enemies food and water. He could make sure of the former, at least.

Out of the dust cloud, he could make out the figures of the Moors, there to rescue their stricken leader. He left his horse where it was, walked through his men until he was with Felicius in the front line. The prefect nodded to his superior, leaning slightly, favouring his good leg. Theodosius knew the man had nursed an old wound in his thigh for a number of years. The months in Africa had done it no favours. 'Form Testudo,' he said to Felicius.

'We'll be surrounded, sir?'

Theodosius nodded. 'I know.'

Felicius barked the order, and trumpets trilled in the dusty air. The Roman force formed up in one giant square, shield overlapping on all sides, raised above their heads in the centre. To their enemy, they were nothing but an unbreakable square of shields. It rained then, not water, but spears and arrows. *Thud. Thud. Thud* to his front and above. Arms straining on his own shield, Theodosius winced. He was not a young man, and war was a young man's game. 'We move north at a walk,' he said to Felicius. He heard the murmurs as his order was passed from front to back and left to right. His pulse thrummed in his ears. He counted its frantic beat. When he got to a hundred, he said: 'Now.'

They moved. Step by step, shuffling sidewards like crabs, moving inexorably north. Men fell, shields giving way beneath the near constant barrage, but the Romans did not stop. Feeling his left bicep cramp, Theodosius changed grip, resting his shield's weight on his right arm. In just a few moments, he felt the same pain there. Huffing breaths through clenched teeth, legs like lead, he tried to catch a glimpse of their progress through a small gap in the shields. All he saw was dust.

'Can't do this for much longer, sir,' Felicius said through a ragged breath.

'We won't have to.' As if on cue, the barrage on their shields seemed to lesson. The thrum of hooves on dirt faded, and Theodosius ordered a halt, though no man risked lowering their shield. 'What's going on?' Felicius croaked, voice as coarse as gravel.

Theodosius grinned. 'The prisoners we took last month. We had them held back from our formation so the men of the town didn't see them.'

'What of them?'

'Our friends out there saw us moving towards them, thought them reinforcements.'

'Why would they think that?' Felicius asked.

'Because I had a centurion dress them all in tunics and mail,' Theodosius said with a wink. Shields lowered, the two men moved out of the formation, over to the huddle of prisoners. There were five hundred in all, each once a loyal citizen turned traitor. They would be executed that night, their hands cut off and then burned alive, by imperial decree. But in their last meaningful act, they had saved the lives of Theodosius' army.

'You really do think of everything, don't you?' Felicius said, a wry grin fixed on his face.

'Not quite everything,' Theodosius tried to swallow after he spoke, but there was no moisture to be found in his mouth.

Firmus was brought out to them as the sun was setting. They'd pillaged food and water from the enemy dead, resumed their positions at the gates of the fort. The bald commander had not held out for long. It seemed Firmus, on hearing of the day's events, had chosen the easy way out and hung himself. Theodosius found he couldn't blame the man, hearing the screams of the prisoners as their hands were chopped from them. Firmus's fate would have been even worse.

'What now?' Felicius asked him, the two sipping water like it had been blessed by the Almighty Himself.

'Now, we put this province to rights,' Theodosius said, smacking his lips in satisfaction.

***

He did that and more in the two years that followed. Restoring peace and the people's faith in the Roman government. He stood on the bay of Carthage and sighed. It should have been one of contentment, instead it was one of sadness and regret.

In his hands was a letter from Gaul. The emperor was dead, his heart giving out after he had got himself into one of his famous rages. He hadn't always seen eye to eye with Valentinian, but the man had come to rely on him after his success in Britannia, and the two had even become friends.

The new Augustus, Gratian, Valentinian's son, seemed to be moving quickly to remove anyone that might consider rivalling him for the purple. Not that Theodosius would have. He was happy with his lot, content with life. It would seem, though, that he would not be given the chance to impress that on the new ruler of the world. Five men stood behind him, from the *scola scutariorum secunda,* part of Gratian's elite guard. They had orders to kill Theodosius, orders the general had just read himself. Their commander, a thick bearded German by the name of Romulus–a ridiculous name given to him on his acceptance of Roman citizenship, could not keep the grin from his face as he'd handed the parchment over.

Theodosius would not give the man the reward of seeing his fear. He was a Roman, a proud man, and a general to boot. He would meet his end with the same dignity he had lived his life. A clamour behind them, as Theodosius' officers demanded to be let through. 'Outrage!' they cried. 'Treachery!' It was not lost on Theodosius that the very man he had sent back to court in disgrace was probably the one that had suggested this order be given. He thought of the rat Romanus then, his face slipping into a leer.

'Sir! Sir! We cannot accept this!' Felicius calling, his body straining against the imperial guardsmen that held him.

'Let him through a moment, would you,' Theodosius said to Romulus, as if he hadn't a care in the world. 'A quick word with my friend here, and you may despatch your orders as you see fit.'

'This cannot be happening!' Felicius said as he reached his commander's side.

'And yet it is, old friend,' Theodosius said through a thin smile. 'Calm yourself, prefect. I have lived a wonderful life, reached heights I could never have dreamed of as a boy. I have seen much of this world, sampled its delights, and now it is time to meet my maker.' He took two deep breaths, composing himself. He'd never been one for grand speeches, would seem odd to change that now. He unbuckled his sword belt, passed it to Felicius. 'Give this to my son, would you? He will take the news hard, I know. Tell him I love him, and that I have missed him these last years. There is greatness in him, Gaius. He will achieve wonders, you mark my words. But promise me something, before I go.'

'Anything,' Felicius said, eyes wet.

'Be there for him when he needs you. This world is full of liars and thieves, men that smile at you whilst the sun is shining and stab you in the back from the shadows. He is young yet, he will need friends around him.'

'I promise. On my life I swear it.'

'That it all a man can ask for. There is one more thing, a letter for Theo, on my desk. You will make sure he gets it?' Felicius nodded, unable to speak. He gripped the younger man by the shoulder, squeezed it, then ushered him away. 'Go now, you don't have to stay.'

He turned back to the bay, to the glistening water swirling lazily beneath him. All was calm, all was quiet, and he breathed deep, one last gulp of sweet air, and closed his eyes. He pictured his wife, their estate back in Spain. The smell of freshly pressed olive oil sprung to mind, a distant memory from his childhood. Finally, he pictured his son. Young Theo, named after him. No longer the child he had been, but a man in his own right. A smile touched his lips. He knew the son would eclipse the father, that he would reach heights unimagined. The world would remember the name Theodosius, but it would be the younger, rather than the elder.

He had no regrets.

I

December, 382 AD. Eastern shore of Britannia

'**H**ave you checked your helmet strap?'

'Twice now, father.'

'Loosen your sword in its scabbard. You don't want it getting stuck.'

'Done it three times now.'

Victorinus shivered. An icy wind swept in from the sea, bringing with it rain that peppered him like a storm of arrows. He shivered again, but it had nothing to do with the cold. 'At all times you stay between Pastor and me.'

'Father, you've said that four times already!' Silvius exclaimed.

Blood pumped thick in Victorinus' ears, his breath coming in shallow gasps. Under the weight of his shield, his left hand trembled, and all he desired was to hide behind the cluster of trees on their left and relieve himself. But that would mean leaving the line and leaving his son. 'When we hit them, keep your shield high. Lean in to it, and lunge low with your sword. Pastor will cover your right flank and-

'Father! You've been repeating the same instructions for an hour or more now! You need to be calm. You're supposed to be commanding this entire wing, not just me!'

He looked right, drinking in the sight of his son. Silvius had seen only seen seventeen summers. A stocky youth with a crop of brown hair. Milky pale skin covering a hairless face, eyes wide with the prospect of his first battle. 'You have trained me well, father. I'm going to be fine.'

Victorinus gulped, but nodded. Looking over his son to Pastor, reassured by the confident nod the younger man gave him. He's going to be fine. He's going to be fine.

They stood atop a small knoll, the sigh of the sea, out of sight over the horizon, a whisper on the wind. Victorinus felt his stomach tighten as he saw their enemy appear. Saxones, Franks, whoever they were, striding out of the distant tree line, the swagger in their step evident even from that distance. But they were so far unaware of the welcome party Rome had planned. 'Silence in the ranks,' he called out, not wanting to give their position away. Around him, hunched behind shields, huddled in dripping wet cloaks, five hundred men of the Heruli, the famed German auxiliaries, stood bristling, eager for battle. Victorinus felt himself relax at the thought. These men were veterans, hardened killers that had first come to Britannia sixteen years before. They'd seen off an invading army, then, put down a rebellion in the process. They were good men, and the gods knew Victorinus needed them to fight well today.

A horn sounded, off in the distance, somewhere to Victorinus' right. 'That's the signal,' he muttered, and turned to the man stood behind him. 'Give the bastards something to look at. We're moving out.' A banner appeared in the skyline at his back, as bright as the day was bleak. There was the collective outtake of breath from the surrounding men, a release from the tension of waiting. They moved off at a walk. Cresting the knoll, Victorinus saw the moment his enemy spotted them. Spears waved in their direction, heads turned, and the odd guttural voice carried to them on the wind. 'Numbers?' he asked his son.

A pause as Silvius squinted, his lips moving silently as he counted. 'Thousand or so,' Silvius said after a time.

'Twelve hundred, I make it,' Pastor piped up.

'How many ships did the scout say landed on the beach?'

'Sixteen, sir,' Pastor answered.

Victorinus nodded. 'Reckon twelve hundred is about right then.' He stopped, the men around him halting with him. 'We wait here for the *Dux* to make his move.'

Groaning behind him, Victorinus smiled. More waiting. He felt their frustration, but knew it was about to get a lot worse for his enemy. 'Best make a show of it, lads!' he called. 'Shields up, spears ready!' With a collective thud, the men of the Heruli dumped their packs, hefted spears and made a wall of shields. They were big shields, heavy, weightier still with the added burden of rain water. Oval shaped, when held aloft, they covered a man from chin to shin, presented together in a line they made for an impressive sight, one to put the fear into an enemy. Victorinus hoped that would prove to be the case today.

The horn sounded once more, closer this time, and Victorinus felt a shiver of anticipation rip through him.

'Steady now,' he said to Silvius, noticing the tremor in his son's arm. There was a rumble beneath their feet. For a moment it seemed as if the earth itself was shaking, and Victorinus looked once more to his son, this time showing him his teeth. 'Here comes your brother!'

The Saxones were charging at the Heruli, screaming war cries and curses. Their mail was dull in the dim light, but there was no mistaking the gleam of their swords. They were sixty paces from Victorinus when the first of them heard the rumble. One warrior stopped, his head swivelling left, then right as he sought the source of the sound. But it was already too late.

In a burst of light and motion, five hundred armoured horsemen rushed from the tree line to Victorinus' left. The *Ala I Hispanorum Asturum*, one of the few of Britannia's fighting units that had stayed loyal throughout the great rebellion of sixteen years previous, thundered across the open grass, long swords held out before them as they prepared to cut down the enemy as they ran. At their head was a man in a glistening coat of mail, a bronzed helmet topped with black feathers, a faded red cloak that billowed behind him. He charged ahead of the rest, urging his mount on, desperate to reach his prey and cut them down. The *Dux Britanniarum*, Flavius Maximus, commander of all Rome's forces in Britain.

'That's our cue, let's be about it!' Victorinus called, stepping off without checking his men were following. He knew they would.

'I see Maurus!' Silvius called out beside him, pointing with his sword. Victorinus followed the blade and didn't know whether to smile or squeal as he recognised his eldest son, clad in mail with his sword waving above him.

'Just focus on you. Maurus has done this before,' he said to Silvius, but he could just as well of been talking to himself. The Spanish horse crashed in to the running Germans, smashing through their disorganised ranks and leaving a host of broken bodies in their wake. Victorinus kept his eyes on Maurus, saw the moment his horse ploughed in to a rushing German, sending the man flailing through the air. With his next action he cleaved down at a neck, blood bright on the iron-grey sky. Victorinus picked up the pace, his laboured breathing clouding the air as his old legs worked as fast as they could. *Too old for this shit*, he thought as he ran, but then he looked to his right once more and remembered why he was there. Must keep him safe. Or his mother will see us both dead. There had been many an argument in the last year, Sarai saying he wasn't old enough to fight, Victorinus insisting it was the lad's right to choose. He'd won in the end – a rare enough event – but he'd had to promise he would be at Silvius' side when he first met with the enemy. Not that he'd have let his son go on his own.

'You don't have to do this,' Pastor called to him, a hint of a smile around his youthful face.

'I'll tell you what I do and don't have to do! Keep that shield up!' but he didn't know if he was talking to Pastor or Silvius – or himself. Ahead of him the Spanish horse were turning, they'd cut through the German raiders like a scythe through barley and were readying to come back at them. The battle field was carnage. Hoof prints carved into frozen mud, blood glistening in pools, sheets of rain whipping in from the sea, drowning the screams of the dying. The raiders had lost perhaps a third of their force to the first devastating charge, and Victorinus could make out a helmetless man, soaking hair plastered across his face, waving his sword around in a fury as he tried to get his men in to some sort of formation. Victorinus took in the space between his men and the Germans left standing and skidded to a halt, wiping lank grey hair from his old eyes, too breathless to shout a command.

'Why are we stopping?' Silvius asked him.

'We're... too... close... to... the... enemy,' he managed to utter through ragged breaths.

'When the horse coming charging back, they could end up hitting us too. Best to let them rip through this lot one more time then we can mop up after,' Pastor said, as if he were reading Victorinus' mind.

'Yes... that.' He wanted to throw his shield on the floor and plant his hands on his knees. Better yet lie down and curl in to a ball. But he was a leader, and this was a battle. And having a lie down midway through a fight probably didn't set the best of examples. Felicius would have led these men better, if only the rogue had got there in time.

The Spanish horse was galloping again, whooping as they went, bloody swords arcing beside them. Victorinus spent an agonising moment searching for his son amongst the horde of flesh and metal, but couldn't make him out. There were ten or so horsemen down. Tangled with the German dead, he prayed to any god that would listen that his son was not among them. With a sickening crunch, the cavalry collided with the raiders once more. They sent men flying - dead before they hit the ground. In a blur, the horsemen galloped past Victorinus and his men, the men of the Heruli barraging them with abuse as they did. Cavalry and infantry, never the best of friends. A horse stopped in front of Victorinus, a fine grey stallion spotted with black. Its rider ripped his helmet off and smiled down at Victorinus. 'Good to see you, old man! Reckon you're up to finishing this lot off?'

Victorinus couldn't help but smile. He may not have always seen eye to eye with the *Dux*, but the man was a born fighter, and there was no doubt about it. 'Aye, *domine*, I reckon we can get it done.' He filled his lungs with icy air and urged his men on. Not that they needed any encouragement. Their enemy was in tatters before them. Over half of their men slain, the remaining stood around in confounded terror. Victorinus could see no leaders, no helmetless man trying to rally them now. They were done. He allowed himself a smile. 'Keep that shield up,' he said once more to his son, and then moved off at a jog.

Rain clanged off his helmet, the frozen ground still solid beneath his feet. He winced as the freezing wind lashed out at him, burning his lungs as he heaved in air. Ten paces and he looked one last time at his son, drinking in the sight of the lad who meant the world to him, just in case he never got to again. And then the slaughter consumed him. He smashed his shield in to the face of his first foe, snapping the man's head back and seeing bright blood spurt from a toothless mouth. Before the man could recover, he plunged his blade through his chest, twisting it as he pulled it free. Silvius was still with him, a light touch on his left shoulder that reassured him more than words could. A snarling man with an axe held high charged him, and Victorinus stepped to his left and swung his sword low, knocking his assailant from his feet and sending the axe spinning in the air. He chopped down, not letting the man find his feet once more, and was already looking for his next opponent before he'd pulled the blade free.

Silvius fought hunched behind his shield. Cautiously, he probed at a warrior with thick braids of black hair and a long knife in each hand. Victorinus snapped his shield next to his son's and watched on as the lad feinted high and right with his sword before smashing his shield in to his opponent's face. Silvius leaped forwards for the killing blow but the knife man was quick on his feet. He danced back two steps, watched as the sword cut nothing but air, then changed the grip on one of his knives so the blade was point down, and jabbed it straight towards Silvius' wrist. Before Victorinus could even yell a warning, Silvius had wrenched his sword arm back and danced back a pace himself. He thrust his shield out once more, this time moving as he did, so his sword snaked out beneath the linden board and buried itself in his opponent's groin.

'That was well done,' Victorinus called, stabbing the man himself just to be sure. Silvius went to move off, lost in the joy of battle for the first time, but Victorinus put his sword arm across him, holding him back. 'A soldier fights, but a commander must see everything.' They stood together as the Heruli marched on, their centurions calling the pace, keeping the line together.

German killed German in a bloody battle that lasted just moments. The raiders had lost their nerve when Maximus and his cavalry hit them. They'd no desire to stand and fight their countrymen. 'Alaric!' Victorinus called to the senior centurion of the Heruli. 'We need prisoners.' The man nodded, just his eyes and beard visible beneath his helmet.

'I'm not a commander!' Silvius said, his face dropping in to a frown. 'I wanted to fight, father.'

'And you did, lad! We will speak more later, but for now just know that you did well. I thought that bastard with the knives was going to get you, but you did for him good and proper. Now come and see what victory looks like.'

Alaric followed his orders to the letter and soon the Heruli were ordered back in to formation, panting like dogs behind their battle-scarred shields. The remnants of the raiders stood in a half circle on blood slick grass, their dead scattered around them.

'You should be grateful it's not summer,' Victorinus said to his son as he waded through the ranks of the Heruli. 'The stench would be horrific.' He strode out in front of his men, wiping clean his sword on the hem of his tunic and sheathing it. He puffed out his chest and tried to strut, to appear more confident than he felt. Felicius would have done a better job of this, he thought again. Where was he, anyway?

'Do any of you speak Latin?' he called out, moving within ten paces of his beaten enemy. There were maybe thirty men left, many wounded, huddling together as if it would save them. The wind howled again, rain spat at his helmet and he wrenched it off to be rid of the noise. He felt his wild hair rise and fall with the wind, allowed himself a small smile at what he must appear. A dishevelled old man, thinning hair too shy of the barber's blade. His haggard, red face all too familiar to the tavern owners of Britannia, ill-fitting mail crammed over a fattening body. A tribune of Rome. Oh, how the mighty fall.

'I can translate, sir?' Alaric probed, moving up beside him. Victorinus was about to agree when a man stepped from the bewildered half circle of the doomed. He was the helmetless man from earlier, and he puffed out his chest as he approached, every bit the proud warrior. He stopped ten paces from Victorinus, threw his sword to the frozen ground and reached across to his round shield. Victorinus took an involuntary step back as the German fiddled with something out of sight, certain a knife or dart was about to be thrown at his chest. But then he heard the sound of a leather clasp undoing, and the shield dropped to the ground, revealing a stump where there should have been a hand.

'I speak your rotten tongue,' the man spat. 'I am Aldhard, chief of the Sturii, and I would bargain for the lives of my men.' He had bright amber eyes that pierced in to Victorinus, a scar across his left cheek, white and livid, an old wound. He spat, then grinned, revealing three missing teeth in the top row of his mouth.

Victorinus checked himself, breathed deep, before responding. 'You are in no position to be bargaining, Aldhard, chief of the Sturii. Your men have trespassed on

Rome's lands, not for the first time this year. You are at the mercy of the *Dux Britanniarum*.'

'What right do you have? Does Rome have? To tell me where I can and cannot go? Your empire lays in tatters. You've had more emperors in the last ten years than I've had warm meals. The sun has set on your glory days, Roman. Mark my words, my raids are just the beginning. A storm is coming, Roman, so vicious, so huge, that even your mighty legions shall tremble before it.'

Victorinus puffed out his cheeks, stopping short of admitting some of what the man said was true. Hoofbeats on the frozen mud behind had him turning, and Maximus dropped down from his horse's back. 'Who is he?' Maximus asked.

'Says his name is Aldhard, chief of the Sturii, whoever they are,' Victorinus said with a shrug.

Maximus nodded, looking from the defeated tribesmen back to his men. 'I see your son fought today, well met, young Silvius.' The lad nodded a wordless greeting. 'Maurus fought well today too. You must be a very proud father,' he clapped Victorinus on the shoulder and moved past him.

Victorinus pondered whether watching your son's kill was a reason to be proud, then figured he'd stick to be grateful they'd lived to see another sunset.

'You there, Aldhard. Do you know who I am?' Maximus called. He had his sword outstretched, pointing to the chief.

'You are Maximus,' Aldhard said, and spat once more. 'I fought you on the Danube, years past. You were fighting for your uncle then.'

Theodosius. The man that had led the relief army that freed Britannia from the grasp a tyrant. A man Victorinus had come to respect. A man he mourned still.

'Aye, likely I did. Fought too many nameless tribes on the border, can't say your name is one I remember. The punishment for raiding my lands is death. Do you understand that?'

Aldhard just shrugged. 'Kill me. A thousand more will follow in my footsteps. Then two thousand, then three. You can kill one man, but you cannot kill the idea. The world is changing, Maximus. Soon it will have no more need of Rome and her empire.'

Maximus grinned. 'So, you're a prophet and a pirate, are you? What happened to your hand?'

Aldhard held up the stump of his left arm, mottled scar tissue a mix of angry red lines and white. 'A small sacrifice to pay for the realisation of my dreams.'

'And what dreams do you have? Do they involved being slaughtered on a freezing day on the east coast of Britannia? Because I have to tell you, Aldhard, that is your reality.'

Aldhard just smiled. It made Victorinus uncomfortable, but he couldn't put a finger on why. 'One day, general, one day soon you shall see. Alas, it seems today is not that day. But mark my words, we shall meet again.'

A pause, just the roaring of the wind. The rain ceased, though it did nothing to stop the chill running through

Victorinus' bones. Too old for this shit. He should be tucked up in his home, with a roaring fire in the hearth and warm food in his belly. Not fighting off raiders by the sea on a freezing winter's day. 'I'm afraid, chief Aldhard, that we will not.' Maximus turned from the defeated chief and met the eye of Alaric. 'Kill him in front of his men. Get a fire going, line the bastards up, then chop their right hands off one by one, but seal the wounds shut with a heated blade. I don't want any of the bastards dying. When that's done, march them back to their ships, set them all alight except for one. Put them on the remaining one, push it out to sea and let them be.'

'Why not just kill them?' Victorinus asked. Seemed like a lot of trouble to go to, just for them to die at sea.

'Because if the curs make it home, their tale will be told from camp fire to camp fire. It will spread fear, will alert the tribes to the fact that Rome is not weak. Rome still has backbone and the means to defend her borders. And if they don't make it back?' Maximus smiled. 'Then they'll die a slow and agonising death at sea, or get caught in a storm and drown. Either way sounds good to me.' And he was gone.

Alaric gave Victorinus a salute before moving off to follow his orders. Victorinus took his son by the shoulder and steered him away. He had become a man that day, claimed his first kill, but he didn't need to see what was about to happen. 'Is it always like this?' the lad asked. He was shaking, blue lips quivering as he tried to control his chattering teeth.

Victorinus unclasped his cloak and wrapped it around the lad. It was old, faded, once the bright proud yellow worn by the *miles areani*, not that they existed anymore. 'Aye, sometimes worse. Come, let's get you some hot food and a warm cup of wine.' He remembered his first engagement with an enemy, off scouting north of the Wall. A Caledonian had come at him with a spear. Victorinus had dodged the blow on instinct alone, before carving a bloody ruin through the man's chest. He hadn't slept for a week after. They made their way back to camp. The Heruli hadn't had time to build a proper marching camp, but there were tents and guards on the perimeter. The medics were ready to treat the wounded, some men already limping in their direction. At the centre of the camp, four open-sided tents were grouped together, and ten slaves worked at cook pots beneath the canopy, the smell of simmering stew as welcome to Victorinus as anything he could remember. He sat his son down, grabbed two bowls from a wooden table and scooped them both in to one of the cook pots. A slave passed him two chunks of bread, another brought over a jug of wine. For a moment, he stared longingly at it. 'Make sure to eat yourselves,' he said to the slaves, feeling the familiar tremor in his fingers. They nodded and thanked him, leaving father and son alone. 'Where has Felicius got to?' he mused as he ate.

'Not like him to miss a battle,' Silvius remarked, mouth half full of bread.

'Aye, that's true enough.' In the distance, back where they had come from, the first screams filled the air. It seemed Maximus's orders were being carried out to the letter. 'Sure he won't mind missing out on that, though.'

II

*To the prefect Gaius Felicius, commander of the Fourth Co-
hort of Gauls, Vindolanda, Britannia. From the Divine
Augustus Flavius Theodosius, lord and protector of Rome's
eastern provinces. Greetings.*

*My old friend, I trust this letter finds you in good health.
My health, which I know must have been a concern to you
and all those who claim citizenship in our fair empire, is
growing haler by the day, and I am once more ready to lead
our armies as we seek to complete victory over Fritigern and
his troublesome rabble.*

*I write to you first and foremost to once more extend my
sincere thanks for the support you and your men provided
me over the course of the last two years. You are an exemplary
officer, and a fine man, one the empire desperately needs. I
have written to my cousin, the Dux Britanniarum Flavius
Maximus, and recommended you for promotion. I see you
reaching the rank of magister militum in the not too distant
future. With an army at your back and Rome's enemies in
your sights, I cannot think of a more worthy man to stand
on the edge of empire and keep our borders safe.*

*I worry for you, back in the west. Even though the east is
still striving to free itself from the clutches of my predecessors'*

great defeat at Hadrianopolis, I feel that once my work is complete, we shall begin to thrive once more. However, I fear that the west is doomed to fall. We have spoken at length, you and I, of the difficult relationship I have with Gratian, my divine counterpart in Gaul. His heart belongs to the One True Faith, which of course sets him apart from those that seek refuge with the false gods, but I fear he has not surrounded himself with trustworthy men. Not a day goes by where I do not hear word of another Germanic 'noble' being promoted to high office in the western army. At a time when our beloved empire is fighting for its very survival, and wave after wave of warriors seek passage across the Rhine or Danube, how can we trust in these men, who we embrace in to our inner circle? There have been warnings throughout our glorious history, have there not? Let us not forget the infamous Arminius, who seemed set to thrive in our army, just to turn traitor and inflict the greatest defeat of the Divine Augustus' reign.

Gratian seems to welcome all in to his court, without thought to these men's past, and what old grievances could lurk there. What would happen if one of these Germans unlocks the key in our defences on the two great rivers that border our lands with theirs? The damage they could do is irreversible. In the five years my colleague has been in power, he seems to move further and further from the path his father trod. Gone are the stalwart generals that defended our lands so admirably, sent in to retirement or – as with my dear father, executed for no reason other than fear they may rise above their station.

I know, dear Gaius, that you were with my father in the last tumultuous months of his life. Fighting alongside him *in Mauritania against Firmus and his Moors, uncovering the plots and manipulations of the despicable governor Romanus – what harm that man did to the fertile provinces of Africa! And this brings me to my point. My dear father, the loyal, fearsome general Theodosius, who took back Britannia against all the odds sixteen years ago, who sailed to Africa and swiftly and absolutely crushed the Moorish rebellion, should lose his life at the word of a governor proven to be disloyal. Just because that envious, greedy little man has the ear of the emperor! What I would give to have Romanus in chains before me, what justice I would inflict on him.*

I never asked you about the last weeks in Carthage, when the order came for my father's death. Truth be told, I never had the courage. He sent me a letter, just before the evil deed was done, delivered to me at our estates in Galliae. In it he wrote of his fierce pride in me, of the bright and prosperous future he foresaw for me, though at the time it was hard to see the truth in his words. Grief blinded me, secluding myself into my private rooms, ignoring all correspondence and hiding from the sun. It was two years after his passing that I read his words once more, saw for the last time the flourish of his hand on the dry ink. And it gave me a new perspective. He told me also of his concerns, his predictions for the future. You will of course be well too aware that after we had vanquished the traitor Lupicinus Valentinus in Britannia, and sent him swinging to a well-earned death, it was his own cousin, Maximinus, the famed and feared lawyer from Rome, that was sent to rule Britannia. My father never saw the logic in the appointment, as did many other influential men at court. When our borders were in constant threat, and the western field army needed all of their strength in both Gaul and Pannonia, why leave Britannia so potentially vulnerable again?

My father had long since feared a potential alliance between Maximinus in Rome, Romanus in Africa, and my cousin, and now the effective ruler of Britannia, Flavius Maximus. Three men, all with significant influence, powerful connections, and spread across the west. What damage could they do between them? These men were in the perfect positions to pounce when Valentinian suddenly passed five years ago, and Gratian was elevated to the throne. Maximus did not have to see out years of exile in his estates like I did, before they thrust him back in to high office. Before my father's bones were even in the ground, they appointed him Dux in Britannia. They found Romanus guilty of bribery and corruption, yet Gratian punishes him how? By recalling him to the comfort of court? They awarded me the appointment as general in the east only in desperation, with Gratian hard pressed on his own borders and his younger brother elevated to Co-Augustus nominally ruling alongside him. He could not afford to lose one of his trusted generals.

I have often wondered if he wanted me to fail, that I was being set up. If that were his intentions, then I am delighted to say they failed spectacularly. I wish my father had lived to see me now, an emperor, holding a court of my own in Thessalonica. It was something I know he never coveted for himself, unlike many other commanders in the army, but by God, he would have burned with pride to see me on the throne. Soon, I hope, I will finally be strong enough to march to Constantinople, and take my seat in Rome's greatest city.

I will think of my father then, as I ride under the great gates
and breathe the air of that fabled place.
I am digressing. My point here, to you, my dearest friend,
is that I want – need – you to be my eyes and ears. I need
to know what my cousin is up to in distant Britannia, if
Gratian is placing his trust in the wrong men. Civil war has
cost our beloved empire so much over our great but scarred
history, it is something we can ill afford to sleep walk in to
again. Can you do this for me? Can I trust you to be discreet?
I have confidence that I can, that you of all men can see the
big picture, and that nothing is more imperative than the
stability of our fragile empire.
Your friend always,
Theo

***

Prefect Gaius Felicius pondered the letter as he crested the ridge of a grassy knoll. It sat folded beneath his mail, snug against his breastbone, the folds of the parchment digging into his skin through his thick woollen tunic.

He squinted at the land rolling away to the slate grey sea, a chill wind biting at his flesh. They'd not made the battle. That much was evident. Corpses littered the frozen ground, both men and horseflesh. The Heruli had stood to attention, two sides of a square formed with a fire roaring at their centre. A clutch of prisoners stood in a huddle, and before Felicius had ordered his men on, he watched as they hauled the first to the fire, his right arm set on a wooden log as an axe flashed down and took his hand.

Roman justice. He didn't know what sickened him more, the sound of the axe thudding in to the wood or the horrified scream of the dismembered prisoner. He felt a shudder run through him, this time not from the cold, and turned back to his men, gesturing them on with a wave.

'Almost glad it's not summer,' centurion Vitulus said. The big man had been Felicius's second in the Fourth Cohort of Gauls for coming on twenty years. The man had fought with him throughout the great rebellion of sixteen years ago, taking a grievous wound to his left shoulder in a viscous battle at sea with German pirates. In true style, he'd shrugged it off to fight in the rest of the campaign. Together, they had left Britannia's blustery shores with the *magister militum* Theodosius, fighting for him on the Danube and Rhine before heading to Africa to take on the Moorish rebellion.

It had been heart wrenching, watching the stoic old general go to the headman's axe with more dignity than some men showed whilst being crowned. He had remained true to himself until the end. 'Huh?' he said, cocking his head to Vitulus, realising his mind had wandered. They approached the waiting Heruli, passing a headless corpse missing a left hand. They had left the head where it landed, a wide-eyed expression above a long-scarred cheek. He shuddered once more, reliving another headless corpse on the bay of Carthage. At least it had been warmer then.

'I said I'm almost glad it ain't summer. This lot would be kicking up a right stink,' Vitulus gestured to the scattered corpses.

'Aye, that they would.' Felicius shifted his weight from his left leg to his right, an old war wound in his thigh that always ached in the cold. Wasn't much better in the summer, truth be told. They had sent him to Britannia and given him command of the Fourth because of the wound. He'd thought it a punishment at the time, a sign that his career was on a downward path before he'd reached the top. Turned out to be the best thing that could have happened to him.

A figure moved out from the ranks of the Heruli and approached and saluted. 'Well met centurion Alaric,' Felicius returned the salute. 'Apologies for our late arrival. Roads weren't great in this weather. Doesn't seem like you missed us though, take many losses?'

'Six dead, five injured, but they'll recover. The cavalry lost a couple, but overall it was a quick fight. Tribune Victorinus is here, took his lad back to the tents.' He threw a thumb over his shoulder, pointing to another grassy ridge to the north.

'Silvius? He wasn't hurt, was he?'

'No sir, he did well, claimed his first kill. I think the tribune just wanted to get him away from the battlefield as quick as he could. You know what it's like your first time.'

'Aye.' Felicius nodded, remembering his own. 'And the *Dux*?'

'With the cavalry, sir. He ordered us to take a hand from each of the survivors, seal the wounds with fire, and send them back on one of their ships. We took the head of their commander.' Alaric gestured to the headless corpse behind Felicius.

'The man with one hand? He was their leader?'

'He was. Had a lot to say for himself, too.' Alaric looked around, then stepped in close to Felicius, murmuring. 'Word is we're going to have a busy winter of it. Trouble with the Caledonians in the north, from what I hear.'

Felicius smiled. In his long career in the army, he had become all too accustomed to junior officers trying to garner information from him. 'Cup of wine sir?' 'Can I get you a meal sir?' 'Does your kit need attending sir? I can get one of my lads on it.' Anything to curry favour. A man with knowledge was a man prepared. Winter wars increased the need for thick leggings, warm boots, extra tunics and waxed cloaks. All things that came at a cost. And low and behold, as soon as the tanners, weavers and cobblers caught wind of a potential increase in demand, the price for everything doubled.

'Centurion Alaric, you and I both know that if my superiors have entrusted me with confidential information and I haven't disclosed it to my men, then that information is considered classified. For the benefit of us all.'

Alaric cast his eyes to his boots, face flushing red. 'I'm sorry sir, just that the men have been talking-

'And counting the coins in their purses, I do not doubt. If the Heruli are needed to march north this winter, then trust in your betters to let you know in good time.' He clapped the shame faced centurion on the shoulder, leaned in close and whispered. 'But if I were you, I'd make sure each man had a spare tunic, a new cloak, and two pairs of leggings as a minimum, just to be sure.' He gave the man a wink before turning back to Vitulus.

'I'm off to find the *Dux*. Get the men helping Alaric here anyway they can. I'll find you when I have news.'

Felicius moved off, away from the screams and the thump of the axe. He felt bad to have missed the battle. As a man and an officer, he had always prided himself on his professionalism, the constant readiness of his men. Word had reached him in Vindolanda that the *Dux* requested him to command an infantry column to repel a band of raiders five days previous. Due to the winter weather, the crumbling roads and one raw messenger who had taken a wrong turn or two, the message had reached him a day later than it should have. Still, he reasoned, he had made good time, covering thirty miles a day to reach the eastern coast. Whether the *Dux* saw it that way, though, was another matter entirely.

He reached the ranks of the Spanish horsemen, the *Ala I Hispanorum Asturum,* one of the finest mounted units in the west. They called them Spanish, but the men that filled their ranks were Britons to the core. The unit had been operating in Britannia for three generations, and the only true Spaniard among them was their commander, Abel Felix. Ten years ago, the prefect received a promotion for his and his men's loyalty during the great rebellion in Britannia, and they played a key role in restoring the provinces to Roman rule. Felix had changed little, the same small wiry frame tucked under his armour, a dusting of grey in his dark beard the only mark the years had left upon him.

'Gaius! We were beginning to think you had got lost!' he called through a grin.

'Not at all, prefect! Me and my lads just decided it was about time you lot did some work. I trust you didn't lose many men?'

'Five, but nothing we won't recover from.' The rain came back with a vengeance, peppering the soldiers and their mounts as they ducked for the cover of the tents. Felicius and Felix made for the nearest, the Spaniard leaving his centurions to organise his unit.

'Where is the *Dux?*' Felicius asked as they removed dripping helmets and wet cloaks.

'He's around somewhere,' Felix shrugged. 'He fought with us today, lead the charge out of the trees. We smashed through them twice, Sixtus and the Heruli finished them off.'

'I didn't even know Sixtus was here. Hasn't he been in the south?' Felicius had been close to Victorinus ever since he first arrived on the island. They were very different people, with careers seemingly going in opposite directions, but a bond had formed almost instantly, and each man knew he would die for the other.

'He was, some errand for Maximus. Not sure he enjoyed having to fight with the men today!'

They laughed, and Felicius was still grinning when Flavius Maximus stalked in to the tent, his face thunderous. 'I see you've time for a laugh and a joke, Felicius. Even if you cannot make it to battle.' The *Dux* threw his sodden cloak at a waiting slave. Spotting a jug of wine left on a table, he picked up the jug and a cup, before pausing to stare at both. With the hint of a smile, he put the cup back on the table and drank deeply from the jug, smacking his lips once he quenched his thirst.

Felicius was at attention, eyes fixed to a point above Maximus' head as he snapped a salute and thought desperately for the right words. 'My apologies, *Domine*. My men received your summons a day late. We made the best time we could.'

'I'm sure you did,' Maximus said, his eyes fixed on Felicius. He drank once more. 'At least Sixtus had the decency to show up on time. You know he even lead the Heruli into battle? Ha! Not sure I've ever seen the miserable old bastard move so fast! Where is he, anyway?'

'He took his son away from the battlefield, *domine,*' Felix cut in. 'It was his first battle today.'

'Ahh, young Silvius! Of course! He survived unscathed, though. Now this Aldhard has been dealt with, we can move on to our biggest threat.' Maximus raised the jug to his lips once more, then lowered it with a frown, evidently disappointed to find he had emptied its contents already.

'Our biggest threat, sir?' Felicius asked.

'The blasted Caledonians, of course! They are stirring once more, and this time I intend to destroy them so utterly that they will never recover.'

Felicius and Felix shared a look. The *Dux,* oblivious, seemed to be scouring the tent with hungry eyes, seeking another wine jar. 'Sir, reports from our contacts north of the Wall say there is no unexpected movement. No suspicious meetings of people, no increase in food production or no signs of weapons being forged,' Felicius said, knowing already what the reply would be.

'You are too reliant on Drost. You forget he is Victorinus' man no longer. He is one of them, one of their leaders even! You cannot trust the man, not when it comes to this.'

Drost had been in the *miles areani* at one point. A word shy youth with a scarred past he kept locked in the dark recesses of his mind, it hadn't been until the events of the great rebellion that he had spoken of being heir to the chiefdom of one of the biggest tribes in Caledonia. He'd won his place as chief, by the sword, as was their way, and since there was no more *areani* scouting north of the Wall, he had become their biggest source of information. 'Yes, *domine.* You are quite right, I'm sure,' Felicius said.

'Well, as long as you are,' Maximus snarled. 'Dusk tomorrow, Eboracum. All senior commanders to be present. Before then Felicius you will ensure our handless prisoners are on their ship and pushed out to sea. Bury our dead, burn theirs, and come the dawn we are gone from here.'

'Aye sir,' Felicius and Felix just had time to mutter, as the *Dux* strutted out in to the rain.

III

The rain still drizzled down in a lazy arc as Victorinus rode through the gates of Eboracum. Amor, his trusty steed, tossed her wet head as they approached the stable, evidently as keen to be under shelter as her rider. The grey mare had been his mount for nearly twenty years. She was not as nimble as she once was, but, Victorinus thought with a wry smile, neither was he. But she had carried him stolidly across the island and back, as he ran errands for the *Dux* in all the provinces of Britannia.

His legs burned from his march with the Heruli, his shoulder sore from bearing the weight of his shield. Wincing, he lowered himself from the saddle, giving Amor a thump on her side as he did. She nuzzled in to him, hot breath on his face. 'I know what you want, old girl,' he said with a smile, reaching for an apple from his pack. Amor snatched it up in an instant. He cast his eyes up towards the command centre at Eboracum and thought about what today's meeting could mean for him. The perils of being a prefect from a defunct unit. Despite the extinction of the *miles areani* after the great rebellion, Victorinus did not lose his rank. Nor had it had really given him a new one.

Maximus used the old officer for whatever he saw fit. Whether it be delivering messages, inspecting forts and military units across the island, or occasionally leading men in to battle. Victorinus had never complained. He hadn't always seen eye to eye with his commander, but he reasoned Maximus had done well by him overall, and the man was a born fighter.

'I might be awhile up there,' he said to Silvius, who was passing his mount over to a stable hand. 'Why don't you head over to the barracks and see if you can find Maurus? Felix said he's approved him a few days leave from tomorrow. I thought I'd take you both home.'

Silvius nodded, lowering his hood and running a hand through his drenched hair. 'Aye. It would be good to see mother.'

Victorinus gave his son a tight smile. 'I thought it would. Off with you then. Pastor, you're with me.'

The young warrior had been trying to fade away in the rain, and groaned when Victorinus said his name. 'I've no rank! Why do I need to be in a meeting with the *Dux*?'

'Because if you're not, you'll slink across the river for two days drinking and you'll be no good to me for the rest of the week! You never know what Maximus will want from us, and I've a feeling I'm going to need you to be sharp in the coming days.'

'Why's that?'

'Just something Felicius said. Come, or we'll be late.'

Brooding, he moved through the fortress, disregarding the guards' salutes. He hadn't seen his friend Felicius for long after the battle on the east coast, but they'd spoken enough for Victorinus to learn of the campaign Maximus wanted to fight this winter. He frowned, hand stroking his straggly beard. As always in times of stress, he felt a yearning for the wine, his age-old nemesis. It had been over ten years since his last drop of the stuff, though his desire for the jug, the shakes whenever he thought of it, had never gone away. He would not go back to the man he used to be.

His iron studded boots grated on the floorboards as he passed two saluting soldiers and in to the command room within the fortress. A clutch of wet men stood around a table; the isle of Britannia laid out on canvas before them. The *Dux* looked resplendent in a dark blue cloak and gold trimmed mail. He'd had his hair trimmed and was clean shaven, his calculating eyes taking in the men gathered around him. 'Sixtus! Good, you're here. We shall begin.'

He leaned over the desk, the other men shuffling closer. Victorinus thought the room smelt of damp wool and sweat, and promised himself that whatever happened there tonight, he would give himself time for a bath before he left. Two braziers cackled and spat in the far corners, a little light leaking in through shuttered windows holding the rain at bay.

'Gentlemen, I thank you for coming here at my summons. We have, in the last few days, dealt with the most recent raiders landing on our eastern coast. We have repelled them, thanks to Victorinus and the Heruli.' Victorinus smiled at the nods and murmured praise that came his way. It wasn't often Maximus singled him out in front of his senior commanders, and he and the Spanish horse had done most of the work. But you take the good where you can, he figured.

'And now we must turn our attention to the biggest threat facing us. The Caledonians are on the move once more, their clans grouping together under a single banner. We haven't witnessed such movement north of the Wall since the great rebellion. They think we will give them the winter to prepare their men, sharpen their spears and haul together food stores. But they are wrong. Winter or not, I plan to ride north and put a stop to them before they can do us any damage.' He thumped the table, emphasising his point.

Victorinus looked left to right, taking in the sombre faces around the table. Eventually they settled on Felicius, and the prefect cleared his throat as their eyes met. '*Domine*, I do not wish to cause offense. But as I said to you before, we have seen no signs that the tribes are readying for war. Their cattle still graze the wild grass. There has been no increase in trade along the Wall. And Drost says-

'Damn what Drost says!' Maximus slammed both palms down on the table, making the whole room shake. 'Drost is one chief of a small tribe far to the north of our border. He has no more idea what the southern tribes are doing than we do. I've had men north of the Wall for the last two months. They tell me there are newly built barns brimming with grain, spears stockpiled in hill forts. They are preparing themselves, on that you can believe me.'

An uncomfortable silence spread like through the room like blood on stone. It seemed no one quite knew where to look and found a sudden fascination in the most innate things. Victorinus cleared his throat. 'Sir, I was unaware you had sent men to the north. Surely you know my knowledge of the lands beyond the Wall is better than any other on this island. Can I ask why you did not send me?'

Maximus turned his head slowly, his piercing eyes hitting Victorinus like a spear. 'You were in the south, checking the food stores in Londinium. I had to send another.'

'Who?' The man next to Victorinus gasped in horror. Felix stepped forwards from where he had been lurking, his eyes pleading with his friend to stop. Every man in that room knew one thing: never challenge the *Dux*.

'I went,' a gruff voice said. Andragathius stepped forwards, rubbing a hand through his thick beard. The big German was the *Dux's magister equitum*, and as the master of horse was Felix's immediate commander. Known for being fiercely loyal to Maximus, he had served with the commander of Britain's forces for all his adult life.

'*You* went?' Victorinus said incredulously. 'What do you know of the geography of the north? Of the tribes and their movements? I know every tribe, every chief, I know which of them has a daughter married to the heir of their neighbour. I know which chief fathers children with another's sister. Everyone knows the tribes are interconnected. There are factions up there in the wilderness that you could not comprehend in an entire year of riding amongst them! Sir,' he said, turning to the *Dux*. 'If you were planning on sending a man north of the Wall, that man should have been me.'

Victorinus could make out Felicius shaking his head slowly, Felix hiding a grin under his hand. He felt his cheeks burn with embarrassment and prepared himself for the inevitable backlash from his lord. 'Tribune Victorinus,' Maximus began, his voice dangerously low. 'You have proven yourself to be both resourceful and loyal in the years we have served together. And I know full well of your experiences in the north. And that is in part why I did not send you.'

Victorinus went to speak, but Maximus silenced him with a raised palm. 'Your judgement in this matter is clouded. Some of those chiefs that would attack us are men you would still consider friends. One of them even served under you for a time.'

'Drost would never attack us!' Victorinus spoke up.

'No. No, maybe he would not. But his tribe is far to the north, three, maybe four days hard riding from the Wall. There are a lot of men and spears between us. Do you really think he would risk all he has to send a man south to warn us? Or would he turn his back, snug under his furs with that new wife of his? Think about it tribune, how many years has it been since he was in our service?'

'Aye, a fair few,' Victorinus slumped, blowing air out of his red cheeks. He had to admit, his commander had a point. And if the southern tribes really were massing, was there anything Drost could realistically do about it? He thought not. Loyalty in the north changed with the wind, and maybe his old friend was doing as the *Dux* said, and looking to his own.

'So what are your orders, sir?' another general asked. This man was Ambrosius Castus, a name given to him upon his enrolment in the army. Victorinus didn't know his birth name. Five years ago, he had come over from one of the Germanic tribes as part of a peace offering. He'd done pretty well for himself, all things considered, serving with distinction in Africa before being posted to Britannia. He commanded three auxiliary units, some fifteen hundred men at full strength, which, of course, they never were.

'Three days from now I will set off north and west, to Maia, on the western edge of the Wall. From there, we shall ride east, taking troops from each fort we pass. Andragathius, you will leave tomorrow, head west to Mediobogdum, and send riders out to as many garrisons as you can on the way. There are still some ten thousand fighting men on this island, and by God, we are going to need them all. I want you to have your full strength of cavalry at Luguvallium in five days. Can you manage it?'

Andragathius snapped a salute. '*Domine*, it shall be done. With your leave I shall prepare.' Dismissed, the German marched from the room, without so much as a word to his peers.

'Are you sure it is wise to strip the garrisons along the Wall?' Castus asked, his face set in a heavy frown. 'I understand well enough, sir, that having a mobile force in the field ready to march gives us an advantage. But surely if we gather our army in the east, then the Caledonians could just cross the Wall in the west?'

Maximus grinned. Victorinus had served under the man for long enough to know that when he did, it was never a good thing. 'A calculated risk. And we won't be stripping the forts entirely. A small garrison of trusted men will stay in each. And each garrison will build a wooden tower, fifty paces south of the Wall. These towers will have bails of dried hay on top. They see an army coming for them, they light their fire. All we need is for one garrison to light their torch, then the next fort in the line,' he ran a finger across the map, stopping at each fort along the Wall, 'will do the same. Wherever we are, we will know within half an hour if we have a potential breach, and we simply follow the fires until we find it.' He slapped the map once more, brought himself up to his full height and drank greedily from a wine cup, smacking his lips in satisfaction once it was drained. 'Any other questions?'

'Where do you want my men to go, sir?' Felicius asked, still frowning at the map, obviously uncertain of the plan.

'Your men will stay in Vindolanda until we reach them. You, on the other hand, will not. I plan on putting upwards of ten thousand men in the field, prefect, and four thousand mounts. We need grain, wine, oil, as much as you can get your hands on. My treasury is open to you, of course. I'll have a letter with my seal sent to your quarters this evening giving you full authority to take what you need.'

'The emperor is aware of this?' Felicius asked, and this time it was Victorinus' turn to squirm as his friend put his neck on the chopping block.

'Not yet, but he will know soon enough,' Maximus waved a careless hand. 'My job here is to keep our provinces safe from invaders, and that is exactly what I am doing. When I have news for the emperor, he shall have it.' There would be imperial spies, of course, the dreaded *agentus in rebus*, working in secret on the emperor's behalf on the island. No doubt there was a slave or two close to Maximus, secretly reporting back everything they saw and heard. It was common enough knowledge that the divine Gratian had little time for Maximus, and that was the main reason for his continued stay in Britannia. The backwater of the west, Victorinus had heard it called. Not that he'd know any different. Born and raised on the island, he was yet to leave.

'I am to be your grain man?' Felicius said through a sour grimace. 'Surely there are men in your command centre for such tasks? I've no notion of how to gather enough provisions to feed ten thousand men!'

'Then it is high time you learned, prefect. I did the same thing for my beloved uncle, God rest his soul, and you shall do this for me. There is one more thing. A ship will arrive in Londinium in the next week, from the east. Its cargo is of the utmost importance to me and our mission here. You will ensure it reaches this fortress in good time, and you *guarantee* they have not tampered it in any form when it does. Am I understood?'

'Yes, sir. Can I ask what it is?'

'No,' Maximus said through his dangerous grin. 'But I shall tell you all when the time is right.' The *Dux's* eyes met with Castus for a moment and both men smiled. Victorinus wondered what private scheme his commander was cooking behind the scenes, hiding from the men whose loyalty he thought he could not fully trust. 'Tribune Victorinus, I've a job for you, too.'

Victorinus swallowed, wondering nervously where he was going to be sent to this time. He thought of his promise to Silvius and hoped he would have the chance to take his son home for a while. 'You will take command of the Heruli once more and lead them to Aesica. The fortress is half empty at the moment, just some two hundred horsemen in there, so you should have no trouble fitting the Heruli in. I want you to send riders out to all the forts east of there, and instruct them to follow the same orders I will leave for the forts in the west. I will meet you there as I journey west. You too shall have a scroll with my seal containing your orders by daybreak.'

'Yes sir,' Victorinus saluted, reasoning his orders could have been much worse. 'My plan, gentlemen, is to gather our forces together, take them north of the Wall and crush the Caledonian tribes once and for all. We shall bring about a victory so great they will toast us in Rome and Constantinople. Are there any more questions? No? Good. You are all dismissed.' Maximus turned from his waiting officers, filled his cup from a jug once more, and tipped back its contents.

The men saluted and together marched out of the chamber and into the murky twilight.

***

The rain had stopped, mercifully, as Victorinus clambered down the steps and on to the cobbled path. Smoke rose lazily from the cooking fires at the edge of the fortress, the night air alive with the jingle of moving mail and the crunch of marching feet. His breath misted in front of him and he pulled his cloak tight, thinking how he felt everything more with age. 'Pastor,' he called to his young companion, who dutifully turned in his tracks and walked back to his lord.

Pastor didn't hold any rank in the army. He was another victim, just like Victorinus, of the disbandment of the *miles areani*. Victorinus, though, had kept his rank. Pastor hadn't had one to start with. He was the bastard son of a hanged traitor, the very traitor that had for a while taken Britannia out of the empire, as he sought to carve one of his own. Pastor had been raised to play a role, a pawn in a game he never fully understood. However, Victorinus had developed a fondness for the lad, and even after his treachery had been exposed and his father hanged, Victorinus had treated the lad kindly and provided him with a wage from his own purse. 'I need to meet with Drost,' the tribune said quietly to the youth.

'Aye, thought you might,' Pastor said through a sigh. He knew what was coming.

'Go north, usual place. Set the meet for six days from tomorrow, at dawn. I'll meet you in Aesica.' Pastor sighed, rubbing the stubble on his chin. 'I know you don't want to ride north in the winter at night, and I know what I'm asking will tear you away from whatever important business you had planned over the river.' He hooked a thumb in the general direction. Eboracum was known for its town being one of the best for soldiers to blow off steam when not on duty. Victorinus had done it himself often enough over the years. 'But this is important. You heard what the Dux said in there, he's planning a war. If the tribes really are massing, I need to know why I'm hearing it from Maximus and not from Drost.'

Pastor sighed again, clicked his tongue. 'Yes, I know. I'll leave within the hour, just need to get some supplies.' Victorinus reached in to his purse and passed the lad some coins. 'Thanks,' he said, clapping Pastor on the shoulder. 'I wouldn't ask you to do it if it were not important.'

'I know.' With that, he was gone.

'At least he hasn't sent you halfway down the country this time!' Victorinus turned to see Felicius coming down the stairs, a grin fixed on his bearded face. 'How was the south, anyway?'

Victorinus shrugged. 'Waste of time. I'm no expert when it comes to food stores and running garrisons. Seemed fine to me, though. Saw Clementius, actually.' The prefect of the Second Augusta, one of the oldest legions in Rome's glorious history, had fought with Victorinus and Felicius before. The man was in his sixties now, refusing to give in to age and hang up his sword for good.

'The old bastard still going strong then!' Felicius looked around as he neared Victorinus, checking to see who was in earshot. 'What do you think is going on, then? We've seen or heard no evidence that the tribes are up to no good. All seems a bit off, don't you think?'

'Aye. Maximus puts too much trust in those German generals, if you ask me. I know he's never fully trusted you and me, but seriously, between the two of us, who doesn't know more about the tribes than us? Years we've fought up here on the Wall, Felix too! And yet we're the last ones to hear of an apparent invasion coming our way.'

Felicius rubbed his beard, and Victorinus had the sense his friend was debating telling him something or not. 'Spit it out, brother,' he said impatiently. 'I'm your oldest friend. If you can't tell me, who can you tell?'

'You might not thank me for it,' Felicius said through a heavy sigh, before reaching under his cloak and producing a roll of parchment. 'It's from Theo.'

'You mean the divine Theodosius, lord and commander of all imperial forces in the eastern empire?'

'He's still Theo to me. Read it.'

Victorinus walked to the nearest brazier, and opened the scroll, leaning it in to the flames light. He was silent for a good while. 'By the fucking gods,' he muttered to himself, rolling the parchment back up and handing it over. 'You should burn that.'

Felicius nodded. 'I will. But read what he says, too much trust in German officers, outsiders infiltrating the highest reaches of the army. Then you have this feud between Maximus and Gratian-

'We don't know there's a feud! We don't know any-thing! For all we know, this is Theo trying to undermine Maximus and Gratian from the east. Think about it. Who ordered the execution of Theo's father?

'Aye, I know that. I was there.' Felicius shivered. 'But what reason does Theo have of causing a wedge between Maximus and the western emperor? Gratian raised him to the eastern throne, after all!'

'Not sure he had much choice, after what happened to Valens.' Hadrianopolis was a city Victorinus had never heard spoken of until four years previously, when the eastern emperor Valens had taken the field against a Gothic army outside its walls and been crushed. The defeat had shaken the empire to its core. Within months, Theo, the son of a disgraced and executed general, had been summoned from his early retirement to take command of the remnants of the eastern field army and drive the Goths back over the Danube. Soon after that, he had been offered the purple. It was a remarkable change in fortunes for a young man who thought his best years were already behind him. 'Have you replied?'

'No,' Felicius shook his head. 'I will, though. I owe him much, after all.'

'Not least if he gives you that promotion he's promised.'

'I'd swap a promotion for peace, and that's the truth. God, Sixtus, what do I know about provisioning an army? Where do you even begin?'

'Grain? I guess. Can't say I've ever had to worry much about that side of things. I'd get yourself into the *praetorium* here tomorrow morning. There's an army of beaurocrats in there from dawn to dusk. One of them must be used to this kind of work.'

Felicius groaned. 'Civil servants, what has my life come to? Why am I doing this whilst you march up the country with the Heruli? You're usually the *Dux's* lackey. Why choose to pick on me now?'

'Don't know, don't care! I'm off to find Alaric, get his men on the road tomorrow, then take Maurus and Silvius to see their mother for a day or so. I can catch Alaric up on the road. I trust Lucia and Marcelina are well?'

Felicius smiled at the mention of his wife and daughter. 'They are. They're at Vindolanda, if you have time to swing by. Marcelina still needs a husband, as Lucia keeps reminding me. She was thinking your Maurus would be a good match? They're of an age, after all.'

Victorinus laughed. 'Sarai said much the same to me last time I saw her. Seems she and Lucia are as firm friends as ever. Maybe we should discuss it further come the spring?' They clasped hands and walked off in opposite directions, Victorinus feeling suddenly lighter. It was good to have friends around. Men he could trust. His mood darkened as looked back up at Maximus's headquarters, for a fleeting moment, he thought he could make out a shadow in an open window, but before his aging eyes could discern what he saw, the shadow was gone, and there was just the flickering light of a candle dancing on the breeze. He turned away from the window, pulling his cloak tight around him once more, and went off to find his sons.

IV

To the Divine Augustus Flavius Theodosius, lord and protector of Rome's eastern provinces, from Gaius Felicius, Prefect of the Fourth Cohort of Gauls, writing from Eboracum,
Britannia. Greetings.

My lord emperor, it does my heart good to hear from you,
and for you to write that your health continues to improve.
I, like all loyal subjects across the breadth of the empire, was
deeply concerned with hearing of your ill health. You have
achieved so much in such a brief space of time, and I have
seen firsthand the surety and comfort you are bringing to
your subjects at a time of their upmost need. I trust the health
of your precious young son, Arcadius, remains strong, and
that of the beloved empress. May God watch over them both.
I must admit, domine, that initially your letter took me a
little off guard. I am a soldier, born and bred, and have
never aspired to be anything more. Thoughts of the inner
goings on at court are of no business to me. I go where I am
stationed, and fight my enemy with a shield and sword, my
men around me. However, your words have been playing
on my mind. You will recall, I am sure, the first time you
and I met. Two groups of mercenaries were fighting each
other instead of digging the defensive ditches as they had

been ordered, and I leaned on the wall at Rutupiae, watching with growing disgust. I stormed from the rampart, you running behind me to confront the warring group. Who was it I found? No low soldier brawling for the fun if it, but none other than Flavius Maximus, nephew of the great general Theodosius, cousin to you, with bloodied knuckles and dirt all over his face. It didn't make for the best of first impressions—for either party!

Since returning to Britannia, I have found our relationship has failed to thaw. He does not fully trust me, or the tribune Sixtus Victorinus — a dear friend of mine, I'm sure you remember. Although the two of us, along with the prefect Clementius of the Second Augusta and prefect Felix of the Spanish horse, have served in Britannia longer than any of the other senior officers he surrounds himself with. These are Germans, as you mentioned in your letter. They are his inner circle, and that circle is as strong as marble.

As for his relations with people at court, I am afraid I have no news. Maximus mentions no correspondence he has from abroad. I am not even sure he is in regular contact with your divine counterpart, Gratian. I can tell you he is planning a winter expedition north of the Wall. He says he has intelligence that the Caledonian tribes are once more massing out there in the vast emptiness, sharpening their spears and readying to march south. I must stress that we have seen no evidence of this from Vindolanda or from Vercovicium, where the main trade gate with our northern neighbours is open daily still. Everything seems normal. You may recall a young man named Drost, who served under Victorinus in the miles areani all those years ago. He is now a tribal leader *in his own right, and his tribe, the Vacomagi, has been loyal to us since he gained leadership over them. If there really was a conspiracy in the north, if the tribes really were massing at the Wall, eager to slip over and ravage our lands, surely he would know?*

Maximus did, to his credit, have reliable intelligence of a raiding party on our east coast just days ago. He mustered a force quickly and slaughtered them before they got a mile inland. The survivors of the battle experienced having their right hands cut off, and they sealed the wounds with fire. Afterward, they were herded back onboard one of their ships and cast out to sea. I very much doubt they'll ever make it home. Maybe they're still out there now, rowing in circles between us and Gaul? May God have mercy on their souls, even if they are heathens.

I digress slightly, but the point I was trying to make is that I believe you are correct. Maximus is up to something, though what that is I do not know. I expect I shall be busy over the coming weeks; I have been charged with finding the supplies for ten thousand men plus some four thousand mounts, how he expects me to find what we need to survive in the field in winter in Britannia I do not know, but as ever, I shall do my best to deliver. I promise you, domine, I shall keep my ears open and report back anything I find. I agree wholeheartedly with your point regarding civil war. Rome has gone through that turmoil too many times. We have too many enemies, not enough manpower. We cannot possibly hope to hold our borders and fight each other. If I can play a small part in preventing that come to pass, I will do it with all my heart.

There is one thing, now I think about it. Maximus has instructed me to take in a ship from the east. He didn't say where, saying it has cargo vital to our cause here in Britannia. I am to ensure its safe delivery and to personally guarantee that it has not been tampered with in any way upon its arrival. I've no notion of what it is, or what it is for. Are you aware of anything? Perhaps you could ask someone to look in to it from your end? I don't know why, but I have a horrid feeling about what it could be.

As to the last days of your dear father's life, I find myself unable to find the words. He was an exemplary man until the end. I know he took comfort that he was going to meet his Lord and Saviour, and that he met his end, certain his son would rise so high that he himself would become a mere footnote in history, if he was remembered at all. He was fiercely proud of you, as he should have been. I know as much as any man that he did nothing to bring about such a wicked and ill-deserved end. He was fiercely loyal to the empire, and whoever sat on the throne, he was always ready to serve.

I continue to be your most loyal servant,

Gaius

***

Felicius pawed at his tired face, frustration getting the better of him. He clicked his tongue, exhaled loudly, and spoke once more. 'Please explain that to me again, one more time.'

The *magister officiorum,* Pericles Abas, shuffled the parchment on his desk, making a show of looking busy. 'I really don't know how many times I need to take you through this, prefect. To acquire that much grain, I shall have to mobilise two ships to Africa. We simply do not have enough produce on the island-

'Africa?! What about Gaul? Hispania? Surely they will have grain they can send us?' Felicius thumped the palm of his hand down on the desk, his patience worn thin. It was dawn, the day after Maximus' meeting with his generals, and Felicius was already cursing the man in his head, promising himself revenge on the *Dux* somehow.

'I have told you twice already!' Abas snapped. 'There is no stock in Gaul or Hispania. We are already two-thirds in to our winter allocation of grain. I cannot just pester my counterpart across the sea for more because the *Dux* has decided on a little expedition north of the Wall! Good God man, it will snow soon. What does he hope to achieve? Why don't you tell him to leave his campaigning to spring like all *sensible* generals do, and he can have all the grain he wants then?'

'Oh aye, I'll just pop around to his quarters now shall I? Wake him up with the good news? What do you think he's going to do when he hears? Pat me on the shoulder, thank me for a job well done and delay the war until April? Whilst I'm at it, I'll send a runner up to the Caledonians, ask them if they can sit on their arses a couple of months, you know, come at us when we're fully provisioned and ready for them. Only fair, hey?'

Abas tutted, rolled his eyes. He was a small man, in mind as well as build, as beaurocrats tended to be. He was somewhere in his middle fifties, clinging on to a hairline that had long since lost its battle, the centre giving way, though to give them credit the wings were still holding their own. As if to make up for his crown's shortcomings, he had enormous bushy eyebrows, and thick grey hairs sprouting from his ears. He squinted up at Felicius. The prefect couldn't make out if it was in disgust or the man really couldn't see him. Seemed a harsh fate, for a man whose job it was to read reports all day, to lose the one thing that gave use to his life.

'Prefect, it is January. We have three great holds of grain on this island. One is in Londinium, the biggest. Our warehouses there are barely half full. Here in Eboracum we are two-thirds of the way through, and Aquae Sulis in the west has already sent word to us they will need topping up by March. The seas are treacherous this time of year. You're looking at a four week turn around *if you are lucky* before the fleet can get two ships to Africa and back. And that's if they have enough at Carthage. If not, they will be required to go further east to Egypt.'

'Egypt! *Jesu* save me. Ok, put the grain to one side for a moment. What about wine?'

'There is plenty of wine.'

'Excellent!' Felicius clapped his hands together in relief.

'In Hispania.'

'Oh for fu-

'There'll be none of your soldiers' language in my chamber, I thank you. Again, as I have said countless times now, we need advance warning of these kinds of expeditions. We don't just sit on the supplies needed for an army in the field if we are not told there is going to be one!'

'You realise we can't just plan to go to war, don't you? This isn't some grand offensive from the history books, this is the *Dux* looking to ensure that you and your family don't get murdered in your sleep by some tattooed barbarian planning on leaping over the Wall!' Felicius stopped, took two deep breaths. 'Can you please at least make some enquiries? Get the wheel in motion. I am expected to feed an army in the coming weeks. I cannot do that without the support of your office.'

'There,' Abas said through a grin. 'A little humility, and a hint of gratitude. Didn't cost you so much after all, did it. Leave it with me, I'll send a runner to you when I have news. You will be in the city?'

Felicius swallowed the urge to bite back, and just about managed it. 'I shall be at Vindolanda by sundown.'

'Then I shall send word there as soon as I can. Was there anything else?'

Felicius puffed out his cheeks in exasperation and picked a roll of parchment out of the pouch at his waist. 'I need ten thousand good winter cloaks for the troops. I can get my hands on another six thousand from a factory in Londinium. Tribune Victorinus has a contact there. Where do I go to source the rest?'

Abas made a show of stroking his chin, his squint deepening. 'I can arrange that, at least. Leave it with me. I shall have them delivered to Vindolanda. There is stock of those here in Eboracum, and the factory owner owes me a favour. What about boots?'

'My thanks. And boots are next on my list.'

'There is a cobbler in the *vicus* at Vercovicium, he is a half year behind with his taxes. I shall write him a letter ordering him to supply you with everything you need. He'll have it by tomorrow. Have you thought about meat? Soldiers need more than grain, after all.'

Felicius looked down at his list, frowned as he saw meat wasn't there. 'I hadn't thought of that. God, I'm not the man for this. You seem to know more about the needs of an army than me! Perhaps you should have joined the military,' he said with a sardonic laugh.

Abas smiled. 'I did. Fifteen years with the Sixth Victrix. I was their quartermaster.'

Felicius didn't know whether to laugh at the apparent joke or if the man was actually being serious. 'Don't suppose you feel like signing back up for a few months, do you?'

Abas chuckled. 'My service was uneventful, to say the least. I spent my time in the offices at base, pushing paper and filling demands, much as I do for the state now.' He adjusted himself in his seat, leaned over the desk and spoke again. 'Not that I do not want to help you, prefect. Much the opposite. I know too well the important job you do, and you do it well, I do not doubt. But you have to understand that when some general clicks his fingers and expects everyone to fulfil his demands in a heartbeat, it is not as straightforward as he would think. I know, I know, before you start another rant, that he thinks nothing of this. That's why he has you. When I was serving, I was told by a general he needed a thousand shields sent up to the Wall in ten days. A thousand shields! Do you know how long it takes to make one? To carve and bend the wood, treat it. That's before you cover it with leather! No prefect, I understand very well the challenges you face. Here, I have something for you.' He rose from his desk, walked at a shuffle to a bookcase. Felicius noted the stoop in his back, the way he favoured his left leg. It was sobering to realise that he was of an age to the *magister officiorum,* and he was suddenly very grateful for the life the military had given him. He was fit and active, marching or riding daily. How easily it could have been him, shuffling from one desk to another, struggling to rise from bed as his blood thickened and slowed in his veins. No, there were upsides to soldiering, more than he could count. He supposed the only downside was the occasional high risk of death. But no job was perfect.

'Here,' Abas said, handing over an old wax tablet. 'This is the list I used as my guide when I was a quartermaster. I know it's been a long time since my service, but I doubt a soldier's needs have changed overly much.'

Felicius opened the tablet, reading the neat, coherent words inside. Abas was right. There, in a list, was everything he needed. Food was first, always the most important. A list of quantities of cattle and sheep that needed to be slaughtered a month to keep the Sixth Victrix fed. Where the cattle came from, what the cost for each purchase was.

Stock on hand for spare swords, shields, javelins, helmets. The cost again for each item, and how much the legion were paying per month to keep their armoury full. On and on it went, right down to spare cooking utensils for those inevitably lost on the road. It was impressive, to say the least. 'My thanks for this,' he muttered, still lost in the words, the organisation of it.

'May I make a suggestion?' Abas asked, gently lowering himself back in to his seat. 'You need a clerk, someone who can help you organise all of this. Supplying an army of ten thousand is not the job of one man. Speak to the *Dux*. I know he is strong-willed but in this I believe he will see reason.'

'I will. And you're right, I need someone to lighten the load. I thank you for your time, *magister* Abas. You will write to me regarding the grain?'

'I shall. The army gets preference, of course. So if need be, I can take the stock from the warehouses here in Britannia and have the ships back fill them when they arrive. You leave that with me. Good luck prefect.'

Overwhelmed, Felicius left without saying goodbye. The sun had risen outside, a weak, pale thing that shed no warmth. The ground had been frozen when he'd left his chamber in the murky half light of pre-dawn. There was no wind, though, and for that he was grateful. When he had first been sent to Britannia all those years ago, he thought he was adept at coping with the cold. He didn't think it would be any worse than what he'd experienced on the Rhine or Danube frontiers. It was the wind that got to him. It blew so cold it would freeze his face solid, and for some reason no physician could ever explain to him, it caused him to have the most terrible jaw ache.

He pawed at his face again, the dire need for sleep fogging his brain. He'd been up most of the night, drafting and re-drafting his reply to the Augustus Theodosius, or just Theo, as Felicius still thought of him. It had been unnerving at his first, seeing in person the power his friend wielded his casual ease. He could still remember standing shoulder to shoulder with a young lad commanding a unit in battle for the first time. How times had changed. Still, it didn't hurt to have friends in high places, even if he doubted he'd see the promotion Theo promised in his letter. Maximus would see to that, Felicius was sure.

Reaching the stables he found his horse saddled, bags filled with provisions to last him the day's ride. He slipped the groom a couple of bronze coins and mounted, before briefly considering if he should wait for Victorinus. His friend would be travelling the same road after all. He paused a moment, lost in the fog of his breath, before deciding he would see the tribune soon enough. Besides, the man would want to spend the day with his sons.

That turned his thoughts to his own family, and for the first time that day, he smiled. He had been away from them too long, marching off to the east coast and then on to Eboracum. If there was a plus side to winter, it was snuggling up with his wife by a fire, their small home within Vindolanda a warming comfort. He would bathe when he got home, drink warm, sweetened wine and take his wife to bed. Marcelina would be off in the *vicus*, causing mischief, no doubt. Before he had left, she had decided she wanted to learn smithing, and was busy chatting up the owner of the local forge, begging to be taken on as an apprentice. He grinned wider at the thought. He'd have to slip the man some coin to make sure she was properly trained, but if that's what his daughter wanted, that's what she would get. He kicked the horse in to motion, and grin still fixed to his face, left the worries of Eboracum behind him.

V

The sun was fading in the west, the sky a purple hue, as Victorinus and his sons rode down the track leading to the farm. He smiled to see it, always did when he'd been away, whether for a day or a month. It wasn't much, just a rundown two-storey house, two rooms downstairs and two up. But it was his home, the home he and Sarai had moved in to after their wedding. He tried to count the years, smile widening as he realised there were too many.

His was one of two homes in the small farmstead. The other, near on identical to theirs, belonged to Publius and Amata, and their daughter, Delphina. The daughter was of an age to Pastor, and Victorinus had on more than one occasion seen the two exchange murmured conversations under deep red blushes. She would make a fine wife for the lad, he thought, making a note to finally broach the subject with Publius. He and Amata were both experiencing their eightieth winter, and Victorinus felt his smile fade at the thought of this isolated community without them. They would want to see their daughter married, he was sure, and Pastor had grown in to a fine young man. He could see Delphina, her long dark hair and pale skin, poking out from a shuttered window at the sound of horses. He smiled and waved to her. She returned the gesture, but even in the half light Victorinus could see her eyes scanning the other two horsemen, looking for Pastor. *He'll be here soon enough.*

They clattered in to the stables, Victorinus ordering the boys to go straight in and see their mother and leave the horses to him. Sarai would have spent the last weeks in a dreadful state of anxiety, with both her sons off to war, the youngest for the first time. It would be good for all three of them to be reunited. He chuckled to himself as the boys—young boys, they seemed once more — sprinted down the path to the house. He paused for a moment, senses tingling in anticipation, before breaking out in to a chuckle as he heard Sarai squeal with joy.

His spirits lifted. He spent an hour rubbing down the horses, freshening up their hay and settling them in for the night, humming to himself the whole time. His thighs burned after a day in the saddle. Another sign of old age, he thought to himself, as if he needed another of those. He stepped outside the barn. The air was freezing, his breath thick in front of him. He was warm though, from the work, and he neglected to put on a cloak as he walked out the barn, away from the house to a small clearing. A large beech tree, its branches bare, stood proudly in the centre of a small fenced off square. Outside the fence the land was wild, weeds sprouting high above thin grass. But inside, all was neat and tidy.

He lifted the latch on the gate, slowly, so the squeaking didn't disturb Publius and Amata. Light sleepers their whole lives. Stepping inside, he walked to the left of the tree, where a gravestone stood in the dim light. Leonius Victorinus, the inscription read. Gone from the world before he could even comprehend how much joy he brought it.

Victorinus sighed, rubbing a hand over the stone. It had taken him years to have one commissioned, another of his many failings, as a husband and a father. But the mason had done him proud once he'd finally got his priorities straight. Little Leo had been just two when he passed, a winter fever gripping him and not letting go. Truly, the world was an evil place. Victorinus had been away when it had happened. He wasn't in the north, working, but in Eboracum, getting drunk and whoring with his friends.

He had never forgiven himself.

'Sorry it's been so long, dear boy,' he said, lowering himself to the ground, oblivious to the wet seeping through his tunic. 'I've been working again. The *Dux* sent me south to Londinium, to inspect the garrison there and parade the men.' He laughed wryly to himself. 'Not that they gave a fig I was there, nor their commander. Just another tick in the box for the mighty Maximus. Got me out the way for a while I suppose.' His thoughts turned to the previous night's meeting, the revelation that the Caledonians were on the warpath. 'Sometimes I am glad you never got to be grown,' he said. 'An odd thing to think, maybe, but the world is full of bastards. All you ever knew in your brief life was unconditional love, and that is a beautiful thing.'

He looked up at the sky. A cloudless night, stars twinkling high above. 'Are you up there, my boy? In heaven? Or Elysium, as our forefathers would believe. My father would rise early each morning, step outside and kiss the two forefingers on his right hand, and hold them up to the rising sun. "Sol Invictus, I salute you," he would say. He'd repeat it each night, as the sun sank behind the western hills. I can't say I've ever put much stock in gods, or God. Perhaps that is what lead me astray.'

He was silent a while, thoughts drifting lazily in and out of his mind. 'Silvius fought for the first time. You'd have been proud to see him. Stood resolute, shield and sword in hand, and killed his first man. Maurus was there too. What a man he has become,' he trailed off with a sigh. Reaching out, he stroked the headstone once more. Leonius was two years older than Silvius, and as always when he sat there, Victorinus wondered what sort of man the world had grown without. 'What would you be doing now, eh? Fighting, like your brothers? Perhaps making your way in the civil service. Ha! My friend Felicius could use you now if you had!' He was silent a moment, still stroking the stone, as if his touch would seep through to the earth and warm his son's body. 'I'm so sorry I wasn't there,' he breathed, almost a whisper. 'Even if it were just to say goodbye. Tell you one last time how loved you were.' Tears rolled down his cheeks, flattening streaks in his straggly beard. 'I've so many regrets in my life. But if there was one thing I could change, if the gods could grant me one wish, I'd hold you in my arms again, breathe in your scent, and never let go.' His hand dropped.

'A wise man told me once that if you fixate on your past, you'll be too late to change your future,' a voice said behind him, and he turned to see Sarai, huddled in a huge cloak.

He rose from the grass, his first instinct being to reach out and hug her, before remembering they didn't do that anymore.

'Got more years behind me than I have in front,' he said with a shrug. 'Reckon I've seen the best of them.' *I was just too blind to see it.* 'How are you? You look well.'

Sarai smiled, her blue eyes suddenly alight in the darkness. 'I'm all the better for seeing my boys home. It's been awful, waiting for news of them.'

Victorinus shivered, pimples forming on his skin. Was a time she'd have worried about him coming home safe; those days were long gone. 'They fought well. Maurus is shaping up to being one hell of a solider, and Silvius handled himself like a veteran.'

Sarai pursed her lips, clearly unhappy with the thought. 'It's not the life I wanted for them. But they are your sons, I suppose. They're talking about a winter campaign north of the Wall? Is it true?'

'Aye, seems so. I'm meeting with Drost, hoping he'll have some news for me.' He rubbed his ill-fitting beard, irritating his skin. Sarai had always preferred him clean shaven. Maybe he should dig out his razor. Wouldn't make any difference now. 'Something isn't right with all this, and I intend to get to the bottom of it.'

Sarai laughed. He loved her laugh, a noise to bring joy to any arena across the empire. 'Last time I heard you say something like that, you were about to bring down one of the biggest rebellions this island has ever seen.'

His turn to flash a smile. 'I bloody did it and all.'

'Yes. Yes, you did.' She looked at him a moment, the way she'd always used to. The moment passed in silence, Victorinus desperately trying to think of something to say to bring it back. It was too late. Sarai's eyes flickered to the wet ground. 'Don't stay out here too long, you'll freeze.' With that, she turned and walked away.

He stayed another hour or so, just long enough to be certain she wasn't coming back. With tears pricking his red-rimmed eyes, he stalked back to the barn. The horses were asleep, didn't even stir as he walked past. His old mount, Amor, would sleep until the sun was well up. She was perhaps the only living thing on the island that disliked mornings more than him. Come to think of it, he didn't much like the nights these days, either.

He and Sarai had made a good go of it, once the rebellion had been crushed and Victorinus had saved her and their boys from certain death. Trouble was, when something was as broken as their marriage, there just wasn't any fixing it. Can't force someone to love you, after all. With an effort, he clawed his way up the ladder at the back of the stable, his hands stiff with cold. Up top was a small space not quite tall enough for him to stand up in, two beds and a chamber pot. He and Pastor bunked together when not on errands for the *Dux*, a temporary arrangement made too many years ago. Like most other things, Victorinus just hadn't got around to building his own house.

Wasn't as if he lacked for coin either. To give him credit, the *Dux* paid him well, better coin than he'd any right to earn, in truth. There were many skilled masons and carpenters in Eboracum that would jump at the work, winter or not. He just needed to get his priorities straight and get it started. Priorities. Always came back to the same thing. He didn't bother to remove his tunic as he laid down on the cot, the scratchy military blanket his protection from the cold. Reaching beneath the cot, he pulled out an old leather purse, the ties fraying at their edges. He played with it a moment, savouring the touch of the rough material. Eventually, he untied it, pulling out a small wooden horse. *Amor*. Maurus had named it, and he'd adopted it for his own mount. He'd made it for Maurus when he was young, and the lad had given it to him all those years ago, when he'd ridden from that very farm to make himself a hero.

'Hmph,' he chuckled, some hero he was. He doubted Maurus even remembered it existed. He'd reached the age of ten when he stopped playing with his toys. They had passed the others down to Silvius before eventually being thrown out. He'd kept this one though, a reminder of when he had a complete family, something to fight for, a purpose. He stroked it for a while, lost in memory. Finally, he fell asleep, the horse still clutched tight in his palm.

***

They laid in the hedgerow, watching the light dance off the ruins of the crumbled watchtower. 'Something doesn't feel right,' Victorinus said, shifting uncomfortably in his mail. They'd tethered their horses a quarter mile to the south in a thicket of trees, approaching the tower with caution.

'Seems fine to me,' Pastor said, scanning the open ground before them.

'There were no issues delivering the message? Nothing different? Off?'

'You asked me this already! No, it was fine. Normal.'

'No, it was fine, *sir*.'

Pastor tutted. 'I don't have any sort of rank. Why should I call you sir?'

'Because I am a tribune of Rome and deserve some respect! You are an ungrateful, insolent child who would be dead without me.'

'Bit harsh.'

'A bit true, I think you'll find. Where *is* he?'

'It's just past dawn. He'll be here.' As if on cue, a man appeared in the watchtower. Tall and broad shouldered, thick dark hair running past his jaw. A single-headed axe rested on his right shoulder. 'See, he's here.'

'Hmmm,' Victorinus muttered, eyes scanning left and right. There was something nagging at him, something off. He couldn't put his finger on what. 'Come on then, let's move.'

They rose from the hedge, Victorinus' body protesting as he scrambled to his feet. Getting old was no fun. His mail seemed heavier each morning when he put it on. Seemed tighter too. He was just beginning to accept he was going to have to get it adjusted. Damned if he was going to let Pastor in on that, though. He'd have to make sure the lad was on an errand when he got it done. He'd never hear the end of it.

They trudged across the open grass, the sky a pale blue overhead. He longed for a bit of cloud, anything to ease the cold from his bones. The wind bit at him, as if it could hear his thoughts. It took all his willpower to stop his teeth chattering. They were at the long abandoned fort of Habitancum, an advert for a crumbling empire if there ever was one. The Caledonians had long since stripped the walls of stone for their own use, and all that remained within was a watchtower with a yawning hole in its south side and two half filled defensive ditches skirting the perimeter.

Drost walked down from the watchtower as they approached, an affable grin fixed on his bearded face. He looked healthy, Victorinus thought, walking with the easy stride of a man half his age. He must have been forty, though he carried the years with a grace Victorinus could not help envy. 'Salve, brother,' Drost called as he approached, his axe still slung carelessly over his shoulder. 'Been a while.'

'Aye, that it has,' Victorinus said, squinting as the wind howled at his face once more. 'I wonder why it has been so long.'

Drost frowned. 'I'm a busy man. Come on, my boys have got a fire going inside. Should even be some warm oats to break our fast.'

They followed him in to the remains of the fortress. It looked even worse from within than it had outside, if that was possible. Shards of stone lay scattered on the overgrown grass, the odd remains of a smashed clay jar, and even a rusted mail shirt lay strewn across the ground. It seemed the Caledonians had not stopped pillaging once they'd taken down the walls. The buildings, all of them, were nothing but rubble. Victorinus could make out where the barracks used to be, the *praetorium* that would have always been a hive of activity, as officers and clerks rushed about, all on the orders of the commander. Stables nestled in the far corner, north of the Wall, it always came in handy to have a troop of horsemen on hand.

He stopped walking and looked around. His foot caught on something. Reaching down, he pulled at an old belt, tugged it from the earth. 'This is the fate of us all,' he said, to no one in particular.

'Huh?' Pastor stopped mid-stride, his stomach guiding him to the cooking fire.

'Look around you, lad. This is what it all comes to in the end. We think ourselves so grand, don't we? The Roman empire, the mightiest force in the world. Ain't no one that can match us, no one who can stand against us. And yet here we are, standing in the ruins of a fortress that was once built on Roman soil.'

Pastor looked around, looked back to Victorinus and rolled his eyes. 'And what was the point in this fortress? There was nothing here for us to conquer, nothing to gain. Just a fact,' he said with a sheepish glance to Drost. 'Nothing wrong with focusing on what adds value.'

'Gods, you know that actually made some sense,' Victorinus scoffed. 'What I'm saying Pastor, is while there are men like Maximus in the world, men like your father even, we'll always be looking over our shoulders, swords pointing at our own, rather than out in to the unknown, as they used to in the glory days.' Victorinus had been raised on stories of the heroes of old. Caesar conquering Gaul, Scipio vanquishing Hannibal, he could go on. They filled their history with famous generals, men who had led vast armies out in to the unchartered world, and forced Rome's rule on them. That was how he, a Briton born to native parents, had been raised a Roman, after all. Nothing lasted forever. He knew that well enough. He just had a sinking feeling Rome was living on borrowed time. The ruined fortress was proof of that in his eyes.

'You going to stand there daydreaming all day, or are we going to eat?' Drost chipped in, turning from them and heading to the fire.

They ate. A thin porridge with less flavour than the water it was cooked in. Victorinus remained sombre, lost in dark thoughts. 'So you going to tell me why I'm here,' Drost said, when he'd finished eating. He licked his wooden spoon dry, eyes not leaving Victorinus.

'I've heard word that your cousins are plotting a move south once more,' Victorinus said, swirling his spoon around his watery porridge. He had no appetite. 'And I was wondering if that were the case why you had not given me a heads up. We're old friends, after all.'

Drost sucked his teeth. He waved off his men after shaking his head. Eight he'd brought with him, couldn't have a chief making his own breakfast, after all. 'I've heard nothing of this,' he said quietly, checking his men were out of earshot. Victorinus doubted they spoke Latin, anyway.

'You sure? No messages have reached you regarding a meet point for the tribes? No signs of anyone stocking up on food, forging more weapons?'

He shook his head. 'Nothing. I would have told you if there had been. Besides, aren't you the go to man with the tribes? Surely Maximus would have sent you north to investigate if he was concerned?'

'I thought so, too. Instead, he sent me to Londinium on some fool's errand and had one of his trusted generals come north. Apparently anyway. Something's going on. I just don't know what it is.'

Drost was silent for a while. Victorinus could tell there was something his old friend was holding back, some hidden truth he was weighing in his mind. He was just thinking of the best way to extract it from him when he heard a sound. 'What was that?' he said, standing suddenly, his porridge falling to the ground.

'Sounded like a horse,' Pastor said through a mouthful of oats, though he rose too.

'Where did you leave your mounts?' Drost asked, his axe once more in hand.

'Down the road in a thicket of trees. Thought it might be best to make a quiet entrance.'

'It maybe you need a quick exit.' Drost turned to his men, calling them to him. Together, the eight warriors jogged to their leader, heads cranking left and right as they sought enemies in the shadows. Victorinus was just beginning to think they were making a fuss over nothing when he heard something *hiss* through the air, and one of Drost's men collapsed, an arrow sticking through his chest.

'Swords!' Victorinus bellowed, rasping his own free and hurling past Drost's men and out in to the open. He knocked over the pot bubbling on the cooking fire as he sprang forward, sparks hissing, flames growing behind him. His eyes squinted with the sudden shock of sunlight. He saw the flash of a blade just in time and rolled away to his left, his shoulder grating on rubble. He staggered back to his feet with a wince. Turning back, he just had time to take in the features of a topless man with long dark hair and a braided beard, sword in one hand, axe in the other. The man swung for him once more, the axe coming down from high. Victorinus took the blow on his shield, grunted as the pain of the impact lanced up his arm to his shoulder. Feeling the axe bite on the wooden board, he twisted the shield, forcing his opponent to relinquish his grip on the axe. With a snarl, he slammed the shield hard in to the warrior's face, before lunging low to high with his sword, burying the blade in the man's stomach.

More warriors streamed through the ruined streets, the air alive with their war cries. Drost leaped past Victorinus, swiping at one man with his axe before turning, twisting in an arc to cleave his blade in to another. Then Pastor was there, his own cry on his lips, driving his sword through a chest before kicking the man to the ground. Drost's warriors joined the fray, hacking and slashing their way to their chief, forming a ring around him.

Victorinus knocked the axe off the front of his shield and raced to catch up with Pastor. He locked his shield together with the younger man's and they moved forward as one. Three enemy warriors spotted them, and fanning apart, approached them in a half crouch. 'You take the one on the right, I'll take the one in the middle,' Victorinus said quietly.

'That leaves one open on your flank,' Pastor said back through a heavy breath.

'You let me worry about him. We go on three. One, two-

'Wait! On three? Or one, two, three, then go?'

'Oh, just go!' Victorinus bellowed and ran forward. He made it three steps before tripping over a wedge of rock half buried in the soil. With a curse he fell forward, his momentum sending him crashing in to the warrior he'd been charging. He bounced off the warrior, tumbled to the ground. Staggering back to his feet, he realised he'd lost the grip of his sword and had just a shield to hand. He heard a cry to his left and turned to see the third of his attackers charging him. He dropped to a crouch, braced, and took the impact of the warrior's charge on his shield. Grunting through gritted teeth, he pushed back on his shield, feeling the give in the other man. Judging the timing, he took a step back, felt the pressure release on his shield, and then lifted the shield up, the bottom rim facing his enemy. Snarling, he rammed the rim in to his opponent's neck, once, twice, three times, crushing the man's windpipe. He dropped to the ground, hands to his throat, gurgling a terrified scream.

Victorinus, still alert, dropped back into a crouch and turned. Where was the man he had fallen in to? Pastor had downed his man, and stood over the corpse, wiping his blade on the dead man's trousers. Victorinus found his missing opponent, eventually. He was lying flat on his back, Victorinus' sword through his chest. Not exactly how he'd planned it, but a win is a win any day.

Drost and his warriors were fighting in a half circle, a crush of men hammering their shields. Victorinus wrenched his blade from the unfortunate corpse and half ran, half staggered, to his friend. He added his shield to the right side of their line, felt Pastor do the same beside him. Then it was the heaving of the shield wall, the spitting and cursing, the impatient wait for an opening. Twice Victorinus tried to bring his sword to bear, but he couldn't get it past Pastor, crushed to his right as he was. With a curse, he flung the sword to the ground behind him, and quick as his old bones would let him, squatted down and hefted a rock from the ground. He tested the weight of it in his hand, and with a grin, punched the rock over the rim of his shield, and felt the satisfying crunch of a nose breaking on the other end.

The warrior with the crushed face fell away, and Pastor, quick as a market thief, slipped in through the gap and drove his sword through the side of his nearest opponent. Victorinus surged forwards too, battering a man with his shield before doing the same with the rock. Then Drost was up with them, and his men were pouring around their flanks, blades scything through the last of their attackers.

Victorinus lowered his shield and leant on it, content to let the younger men finish the job. He sucked in air, spat blood from a blow to the face he didn't remember taking, and felt the muscles in his left shoulder spasm. *Too old for this shit.*

Pastor handed him his sword. The lad had cleaned the blade, which was good of him. 'The fuck was that all about?' Drost said, oddly cheery. 'I'm all for a good scrap in the morning, but I've got to say I wasn't expecting that!' He pulled the stopper from a wineskin, took a long drink before offering it to Victorinus. 'Not my thing these days,' he said with a shake of the head.

'Gods below, you really have changed, haven't you?' Drost said, a wry grin fixed on his bloody face.

'For the better, I hope.' Victorinus winced as he straightened himself back up, his back protesting. 'Who do we think these are, then?'

Drost stood over a corpse, prodding it with his axe. 'They're not Caledonians, that's for sure. No tattoos, no tribal markings. Plus, their skin is fairer, and our men don't wear long beards like these.'

'So they're not your people, they're not our people. Who are they? And what are they doing here?' Victorinus spoke, but in his mind he was back in Maximus' command room, the *Dux's* eyes twinkling as he shared a look with one of his German generals. 'And how did they know we were going to be here?'

One of Drost's warriors was speaking, pointing and shouting to his chief. 'My man there says they came from the east. There's a bunch of horses tethered outside the walls. Looks like they knew where they were going, and who they were looking for.'

Victorinus shook his head to clear it before nodding. 'Any of your lads here a tracker?'

'Aye,' Drost said. 'Alec here is one of our best. We have none to match the great Halfhand, mind. But Alec could follow their trail back, see where they came from.'

'Then let's pack up and be gone. I need to know who these bastards were, and who they're working for.'

Drost laughed. 'I'm not some trooper for you to order around any more, *sir*. I've a tribe to lead. People look up to me.'

'How lost they must be,' Victorinus said, and they both laughed. 'Drost, if there are men north of the Wall, Saxones, Franks, whoever, then we *both* need to know.'

Drost nodded with a sigh, rubbing a hand through his beard. 'Aye. I suppose you're right. And the gods themselves know who that smoke is going to attract,' he pointed back to their cooking fire, now a raging torrent of heat, thick black smoke billowing up in to the air. Wood must have got caught in the blaze when Victorinus hurled the cooking pot over. 'You two get yourselves ready, and go fetch your horses,' he said to Victorinus and Pastor. 'I'll get my boys ready to go. Looks like we've a long day ahead of us.'

'A long year, potentially,' Victorinus said quietly, before sheathing his sword and heading south, off to get Amor.

VI

'So how many mules do we need for all the carts?'

'Let me see. We have nine thousand pounds of grain, with approximately five hundred pounds on a cart, so eighteen in total. Two mules per cart but remember they won't travel fast lugging that much weight, and you're looking at thirty-six mules.'

Felicius sighed, rubbed at his face. Felt like all he did these days was sigh and rub his face. 'And if we need them to travel faster?'

'Well, we can purchase double the amount of mules, though I'm told that they are in high demand at the moment.'

'Are they really?' Felicius remarked sarcastically. 'Funny how everything we need is suddenly in *high demand* right now. Ain't that just fucking hilarious!' He kicked at a stool before remembering he was barefooted, and winced at the shard of pain that rippled from his toes and shot up his leg. 'Fuck it!'

'Yes indeed. By the way, mother has asked me to remind you to watch your language when you are around me,'

Marcelina said sweetly, an angelic smile fixed to her face. 'And we wouldn't want her to be offended, would we?'

Felicius had spent three days in Vindolanda interviewing clerks for the role of his assistant. He'd discarded a retired teacher as being too old, a pox marked youth who was the son of some high born that sat on a council in Londinium as being too young, and a host of other applicants just for being irritating. In the end, just as he thought the ordeal was over, one last applicant had knocked on his door. His daughter.

'You sure you don't want to learn the ways of a smithy? You know Marcus out in the *vicus* owes me a favour or two. I could have you as his apprentice in no time.'

Marcelina pursed her lips in to a perfect little pout. 'And miss out on all this valuable father daughter time? Honestly, father there is nowhere else I'd rather be.' She fixed that sweet smile of hers back on her face, twiddled with the stylus she was using to write on the wax tablet.

Felicius sighed again, rubbed his face again. 'Buy the mules at whatever price you can get them. At least I'll have the grain sorted for when the *Dux* gets here tomorrow. We will have the mules here by tomorrow, right?'

'Father, I've already bought them.'

'You're a good girl,' he said, and ruffled her hair. If he was honest, it seemed to work out well having her around. She was smart, articulate, good at math, and meticulous in her accounts. In the satchel she wore over her shoulder were six tablets, each one documenting one thing or another, whether it be food stores or weapons. Also, it seemed having a young lady with a winning smile negotiate with the various farmers and traders to top up their supplies worked a treat. She'd got much better prices for spare swords, shields, cloaks and boots than he ever would had he haggled alone. She'd taken some of the weight that had been burying him, and for that, he was eternally grateful.

'The one issue we still have is spare tunics. Seems they can't produce them quick enough. Plus, there's the obvious supply issue with the wool.'

Felicius arched an eyebrow. 'Obvious?'

Marcelina's turn to sigh. 'Father, where do you think we get most of our wool from in Britannia?'

'Good God girl, have you not spent enough time with me over the last few days to realise I've no idea where anything comes from! I train men for war, all of,' he flapped his hands, '*this* has never been my problem before!'

Marcelina tutted. 'Honestly, father I am surprised. All my life you've seemed so in control. Turns out you've no idea what was going on half the time.'

'I am in control of my cohort!'

'You are? Where did all their food come from? The clothes they wore? The shields they battered to kindling under your command?'

He puffed out his cheeks. 'Honestly, never given it much thought before.'

'They came from your quartermaster, who retired last year. Your new one is young and in no way ready to fill in for him, not that you've noticed. Vitulus had to step in last month when he noticed there were no spare spears in the armoury.'

'He did? He's a good man.'

'Better than you deserve, I'd wager. Now back to the wool. It comes from the Caledonians, of course! We trade it with them at the gates along the Wall. They take silver and iron, pelts of fur or basic utensils they cannot make themselves in return. It is the way it has worked for a generation or more. And obviously we are planning a war against the Caledonians...'

'So they have stopped bringing their wool south. How long has this been going on for?'

'Supply dried up in the middle of summer, apparently.'

'How do you know this and I don't?'

'I asked,' she said with a shrug. 'If you don't ask the right questions, you won't get the right answers. Isn't that what you always told me?' She had that sweet smile on her face again, though this time Felicius didn't think she looked quite so cute.

'Back to the wool. Has anyone actually spoken to the traders along the Wall? Asked if they've seen anything different, heard anything?'

'Pretty sure that isn't my job. And wouldn't Maximus have got someone to do that? How did he find out about the planned attacks in the first place?'

'Hmm,' Felicius mused. 'That's what concerns me.' He walked, still barefoot, across the chamber and opened the door. Sunlight spilled in. He glanced up at the sky, judging the position of the sun. It was early yet. 'Go prepare a couple of horses. You and I are going north.'

***

The fortress of Aesica loomed before them as a weak afternoon sun fought a losing battle to exert dominance in the clear sky. It was bitterly cold; the wind howling from the north, rolling off the slope their horses climbed at a walk. Felicius had a century of men with him, under the command of centurion Vitulus. It had been a spur of the moment decision, and he wasn't entirely sure why he made it. But something made him feel uncomfortable about being this close to the frontier with just his daughter.

'Your orders once we are inside, sir?' Vitulus asked, wheezing as he climbed.

Felicius smiled down at his second in command. 'You're not out of breath, are you centurion? Don't let the men see, they might begin to think you're mortal after all.' The men could hear him well enough, and Felicius knew it. He smiled as he heard the muffled laughs of the auxiliaries. It was good for morale, he'd always thought, for the common soldiers to know their officers as men as well as superiors. He knew the name of every soldier in his cohort, their backgrounds, the names of their families. Every day he spent at least an hour mingling, shaking hands and making small talk. He was well respected, he knew, and he thought that made them fight all the harder when called upon. Though he was not perfect, he thought, and clearly he needed to invest some more of his time with his new quartermaster, as well as the many clerks that kept the administration of the cohort ticking over. How long would the respect from his men last if their pay was late, or there was no equipment for them, after all? He looked over at his daughter, riding easily beside him, and his smile came back. He was learning from her already.

'I need to speak with the traders. I assume they'll have their stalls up around the gate. I want you to speak with the decurion, or someone higher if there is. I need to know if the man has seen anything suspicious recently, anything out of place. The decurion, what's his name again?' The unit at Aesica was the *Ala II Asturum,* another wing of Spanish horse, like Felix's own *Ala I Hispanorum Asturum.* Though as Felix was fond of saying, his men were the First Asturians, and those at Aesica were the second.

'Avius Tullus, sir. We dined with him last year when his men came south on rotation.'

Felicius clicked his fingers. 'Aye, that's the man! Seemed a decent sort, don't you think? Felix spoke well of him too, if I remember rightly.'

'He fought for Valentinus in the rebellion,' Vitulus said.

'Aye, though, so did most of the units in the north. Besides, that was sixteen years ago or more, and we won! They were lied to, misinformed, and led astray. Do not hold that against him.'

'I'll do my best, sir,' Vitulus said through ragged breaths.

Felicius' face sagged to a frown as he looked at his senior centurion. He was old, Felicius realised, perhaps for the first time. God, Felicius himself was the wrong side of fifty, his body sitting snug under his armour, coated in an extra layer of fat. In the past, a brewing war would have stirred excitement within him. A chance to prove himself, to claim the next promotion, climb another rung up the never ending ladder. In his latter years, though, it just filled him with fear. His stomach knotted in worry for his wife and daughter. What would happen to them if he were to fall in battle? Maximus would do nothing for them, that much he knew. Sixtus would see they were ok, but what if he were not around also? He looked once more to his daughter. He would need to speak to her about marriage at some point. A young lady needed a husband.

The south gate of Aesica opened as they approached, a sentry on the battlement waving them in. *They don't look concerned,* Felicius thought as he rode under the arch. Inside was a picture of serenity, as familiar to a soldier as the face of his mother. Smoke curled up into the freezing air from the ovens lining the south wall. The stables were a bustle of activity, two hundred horses or more kicking up dust. No one came to greet them, which Felicius at first thought odd, and then a little rude. He was a prefect of Rome, after all.

He was about to dismount and march to the *praetorium*, give decurion Tullus a piece of his mind when a clutch of men appeared around a corner, shuffling hurriedly towards them. 'Prefect Felicius, what a pleasant surprise!' the lead man called. He was short and slim, sand coloured hair trimmed short and a livid scar running down his right arm. 'My apologies sir, I was taking a bath, had the men out on drill all morning.'

Felicius smiled and relaxed, relieved to see some form of discipline in evidence after all. 'No apology necessary, decurion. It is good to see you again. I would have sent word ahead of my arrival, but I'm rather acting on a whim.'

The decurion saluted once Felicius had dismounted, and the prefect saw with amusement the damp patches on the man's tunic. They had clearly summoned him straight from the bath. 'You remember my centurion, Vitulus, I assume? Good. He has some questions for you, if that's alright. You're not in trouble,' Felicius held out a calming hand as Tullus was about to speak. 'But we've heard rumours of trouble brewing in the north. I'm here to follow up some leads. Do you have a local man? Someone that could accompany me if I go and speak to some of the tradesmen?'

'Y-yes sir,' Tullus stumbled. 'We've a lad called Kinnid. He's the son of our cartwright. He can show you who's who.'

'Fetch him for me, would you? I've heard many good things about the Second Asturians. I'll be pleased to report back to the *Dux* that they're all true,' he said with a wink, hoping to calm the man.

The decurion hurried off, revealing another large damp patch on the back of his tunic. Vitulus stood the men down and told them to find themselves some food and drink. 'No getting pissed though, you're still on duty,' he said to a resounding groan. Felicius grinned. Before long, a gangly youth with a crop of blonde hair and a freckle covered face was ushered in front of him.

'You are Kinnid?' Felicius asked. The youth nodded, wide blue eyes quivering as his hands fidgeted nervously. 'Tullus tells me you know your way around this fort, I'd like you to be my guide if that's ok? There's a few coins in it for you.' Kinnid relaxed at this, showing two rows of crooked yellow teeth between his smile. 'Take me to the market stalls.'

He and Marcelina left their mounts with a groom, and followed Kinnid through the narrow streets of Aesica. Men and horses bustled across the cobbles. Felicius caught the aroma of spices, saw the colours of them in the open jars, tanned skinned traders making their way back south, their business for the day concluded. Ox carts laden with pelts and furs trundled north, the air alive with the sounds of the traders' greetings, both good natured and explicit. He smiled at it all, at the business of it. This was frontier life as he knew and loved. Back when serving in the western field army, he'd seen entire flotillas of traders meet in the middle of the Danube. Men from the far east exchanging good natured banter with their German counterparts, standing as equals and exchanging their wares, before going home knowing they'd done a good day's work. This was the Rome he knew and loved. This was how they conquered, how they 'Romanised' those on the outside. The army was there for when this option failed, of course, but in his mind, it should only be used as a second option. Peace should always be the priority.

'Tell me about this place, Kinnid,' he said as they passed the worst of the traffic.

The lad shrugged. 'Not much to tell, really.'

'Tell me about all this!' Felicius waved his hands at the multitude of people pressing around them. 'I want to know everything. Who are all these people? How long do they stay for? When's the busiest time of year?'

Kinnid coughed, Felicius thought he looked a little overwhelmed. He guessed it would be the same as him explaining the role of a prefect to a child. Where would you begin?

'Well sir, we do a lot of trade with the Caledonians, obviously.'

'What do they like to buy?' Marcelina cut in.

Kinnid puffed out his cheeks. 'All sorts, really. They buy tin and iron from the mines here in Britannia, though as I'm sure you know, we're only allowed to sell them a certain amount a year.'

'Why?' Marcelina asked.

'So they can't make too many weapons, keep up kid,' Felicius said with a wink. 'You're meant to be the clever one.' She screwed up her face and stuck out her tongue.

'Herbs and spices are always popular. Some of the traders come all the way from Persia! Takes them months to get here, so they say. Not much call for jewellery or pretty stuff in general. The tribes ain't bothered about that stuff. They're more interested in grain, and you know, practical things.'

'Go on,' Felicius encouraged him, pleased the lad was speaking with more confidence.

'Well, you know, ploughs and wagons, spare axles and wheels—that's where my papa earns most of his coin. Said he's never been as busy as he has the last year or so.'

Felicius shared a look with Marcelina, clicked his tongue before speaking. 'So the Caledonians have a sudden need for carts, do they?'

Kinnid shrugged. 'Can't say I know for certain, sir, but that's what my papa says. We've even got a new roof on our house now. Barely any water gets in when it rains,' he said through a grin. 'Papa says he's never been so busy.'

'How much iron is on a plough?' Marcelina asked, her eyes locked on her father. Felicius raised his eyebrows. The thought hadn't even occurred to him. 'Quite a bit, I think,' Kinnid said. 'Weighs a ton when you're putting one together.'

'Your father makes those too?'

'Not so much. He does the framework occasionally, but mainly he makes carts.'

They were at the north gate, the tide of people ebbing. Felicius noted more people were moving south than north, the sun beginning its descent in the west. He hoped he wasn't too late. 'Take us to your father,' he said to Kinnid, thinking it a good start point.

Kinnid's father was a round bellied man named Marroc, with thinning hair and yellow stumps for teeth. He showed them off proudly as he grinned at his son, wiping a dirty hand on the front of his tunic before offering it out to Felicius. 'Pleased to meet you, sir. Rarely we have men of your class up this way. Can I offer you anything? Ale? No wine, I'm afraid, not on my wages!'

Felicius took the man's hand and returned the smile, politely declining the offered drink. 'I have a few questions for you, if you don't mind. About your work.'

Marroc puffed out his cheeks, an edge of concern in his voice as he spoke. 'All above board, I can assure you, sir. Pay my taxes on time every year.'

'I have no doubt, and I am not accusing you of doing anything wrong. The military has received concerning reports about a possible tribal army moving south. I need to know if you've seen or heard anything suspicious. Your son says you've recently had an uptake in work?'

'Aye, haven't I just.' Marroc put his hands on his hips, rocked back and forth on his feet. 'Picked up end of spring last year and hasn't stopped, really. Most years me and the wife make sure to put a bit of coin aside each month in the summer. Work usually dries up as the weather turns and the rain sets in. Fewer people out on the road, see. Less people on the road, less carts are damaged. I usually make less than half in the winter what I do in summer. But this year,' he whistled, rocked back and forth once more, 'I've not stopped. If it wasn't for young Kinnid here helping me out, not sure I'd have kept up.'

'And is there any reason for the upturn in work? What are the tribesmen saying?'

'Is it the same people coming back to you? Or people from the same tribe?' Marcelina cut in.

Marroc rocked again, hands still on hips. 'Now, the Caledonians don't exactly speak our tongue, and I don't exactly speak theirs. We can communicate enough for me to understand what they need, and for them to understand the price. But any more than that,' he shrugged, face set in a thin smile. 'As for who they are, can't say I pay too much attention, to be honest. Lot of the work has been for new carts, though, big ones too.'

'Was it more repair work before last spring?' Felicius probed.

'Aye, people out there,' he pointed to the vast expanse of the north, 'they've never seen the value in coin. Used to be I'd repair a cart in exchange for wool, or live sheep even! I'd sell them on in the markets here, and that's how I earned my grain. Now though, now they seem to have realised the worth of silver.'

Felicius pursed his lips, his mind racing. 'What sort of silver?'

'Well, *denarii*, of course. Wouldn't take any other kind. They're new coins too. Have the divine Gratian on them.'

That took Felicius by surprise. Even he wasn't paid in coins stamped with the face of the newest ruler of the west. 'Could I see one?'

Marroc, thoroughly confused, reached in to a pouch at his waist and handed it over. Felicius felt the weight in his hand, turning it to see the imprint of the emperor. He grabbed an end in each finger, and gently as he could, tried to bend the coin. He felt the give immediately. With a smile, he handed it back. 'Where do you think they're getting these coins from?' he asked.

Marroc frowned. 'Well, from us, surely?'

'How do you mean?'

'They give us wool, we pay them with coin? Sorry, sir, I'm a simple cartwright. I don't think I follow your lead?'

Felicius reached out and clapped the man on the shoulder. 'Not to worry, you've been very helpful.' He reached in to his own purse, pulled out four coins and handed them to Marroc. 'For your time. I need your son for a while longer. I trust you can spare him?'

They walked amongst the stalls and merchants, sparing a word here, a coin there. The local *sutore,* a cobbler with a face as hard as the iron nails he forged and sold, told them that supply was all but drying up after the Caledonians had cleared his stockroom. 'If there's no more iron brought up soon, I'll struggle to see next winter,' the man grumbled in to his beard, back hunched over a small fire to keep him warm.

They walked and talked for another hour or so, listening to each tradesman tell their own story. The *scutarius,* the resident shield maker for the Second Asturians, said that stock of hides was so low he couldn't make another ten shields even if ordered by the *cornicularius,* the chief administrator of Aesica. 'Where has it all gone?' Felicius asked, puzzled.

'North,' the man said with a shrug. 'Hides are used for covers on carts, as well as a hundred other things. For all I know, they use them to keep the rain from their huts.'

'Can you not get more stock from elsewhere on the island? Surely we have warehouses full of them in Londinium?'

Another shrug. 'The *cornicularius* says no. Forgive me sir, but I can only go with what I'm told.'

The weak sun waned in the west as they made their final tour of the stalls outside the north gate. Felicius was pleasantly surprised to see Centurion Alaric of the Heruli wander out, his face set in a frown as he scanned the northern horizon. 'Alaric, good to see you, man!' Felicius said, feeling his spirits rise. If the Heruli were here, then so was Victorinus, and he could do with seeing his old friend, sharing some of the weight that sat heavy on his shoulders. 'Whatever is the matter? You look like you've not passed a turd in weeks! Where is Sixtus?'

Alaric did not reply at first, just extended an arm and pointed north. A black column of smoke rose lazily into the winter air, curling its way up to the darkening sky. 'The prefect went north, with just his lad Pastor. Told me he'd meet me here tonight. But he ain't here, and...' he trailed off, arm still pointing north.

Felicius felt a sense of foreboding wash over him, seeing the dark smoke rise. It brought back memories of a rebellion sixteen years ago, of a land ravaged by war. 'Sixtus,' he whispered, praying to every god he could think of that his friend was unhurt. 'Ready your men, centurion,' he said, turning to Alaric. 'We're going north.'

VII

They'd been riding three days. Victorinus was sore from his neck to his toes, his legs tingling as the feeling in them came and went. He was old, too old, and unfit. Despite the freezing temperatures and bitter winds, he sweated by the bucket under his armour, and could already feel a bit more give in the tight space between his mail and skin. *Least I'm losing weight*, he thought to himself as his stomach growled in hunger once more.

They'd not brought provisions for a long trip, Pastor and he, and it seemed Drost hadn't either. Game was thin along the northern border of the Wall, the odd hare appearing from the bare branches of the woodland. What they found they killed. Drost's men setting traps as they camped each night.

Their trail had gone cold the evening before. Alec, the tracker, said there was no trace of riders once they'd ridden past Condercum, the former home of Felix and his Spanish horsemen. Victorinus had smiled to see the fortress in the south as he rode, remembering seeing Halfhand on the battlement as he'd ridden up to the gate, right at the start of the great rebellion that had changed their world forever. He missed his friend dearly. Halfhand had been his rock, his closest confident. When his son had died, Halfhand had been there. When Sarai had finally had enough of him, Halfhand had been there. If his life were a raging storm, Halfhand was a rock in the ocean; solid, unmoving, always calm.

He'd not had the time to grieve when his friend died. He'd been too busy trying to stay alive himself. But the tears had come once the fighting stopped. His elation in victory, his moment of triumph, had been taken from him as he mourned the passing of his greatest friend. He grieved for Severus too. The one time marine that had swapped the Rhine flotilla for the northern mountains, another good man, taken too soon. He remembered them both, seeing the walls of Condercum for the first time since their deaths.

Pastor had seen those walls, and Victorinus knew the same thoughts crossed the young man's mind. He'd stared for an age, his expression passing from sadness to anger. He'd had a part in their deaths, after all. Victorinus had tried to summon the words for the lad then, but tiredness and hunger gnawed at his brain, and he could think of nothing worth speaking out loud.

'We'll have to stop soon,' Drost said to him, the chief reigning in his horse so it cantered alongside Victorinus.

'Aye, guess we will,' he said absently, stroking Amor's head as the horse ambled on. She would be hungry too, Victorinus knew, the oats he'd had in the pouch of his saddle long gone now. 'We need food and shelter, not sure I can take another night out in the cold.'

He felt his spirits sag. There had been a purpose to their journey at the start; a trail to follow, an enemy to hunt. Now it seemed pointless. Looking north, to his left, the grass lands swept on for an eternity. Who was it they were even looking for? An errant tribe of Saxones that had ventured too far inland? Might as well throw a nail in the forest, there'd be more chance of finding the nail.

He was halfway to giving in to the despair that weaved dark thoughts through his mind when Pastor came hurtling down the road at the gallop. 'Sir!' he said excitedly through heavy breaths. 'Alec and I have found a small farmstead up ahead. They're willing to let us pay for food and wine, and said there's an empty barn for us to shelter in for the night.' He beamed at Victorinus, and the tribune couldn't help but smile back at the lad. Happiness was infectious, after all.

'Damn fine work, Pastor!' Victorinus said, reaching over and slapping the lad on the shoulder. 'Just like you to pull something out the bag when we need it most!'

'Let us not dally, then!' Drost said, a grin fixed to his own face. 'Warm food, a fire, and wine! Come, Pastor, lead the way!'

It was a mile or so to the farmhouse. They covered it at the gallop. Before the sun had set, they had their mounts brushed down, nuzzles buried in troughs of oats. Amor's tail swished from side to side as she ate greedily, and Victorinus rejoiced at the sight. The food on offer was meagre enough, just stale bread, hard cheese and a couple of hares the farmer had snared, but spirits were high around the cooking fire, as flagons of cheap wine were passed from warrior to warrior, each man at a loss for when they had last eaten so well.

Victorinus abstained from the wine, hard as it was. He didn't think there would ever be a time his brain wouldn't urge him to relapse, to become the drunken failure of a man he had once been. He just smiled at the familiar ache, the tremble in his fingers. He was the master of his own destiny, no longer a slave to his desires. He thought of his sons, back home with their mother, if they'd not set off for the Wall yet. Everything he did, whether declining the offer of a cup, or fighting a rebellion, he did for them. Might have been too late for him and Sarai, but it would never be too late to be a father to his children. He contended himself with an extra piece of bread and walked off in to the night to a nearby stream to fill his water skin.

It was pleasantly mild for a winter's night, the absence of the wind a welcome change. The farmhouse was in a small valley, and Victorinus could appreciate why it had been built there. No wind in the winter, less of the harsh sun in the summer. He breathed in deep and savoured the taste of the night air. He could make out the silhouette of the farmer, edging out of his home to check on the barn. Victorinus smiled. The man was probably nervous at what state it would be left in come daybreak. He knew he would have been, after all. The farmer watched the barn for what seemed a long while, then walked off back to his home. He did not enter it though, but walked past his door and around the back. Victorinus frowned, skin prickling on the back of his neck.

After a moment of contemplation, he scoffed a laugh at himself. The man could be doing any number of things, checking on live stock, getting more wood for his fire, anything. It was no business of his. The farmer had given up his barn, his hard earned food and wine, and Victorinus had seen him well paid for it. The man had seemed a decent sort, though his Latin was clumsy and conversation had been limited. Shaking his head at himself, he put the stopper in his water skin and trudged back to the barn, suddenly bone weary. Stifling a yawn, he was just entering when something stopped in his tracks. Or more to the point, the *absence* of something. Noise.

The night was as still as stone. From within, he could hear the crackling of the fire, but nothing else. Where were the shouts and chatter of the men? The snorts and grunts of the mounts? Alarmed, he heaved open the door and almost fell inside. Looking around, he found himself frozen in confusion. It seemed in the short time it had taken him to walk to the stream, everyone had passed out.

It's not possible, he thought, looking at the sleeping forms of Drost and his men. He had been gone no time at all, a quarter of an hour at most. Surely it wasn't possible? They were all tired, for sure, weary from their long days in the saddle. But for them all to pass out, at the same time, just moments after Victorinus left them? Impossible.

A noise outside alerted him, the crunch of footsteps on the frozen ground. Quick as thought, Victorinus shuffled through the barn, in to the small stall that housed Amor. He leaped over his sleeping steed and buried himself into her, concealing himself from the door. He focused on his breathing, heart thumping so hard and fast he could hear it. Slowly, breath after breath, he got himself under control. With a squeal of hinges, the barn door opened, and the footsteps moved inside. He tried to make out how many men there were, but it was too many to count.

'How long will they sleep for?' a deep voice said in heavily accented Latin.

'Five or six hours at least,' another replied. The farmer, Victorinus realised. He cursed. So that's what the farmer was checking on when he'd walked over to the barn. These men must have been hidden the other side of his house. So now he knew where the farmer had gone afterwards. The only positive thing Victorinus could think of was that the farmer had not seen him.

'Get the carts,' the first voice spoke again. 'You did the mounts too?'

'I... I wasn't sure if I was meant to,' the farmer said, a quiver in his voice.

The first man laughed. 'Will they die? No? Well, I have no need of them. Butcher them for meat if you wish, keep them, whatever.'

Instinctively, Victorinus reached out and stroked Amor. He could feel her heartbeat, strong and steady. No one would be butchering her. He forced himself to stay perfectly still, feeling the cold seep in to his bones. His hands grew stiff, his left leg numb as he lay on it awkwardly, though he dare not move. He heard the cart brought up, the restlessness of the horses that pulled it. Men walked in to the barn, and one by one Drost and his warriors were picked up and thrown on to the cart. 'How many are there?' the first man spoke again.

'Nine,' another replied.

'We were expecting ten?' Victorinus could sense all eyes going to the farmer, and he imagined the man squirming under their gaze. 'I was told ten men entered this barn?'

'None have left. I've kept an eye on them, as you ordered,' the farmer replied, his voice a terrified squeak.

The first man spoke again, this time in a language Victorinus did not understand, and once more he heard the shuffle of feet on the frozen ground outside as they searched for the missing man. For him. Then he had a fresh fear. The crunch of feet on the frozen grass. Had Victorinus left footprints on his walk to the stream and back? If he had, there was nothing he could do about it now. He tried to calm his panicked thoughts. There would be a multitude of prints on the ground leading to the barn now. It would not be possible for them to determine which was which. He hoped.

The men were back before long. Another conversation in the foreign tongue followed. 'You are certain none left?' this directed at the farmer.

'Y-yes. I was watching the barn the whole time.'

Silence spread through the barn. Victorinus held his breath, blood thumping thick in his ears. What if they searched the barn? How long until they found him? As slowly as he could, he moved his right hand down to his hip, grasping for the hilt of his sword. It wasn't there. With a silent curse, he remembered leaving it on the barn floor, next to where he and Pastor had been sitting. He had a short sword, an old style *gladius* strapped to the side of Amor's saddle. But her saddle had been removed, thrown over a hook by by the barn door. 'Then we have made a mistake. Maybe we killed one more of them at that fort than we thought!' the voice said, though Victorinus could tell there was an edge to it still, as if the man didn't quite believe what he was saying. 'We will leave now, but do not forget what we have. If any Romans come this way asking questions, what will you say?'

'I-I have seen no one, nothing,' the farmer said in a quivering voice. 'Please, my family-

'Will stay where they are safe. We shall return them to you when we are done, as promised.'

With that, the cart stirred into movement, and Victorinus listened once more to the crunch of feet on the ground as his friends were taken away.

The farmer sobbed when they were gone. Victorinus heard the man slump to his knees as he wailed, cursing every god under the sun. Seemed like an age passed, Victorinus still lying on the sleeping Amor. His right leg had gone fully numb, his hands bone white and shivering. He needed to move. As quietly as he could, he shuffled away from Amor, a sharp intake of breath as he was parted from her warmth. Tingling in his dead leg, then acute pain as his blood started moving again, he inched away from the sleeping horse, his back against the barn wall.

Still, the farmer sobbed, sniffing and cursing, banging his hands on the ground. Victorinus' emotions flickered from sadness for the man to anger. He knew all too well the pain it caused having your family taken from you. He had lived through that anguish sixteen years ago. But this man could have done something, *anything*, rather than comply with an enemy of Rome, and see good men taken away to who knew where. He felt his resolve strengthen. He needed to know where his friends were being taken, and quickly.

He slithered out of the stall, boots silent on the barn floor. Edging closer to the farmer in the darkness, he spied his sword lying where he'd left it. At least they hadn't taken that. He crept over to it, the oblivious farmer with his back to him, hunched over on all fours, still crying uncontrollably. Victorinus picked up the sword, sliding it silently from its blue scabbard.

'I suppose you're going to kill me,' the farmer said without turning.

Victorinus paused, taken aback by the words. He'd thought he'd been silent, but then he figured no man, stiff with cold and clad in armour as he was, could truly move silently. 'Reckon I've got a good reason to,' he said, lowering the sword and approaching, stopping when he was three paces from the farmer. Wouldn't do to give the man hope of snatching his blade. 'You poisoned the wine, I assume?'

The farmer sniffed, wiping tears away with the cuff of his tunic. 'Henbane,' he confirmed.

'A dangerous plant to be messing with,' Victorinus said. 'How do you know you've not killed them?'

'M-my wife, she has pain in her back, a curve in her spine no doctor can fix. She uses it to help her sleep. I gave your friends the same dose she takes. They will wake fine and rain, on my word.'

'And the horses?'

The farmer turned, wincing. He was a balding man in his middle fifties, a body run to fat under his tunic and trousers. Strong arms though, Victorinus noticed, the arms of a man that had toiled for a living. 'Never used it on horses before. I had to make a judgement call.' He had ruddy cheeks and a squashed nose, two day stubble on his chin.

'My horse,' Victorinus said, in a quiet, menacing voice, 'is precious to me. If she is to die because of what you have done, I will kill you slowly indeed.'

'So you will not kill me now, lord?' Hope flashed in his eyes. It was the most life Victorinus had seen in him the whole time he'd been there.

'I am no one's lord. What is your name?' Victorinus lowered his sword, taking another step back.

'Darrow, sir,' he said, rising slowly to his feet.

'If you are to live to see another sunrise, you will answer every question I ask with nothing but the truth. Do you understand?' Darrow nodded. 'Who are those men that took my friends?'

'I-I don't rightly know, sir. They came here three days ago, hundreds of them. There were Caledonians too, men with the tribal tattoos on their arms and faces. They took my family from me, said I would get them back if I helped them.'

'You have children?'

'Five sir. A son and four daughters. My wife, she struggles so much with her back. I don't know how she is going to cope without her medication. Do you think they've given her a proper bed to sleep on at least?' Victorinus could see the anguish etched on the man's face, the sheer terror of not knowing. Again, it was something he could sympathise with, but he had to quash that down for now.

'I do not know Darrow. Do you know where they have taken them?'

Darrow shook his head. 'I walked out east, the way they left, the day after they took them. Tracks seemed to go on forever. I was worried they'd find me, think me spying on them, so I came home.'

Victorinus felt an assurance that his early thoughts and Darrow's words were leading him in the same direction. The men were Saxone, or Franks, some tribe or another out of eastern Germania. If they were based in the east, it was likely near the coast, their ships ready to sail at a moment's notice. As to what they were doing landing north of the Wall, he didn't know. Not in his lifetime had he known the Caledonians to suffer raids from across the Narrow Sea, nor for the tribes of Britannia and Germania to share any sort of relationship. There was one other thing bugging him, though. 'How did they know that there would be men coming this way today?'

Darrow shrugged. 'A group of them came by yesterday. Said it was likely there would be men following them back east. When they asked for lodgings for the night, I was to give them what they wanted, and then send them to sleep with the henbane.'

'How did they know about the henbane?'

Darrow hung his head. 'I told them. When they took my Martha, I tried to explain she needed her medicine, but they didn't listen.'

'They heard enough to know it sends a person to sleep, though.'

'Aye, guess they did,' Darrow sighed.

'And they waited, just out of sight, and when you saw my friends were sleeping, you went to get them. That about right?'

Darrow nodded, but said nothing.

'What was it they wanted? Why do they want my friends so badly?'

'Wasn't all of them they wanted, sir. Just one man. Let me think, a tribune, yes, that's it! Said they wanted tribune Sixtus Victorinus, and if I wanted my family back, I was to help them get him.'

Victorinus felt his blood run to ice. He tried and failed to catch his breath, felt himself stagger a step. He hadn't told Darrow his name, hadn't even told him his rank. So if Darrow didn't know who he was, how could some foreign raider from across the sea? 'Sir, are you ok?' Darrow asked, but his voice was distant, an echo in dense fog. Victorinus staggered outside the barn and threw up, the vomit steaming on the frozen ground.

It appeared once again that his homeland was involved in some complex plot. And he was once more at the heart of it.

VIII

The smoke had gone when they arrived. Felicius had wanted to leave immediately, rampaging through Aesica with a worried Alaric scurrying in his wake. Avius Tullus had seemed mortified at the prospect of sending his men out so close to nightfall and had begged Felicius to reconsider and go in the morning. Reluctantly, he had agreed.

He had at his back the full might of the Heruli and the Second Asturians, plus the century of his own men commanded by Vitulus. Still, he felt uneasy. Dawn had broken somewhere, the sun hiding from them behind thick black clouds that rolled in from the east. The cold seeped through his bones, chilling him from the inside out. He shivered, cloak wet through from the rain that had assailed them as they'd left Aesica in the darkness. 'Well, they're not here,' he said, more to distract himself than anything. His wounded thigh ached in the cold, and for a while on the ride up, it was all he could do not to let the pain consume him. He looked back to Vitulus, standing in front of his men, and once more thought of the cruelty of age.

'They were, though,' Marcelina said, moving her horse up beside him. He'd ordered, then pleaded with her to stay at Aesica, and let him ride out without her. He didn't know what they were riding in to, for all he knew there could have been a horde of Caledonians waiting at the fort, swords glinting in the half light. But she was his daughter through and through, and in the end, her persistence, coupled with his desire to be on the road, had paid off.

'How can we know that?'

'Load of dead bodies over there. Reckon that's our first clue.'

'Shit,' he muttered, squinting in to the distance. The fort of Habitancum sprawled before them. Or what was left of it, at least. Felicius had never been there before, and for a moment he thought of how it must have looked in its pomp. A sardonic smile touched his lips as he once more remembered he wasn't exactly in his prime himself. Dismounting, he left his horse with one of the Heruli, and moved slowly amongst the dead. 'Saxone,' a voice said from behind him.

Felicius turned to Alaric, the centurion three paces behind him. 'How can you be sure?'

Alaric shrugged. 'The style of their hair, their clothes. See their faces? Most have heavy moustaches and no beard. They are Saxone, I would wager my life on it.'

Felicius nodded. He knew enough about Alaric to know that if was certain of something, then he didn't need to question it. But what were Saxones doing north of the Wall? 'How long until the *Dux* reaches Aesica?' he asked Alaric.

'Tomorrow afternoon, I would have thought,' Alaric said without hesitation. 'Whether he will want to linger there is another matter.'

Felicius cursed, his mind caught in a vice. Clearly, his friend was in trouble. He had been involved in some sort of fight, and had gone off God knew where. If he was even still alive. He wanted nothing more than to ride off after him, hunt until they were reunited. But on the other hand, he knew the *Dux* would be expecting him at Aesica, and worse, would want reports on the progress Felicius had made on supplying the army. It would be a brief report indeed. *If only I could split myself in two.*

'Vitulus, a word!' he called to his centurion, dismounting and walking to the corpses. 'You stay where you are,' he said to his daughter, wanting to keep her away from as many dead bodies as he could. With Vitulus beside him, they walked the amongst the dead. A warrior with a deep, nine inch cut on his chest lay flat on his back, shield still gripped in a numb hand. "A sword didn't do that," Felicius said.

'Axe,' Vitulus said with a nod. 'Drost,' he added, almost as an afterthought.

'Aye, I was just thinking the same thing.' They walked on further, to a clutch of bodies sprawled almost on top of each other. There were footprints in the mud facing them, three feet away. 'A shield wall stood here,' Felicius said, pointing to the footprints. On the right-hand side of the line of prints, two caught Felicius' eye. 'See the hobnails imprinted on the ground?'

Vitulus moved over, squatted down above them. 'Victorinus here,' he said, pointing out the ones on the left. 'Young Pastor here.'

'So Sixtus came here to meet Drost, a meeting I assume he set up via Pastor. I think that's how they normally do it. Where was the fire?'

'There, sir,' Vitulus pointed to the ruined watchtower, and together they walked towards it. They passed the body of a dead tribesman, marked out by the blue tattoos on the man's head and body. An arrow stuck out of his chest, dried blood staining his belly. Inside the watchtower Felicius could see where the smoke had come from. Someone knocked over a cooking pot, and the flames caught discarded timber and what appeared to be the remains of a fur cloak. 'There are no more dead, I assume?'

'Not that we've found, sir,' Vitulus said.

'So if these men are Saxone, and I've no reason to doubt Alaric, then what are they doing up here? And where have they come from?'

'Must've landed east at some point. Why don't I take some lads and see what I can find?'

Felicius smiled. His old friend was ahead of the curve, as always. 'Just what I was about to say. Take a tent party. Nine of you should be just the right number to do some snooping. Once you have something to report, head to the nearest Wall fort you can. Once you're on our side, you can find out where I am and make a report. Sure you're up to this?'

'Of course, sir,' Vitulus said and sniffed, bringing himself up to his full height.

'I never doubted it, old friend,' he slapped Vitulus on the shoulder, but his smile slipped as the centurion moved away, shouting orders for the men that would accompany him.

'You sure this is wise?' Marcelina at his shoulder. He hadn't heard her approach.

'No. But I don't know what else I'm supposed to do. Did I not tell you to wait back there?'

She shrugged. 'You did.'

'You shouldn't be seeing all of this,' he waved a hand at the bodies littering the ground.

'I've a feeling I'm going to be seeing more of them soon.' She paused, eyes scanning the corpses. 'We should focus on your job,' she said, trying to sound upbeat.

'My job?'

'Supplying ten thousand men and four thousand horse for a winter campaign. Or had you forgotten?'

Felicius sighed. 'How could I? Come on then, let's talk on the road. You can bore me with the details as we ride.'

***

Storm clouds ruled the sky as they rode back through the gate of Aesica. Thunder crackled, lightning following, though there was a reassuring pause between the two. The wind had battered them throughout their ride, with such ferocity even Marcelina had given up trying to speak.

In a warm office, their cloaks drying over a brazier, father and daughter sat down at a desk, sharing a flagon of heated wine. 'So we have enough grain?'

Marcelina nodded. 'We have enough for four weeks. We need any more we are at the mercy of the ships sent to Africa.'

'Have we heard from the *magister officiorum* Pericles Abas?'

'Only to say the ships have departed, but we should not expect them back for two months.'

Felicius clicked his tongue, leaning back in his chair. 'Fine, put grain to one side for the minute. What about shields?'

'Five thousand spares being stored in Eboracum, ready to move north when we need them. They're a mix of oval and round, none of them painted, though I figured that wasn't an immediate concern.' Felicius grunted. 'Our biggest issue now is weapons.'

'How so?'

'There's a shortage of iron. Seems the mines on the island are drying up, and we're awaiting shipments from abroad to deliver more. We have two thousand spare swords, though most are longer cavalry blades. Half of those have no hilt, but we've a blade smith who can do that for us. I've promised him double pay if he gets them all done by the end of next week.'

'Is that even possible?'

Marcelina shrugged. 'No idea. I'm working on the assumption he's sub contracting out some of the work.

Makes sense for him and us. I didn't ask too many questions.'

'Fair enough. Well, each man has a sword. We'll just need to make sure they don't lose them. We can strip them off any we lose in battle, too.'

'An optimistic thought,' Marcelina said, eyebrow arched in amusement.

'If there's a shortage in iron, does that mean there's a shortage of armour?' Can't make mail without it.'

Marcelina nodded. 'Same issue, though we have two thousand spares, and just as each soldier has a sword, they have armour.'

'And we can strip the dead,' Felicius added with a wry grin. He rose from his chair, pulled back the shutter to the window, and recoiled as the wind assaulted him. The rain had not abated, striking the stoned pathway with a fury. 'Best make sure each man knows to take extra care of his kit,' he said, more to himself than Marcelina. He knew too well from experience that winter campaigns were a nightmare for every soldier. Keeping mail and helmets, swords and spear tips rust free was hard enough at the best of times, let alone in the freezing cold when there was a high probability of rain every day. He closed the shutter, slamming it when it didn't close the first time.

Sitting back down, his thoughts turned once more to Victorinus, and the apparent peril he was in. He had almost chewed through his bottom lip on the ride back to Aesica, his mind tumbling with what could have happened to his friend. *Vitulus will find him*, he reassured himself, and tried to make himself focus on what he could control.

'Clothing? Tunics and cloaks? Trousers and socks? Boots too!' he cursed to himself. So much to keep track of.

'We've leather enough for boots, and we've twenty cobblers across the north, hard at work producing as much as they can. They're making two different sizes, so the men will have to make do with whichever fits best. Tunics we now have in abundance, thanks to Abas and his connections in Gaul. Cloaks we have...' Marcelina trailed off.

'I feel a 'but' coming on here,' Felicius said, already grimacing.

'They're not waxed, and we don't have the supplies on the island to get it done.'

'Good God,' Felicius leaned forwards and banged his head on the table. 'I'm going to need more wine.'

'I've written to Abas and asked if he can secure us a supply. We have trained people here that can do the waxing-

'They just need the bloody wax.' Felicius finished his daughter's sentence. 'For every step forward we take, I feel we take another three back. He wondered how many candles there must be in Britannia. Couldn't he just confiscate them all?

'That's because we do,' Marcelina added, winking at her father. 'Surely we can pass on some of this load? Men like Abas, this is their job, right? Why not dump it all on his desk and march off in to the sunset with your men?'

Felicius sighed. 'Because the *Dux* has made it my responsibility, and I need to be aware of everything when he asks—which he will do, either tonight or tomorrow when he arrives.'

'What *exactly* did you do to piss him off? Is this because you were late to repel the raiders in the east?'

Felicius puffed out his cheeks. 'Not sure exactly, but he doesn't seem keen on me or Victorinus. We're not *his* men, if you get my meaning. The generals he surrounds himself with, they're all men he made up. They owe their careers to him, and therefore, in his mind, their loyalty is without question. Sixtus and I, we serve Rome. I have a relationship with Theo in the east, and Maximus and his cousin have never seen eye to eye.'

'Oh, you're friends with the Divine Augustus?' Marcelina mocked a shocked expression. 'You've never mentioned that before!'

'Oh, shut up! You know the two of us are close.'

'Has he replied to the letter you sent him?' Felicius had told his daughter of the correspondence he had been having with Theodosius in the east.

'Not yet. Though I only sent my letter a couple of days ago. He wouldn't have received it yet. What about this mysterious shipment coming in from the east? The one that *Dux* has ordered me to ensure arrives safely in the north. Should have reached Londinium today. Should know by tomorrow, assuming the roads are clear.'

'I wonder what it is,' Marcelina mused. Felicius' own thoughts had strayed to it often in the past days. What could the *Dux* be up to? Clearly it was something Maximus wanted keeping quiet. For the life of him though, Felicius couldn't work out what it could be.

'Wax and iron hopefully,' Marcelina said, and they both laughed.

It was an hour before dawn the next day when Maximus rode through Aesica's southern gate. The *Dux* was bleary-eyed and to Felicius' eye a shade paler than he had been a couple of days before. A rag tag of exhausted men dismounted behind him, Felicius counting three of the men that had been in Eboracum for their briefing. 'Tell me what you've organised so far,' the *Dux* said as a way of greeting. Felicius saluted and filled in his commander on what was organised and what wasn't in Aescia's courtyard, Maximus showing no signs of wanting to get out of the cold. When he was finished, he got nothing but a grunt and a nod before Maximus moved away, already barking orders at someone else.

'I'd take that as a compliment,' Felix said, the Spaniard giving Felicius a weary smile. 'He's been relentless since we set off.'

'When isn't he?' Felicius said. 'How goes it gathering the army?'

Felix grimaced. 'We have two-thirds of the numbers we'd hoped for. Turns out the *Dux* was taking the strength of each unit from the reports the commanders were sending him.'

Felicius scoffed an ironic laugh. 'Surely you're not about to tell me some of our brother officers have been lying about the strength of their men? And therefore the size of the pay chest they require?'

'Who'd have thought it?' Felix grinned. 'Safe to say those officers have been taught a lesson in honesty.'

'I'm surprised they're still casting a shadow.'

'Not sure they would be if it wasn't for the impending war. How goes it with the supplies? Enjoying your role as a grain man?'

Felicius let out a string of expletives strong enough to have Felix recoil. 'You can take that as a no,' he said when he was finished. 'Still, seems I'm doing better than Sixtus is.' He spoke of his trip north of the Wall and what he had found.

'Have you told the *Dux*?'

'No,' Felicius paused. 'Something inside me is telling me not to. Can you think why there would potentially be Saxones north of the Wall? Hardly prime raiding country, is it?'

Felix narrowed his eyes. 'Could have beached further north than they planned? But you're right, the tribes have nothing worth raiding for, especially risking a winter crossing.'

'My thoughts exactly. There is something at play here, and Maximus knows more than he is letting us know.' The two men shared a knowing glance, before Felix declared he was off to the baths. Felicius had half a mind to join him, but was disturbed by a runner making right for him.

'Prefect, sir. Orders from the *Dux*, you are to report to him immediately.'

Felicius scowled. 'I've literally just reported to him, right here, and then he walked off.'

The messenger gave a thin smile and a shrug. 'Just passing on the order, sir.'

With a sigh Felicius gestured for the man to lead the way, and moments later he was back in the office he'd shared with Marcelina. She was there, cowering in the corner, the *Dux* pouring over the notebook she had been keeping. 'Sir, is everything ok?' Felicius asked, throwing a concerned look at Marcelina.

Maximus looked up from the ledger and smiled, though it was as warm as the weather. 'Bumped in to your daughter here. She's been telling me about how she's helping you with your duties.'

Felicius swallowed. 'Aye sir, Marcelina has been keeping records for me, even acting as a go between for myself and some local traders and craftsmen.'

Maximus' smile hadn't dropped. 'I hope you're not slacking in this matter, prefect. Did I not make it clear how important your role was? An army cannot march on an empty stomach, as the old saying goes.'

'Aye, sir. Neither can they march without boots or cloaks, tunics, and helmets. If I'm honest, sir, I found myself a little out of my depth when I started. I was interviewing for a clerk to assist me when Marcelina volunteered for the job. As I said, she has been most useful.'

Still the smile below the cold eyes. 'This seems to match up with what you told me in the courtyard,' he said, gesturing to the ledger.

'Should do, sir. It won't be exact until we have our hands on the promised supplies, but as I said to you outside, we're doing all we can.'

Maximus nodded. With a wave of his hand he dismissed the messenger, who had stood nervously in the corner. He didn't speak until the man shut the door behind him. 'Sit, prefect, and you child,' he said to Marcelina. 'Is there wine? Ahh good,' he smiled again as Felicius passed him a jug. This one at least appeared genuine. 'I find myself exasperated, prefect, and we are just a few days in to this venture.'

Felicius raised his eyebrows, surprised at the admission. He wasn't sure if he was expected to speak. Luckily for him, Maximus carried on. 'We have commanders exaggerating the strength of their men, taking extra coin and leaving their units grossly under manned. The men's kit is in poor repair. Again, money has been issued to replace it, the coin has disappeared, and the broken kit has remained. When did we allow ourselves to fall so low? To become so complacent?' He necked his cup of wine, poured himself another. 'But you at least, are an honest man, are you not, prefect?'

Felicius cleared his throat. 'Yes sir, I try to be.'

'So I can see,' Maximus gestured to the ledger once more. 'Is your daughter aware of the other matter I charged you with?'

'She is, sir,' Felicius nodded. 'The ship should have reached Londinium this morning. We are awaiting confirmation.'

'What are we to do with it once it arrives?' Marcelina chipped in, unable to stay silent any longer.

'That is the question,' Maximus said, a sly grin splitting his face. 'It is rather large, cumbersome.' He necked a second cup of wine and sprang to his feet. 'Here's what we shall do. You two will hand over everything you organised so far to the *magister officiorum* Pericles Abas. You have met him I assume? Good, he and his men will take control of supplying the army.' It's his job anyway, Felicius thought to himself. He could feel Marcelina smile next to him, knew she was thinking the same thing. 'Then you will travel south to Londinium by the quickest route. You will take my delivery into your charge and bring it north. I'll leave you to work out the best way to do it. But I want it in Eboracum within the month, you understand?'

Speechless, Felicius just nodded. 'Good!' Maximus poured more wine, drained it again. Felicius thought he could see some of the tension drain out of the man, a patch of colour return to his cheeks. 'How soon can you be on the road?'

'By tomorrow, sir. What am I to do with my men when I'm gone? I assume you will want them to stay in the north?'

Maximus seemed to chew over the matter. 'Leave them here. Your senior centurion, Vitulus is it? Yes, he's an excellent officer. Leave the command to him.'

'Vitulus is... confined to the hospital at the moment, sir. Having trouble with his stomach. But I have a centurion named Serenas who is very experienced and reliable,' Felicius said with just the slightest pause. He hoped it wouldn't betray his lie.

'Well, send him my best. Vitulus is a fine fighting man. We're going to need him on his feet before too long. Serenas I remember, I'm sure he'll be fine for a week or two. Now you have your orders, get to it prefect.'

And with that, he was dismissed.

IX

They looked like ants from where he crouched. Miniature men scurrying around the shallows in harsh winter waves.

Three days Victorinus had walked east. Hunger gnawed at him, tormented by thirst, but he'd made it to the coast—more or less in one piece. He'd not had the presence of mind to commandeer supplies from Darrow. He'd just left in the darkness, numb hand in a white knuckled grip on his sword.

The wind whipped up at him, causing him to squint as he took in the scene below. A grey beach, brown water lapping in on white-topped waves. That was normal enough. What wasn't was the three ships rocking in the shallows, nor the hundreds of barbarian warriors that scuttled across the sand like bugs discovered hiding beneath a rock.

He laid there an hour or more, the passage of time hard to determine with the sun hidden behind a slate grey sky. Caught in two minds, did he get closer and try to find Pastor and Drost? Or he did he run south, find the *Dux* and come back with an army? Indecision ate in to his mind.

In the end, it was made for him. Eyes streaming in the wind, he saw what looked to be a clutch of prisoners led from a tent in single file. They tripped and staggered as they walked—rope tied around their ankles and wrists. One fell, an audible *thwack* of a whip on his back, delivered before he had the chance to rise. Pastor. Even from that distance, Victorinus could make out his young friend.

He felt a surge of energy build within him, a wave of anger that seemed to warm his blood. Pastor was like a son to him, and there was nothing he would not do to see him safe. Edging back from the clearing he had been watching from, he retreated in to a clutch of trees. It was silent within, eerily so, the wind not strong enough to penetrate the woodland. Victorinus moved slowly over the detritus, his tired mind worried they would hear him even from a great distance. His resurgence of energy lasted fifty paces before his legs failed him and he slumped to the ground. Broken branches littered the ground, one piercing the skin on his left hand as he tried to stagger back to his feet. He cursed, watching in confused terror the blood flowing from the wound. He felt dizzy, nauseous, vision blurring he lay back down, blinking rapidly to clear his eyes.

'Well, look what we've found,' a voice said, the sound thick in his ears. He scrunched his eyes closed, then opened them again, but all he could see was blinding light, a blurred head appearing as if it had floated down from the clouds. 'My commander is going to be well happy with me,' the voice said, and Victorinus could just make out a set of crooked teeth as the head smiled. *No*, he tried to speak, but couldn't. Tried to get up, but a hand on his shoulder held him in place. 'You just stay here. We'll get you to where you need to be.'

He thought of his friends staggering across the beach, their feet tied. He saw Pastor fall again, felt the hot pain of the whip on his back. *No.* He lifted his head a fraction, but it felt like it was made of stone. He slumped back once more, helpless. The last thing he heard was the crunch of feet on the frozen debris, and then he knew no more.

***

He woke to the crackle of a fire, the smell of roasting meat.

For a moment, there was nothing but the disorientation of waking somewhere unfamiliar, his brain working backwards as he tried to remember how he got there. He remembered the barn, the agonising journey east. The hunger, thirst, Pastor being struck with a whip. With a start, he surged up, leaping from the ground, right hand searching his waist for his sword. It wasn't there.

A knife lay by the fire, the bone handle glowing orange in its light. He scrambled forwards and picked it up, eyes wide as he scanned his surroundings, mouth set in a snarl. 'Peace!' a voice called from the darkness. 'Tribune Victorinus, sir! It's ok, you're among friends.'

A figure approached from the shadows, cloaked in blue, armour glistening beneath. Took Victorinus a moment or two to realise he was being spoken to in Latin, and that was probably a good sign. A short time later, he was letting the knife fall to the ground, a shaky smile splitting his cracked lips. 'Vitulus,' he stammered, hands suddenly shaking.

'Aye sir, it's me,' Vitulus said, moving a step closer. Victorinus could see him properly now in the light, his balding head and cheeks covered in two-day grey stubble. His broken nose that seemed almost painted onto his weather-beaten face. 'We found you this afternoon. You seemed in pretty awful shape. Got some water in to you and then me and the lads changed you in to dry clothes, cleaned your armour too. You hungry, sir?'

He was starving. Weak as a babe, he nodded, before slumping down on his arse. 'Thankyou,' he said as another soldier approached him, offered him a steaming bowl and a spoon. 'Meat stew sir, not my best, but it will serve,' the soldier said, moving off with a nod of his head. Victorinus devoured the food, oblivious to the burns on his tongue and gums. He had to remind himself he was a tribune of Rome when he finished, and should not allow a troop of soldiers to see him licking a bowl clean.

'I'd offer you bread if we had any,' Vitulus said as he sat down next to him. 'Can you tell us what happened, sir?'

That drew the others out from the shadows. Victorinus met nine sets of eyes, his face sagging into a frown. 'I set up a meet with Drost. I'm sure you all remember him. We met at Habitancum. Everything seemed normal. We broke our fast, talked... and then...' he trailed off for a moment, eyes lost in the past. 'We were ambushed, poorly thankfully. Drost lost a man to an arrow, but other than that, the rest of us saw them off. Funny thing was, they weren't from the tribes, and they weren't Roman. What would a group of Germans be doing all the way up there?'

'They're Saxone,' Vitulus said, and then filled in Victorinus of his own journey north with Felicius. 'Alaric was certain they were Saxones, the prefect had no reason to doubt him.'

'So Felicius sent you after me?' Vitulus nodded. 'Good to have friends, eh? I'm mighty grateful you lads came for me. It's a service I won't forget.' He met the eye of the nine men again, nodding in gratitude. He then spoke of their journey east, to the small farmstead owned by Darrow, and what happened there. Not wanting to dwell on it, he pressed on. 'So, let's establish the facts. We have a band of Saxones, a large band, no mere raiding party, beached north of the Wall. They've taken hostages, Drost and his men, plus Pastor. And according to Darrow the farmer, these raiders have been tasked with finding me.'

Silence among the nine soldiers, nothing but the hiss of the wind and crackle of flames. 'How would they know where to find you?' Vitulus said after a while.

'That was my first thought. The only person who knew about the meet with Drost was Pastor, and seeing as they have captured him, I hardly think it was him that ratted me out. The other question, the more pressing one, as far as I'm concerned, is why?'

Vitulus shifted, clearly wanting to say something but unsure of himself. 'You can speak freely in front of me, Vitulus. We're old friends, you and I.'

The centurion nodded. 'I know that, sir, but what I have to say is... sensitive.' With a start, he surged to his feet.

'Right lads! Look lively, I want a two-man watch throughout the night to be changed every three hours. You two, yes you Demetrius, don't gawp at me like some fool, you're first watch. The rest of you roll up in your cloaks and get some rest. We've a long day ahead of us tomorrow.'

The men unquestionably dismissed, Vitulus sat back down next to Victorinus, edging closer than he was before. 'Remind me never to get on the wrong side of you,' Victorinus said with a smirk. He noted the unfortunate soldier on the end of Vitulus' tongue lashing was the one who handed him the stew. He made a note to comfort the man first chance he got. 'What is it you need to say?'

'Are you aware that the prefect has been in correspondence with the Divine Augustus Theodosius?'

Victorinus nodded. 'I am, though there is nothing overly suspicious about that. The two are firm friends, as you well know. Gods! It's not been that long since you were away fighting for him.'

'Aye, true enough. But do you know what the two of them speak about?'

Victorinus felt his lips tug in to a smile. He knew where this was going. ''Centurion, our thoughts align,' Victorinus said. 'Theo is worried about the influence the Germans have in the west. We are taking in more and more of them to fill out our army. We promote men from among them to the highest offices in the military. They know our strengths, our weaknesses.'

'And there are some that are as brothers to Maximus.'

'Aye. And Maximus is no friend to Gratian, our divine ruler in the west. I am aware of that too.'

'Felicius thinks, that is the prefect-

'No need to stand on ceremony with me, Vitulus. Felicius and I may outrank you, but you know you are a brother to us both.'

'Thank you, sir. Well Felicius thinks Maximus could be up to something. And if you don't mind me saying sir, we all know Maximus ain't too fond of you and the prefect.'

'Hmm, aye,' Victorinus pondered. 'But do you really believe the *Dux* would go to these limits to rid himself of me? Gods, he could just chuck me a purse of coin, tell me it was my retirement fund and tell me to fuck off! I'd be quite happy with that, to be fair.'

'Just trying to make it make sense,' Vitulus said, puffing out his cheeks.

'Aye. What's with your mistrust of Germans, by the way?' Got enough of them in your ranks these days, don't you?'

'Haven't we all? You remember the rebellion?'

'Not likely to forget it.'

'Aye, well. When the prefect and I took the lads to Bononia, we sailed across the channel on a ship.'

'Didn't think you'd swum it.'

Vitulus scoffed a laugh. 'The captain of the ship, Fidelis, had a new crew, mostly made up of Germans.'

'And they betrayed you. I remember the story well,' Victorinus finished.

'Aye. One little bastard was reflecting the sunlight from a little bronze disc, must have marked us out for miles. Never been so scared as I was in that fight.'

'The infamous centurion Vitulus, scared of a fight! Now I've heard it all!'

Vitulus shook his head. 'You should have seen it, sir. When the ships rammed together, it was like the whole world shook. Water pouring over the sides, our ship near on split in two. Never been so sure I was going to die.'

Victorinus cleared his throat, thinking of something to say. Could he admit to a centurion that he felt that fear every time he marched in to battle? Even a centurion as close to him as Vitulus was? He didn't think that was how he should conduct himself, so he pushed the thought away. 'Never been to sea, can't say I've much enthusiasm to do so. But I think you are being harsh, generalising an entire people because of the actions of a few. I think that's where we go wrong sometimes, perhaps how some wars begin.'

'You might be right there,' Vitulus said after a pause. 'I'll try to do better. Now, as to our situation, what do you suggest we do?'

Victorinus got slowly to his feet, walked to the cooking pot atop the fire, and helped himself to a second portion of stew. 'I thought that was obvious,' he said as he sat back down. 'We rescue our friends, of course.'

***

Darkness cloaked them as they crept down the slope. The wind buffeted the noise of their armour, the grunts as they blindly sought sure footing, the chinks of their mail. Ten men against a couple of hundred. It was madness. But Victorinus had always been one to roll the dice. Figured it had worked well for him once before, when he had risked it all to save his family and an empire. Besides, he was an old dog, and it was too late for him to learn new tricks.

He'd slept like the dead after filling his belly with stew, and awoke a new man come dawn. He and Vitulus had spent the day observing the warriors on the beach, getting an estimate of their numbers and routine. The only positive Victorinus could find was that their enemy were clearly not expecting an attack. There were never more than five men on watch, and those men did not venture far from the wind breaks they'd set up to shelter in. It was freezing, a cold so fierce Victorinus thought he would never feel the sun's warmth again.

His nose streamed as he clambered down the slippery bank, chest burning with every in breath as the icy air assaulted his lungs. His sword rattled in its hilt and he had to free a hand to hold it up to keep it from clanging on the rocky ground. In what felt like an age, but in reality was only moments, the ten men reached the bottom of the slope and laid down on the grass at the edge of the beach. Immediately, he felt wetness on his tunic as the moisture on the grass seeped through his mail. Silently, he cursed. He'd never get warm now.

'All here, sir,' Vitulus whispered from somewhere off to his left. Together they had decided each man would leave his shield behind in the small makeshift camp on the other side of the woodland. They would have been an encumbrance in their descent down the hillside and if everything went according to plan, they wouldn't be needing them, anyway.

'You remember where you need to go?' Victorinus replied.

They'd discussed it earlier. Most of the warriors were still based on their ships. There were fifty or so on the beach, ten men to a tent, plus what seemed to be a couple of guards in the tent with the prisoners. They hadn't done everything wrong though, these raiders, and the tent Victorinus needed to get to was the one closest to the shoreline.

'We'll create a distraction for you. You just get to our guys.'

With that, they moved off. Vitulus and five of his men went right, away from the lapping waves. Victorinus and three men headed right for them. They reached the first tent, their feet crunching on the sand and stone beneath them. Victorinus winced with every step, but the wind howled and the waves hissed as they crashed inland. He had to hope it was enough. They paused again at the tent, squatting down, enjoying a break from the wind. They waited, each of them willing Vitulus to give them the signal.

They didn't have to wait long. A cry behind them and Victorinus turned to see the tent furthest inland ablaze. Vitulus and his men formed a half circle around the tent's entrance, and out of the smoke and flames emerged staggering silhouettes, swiftly chopped down as they sought the refuge of fresh air.

'Move,' Victorinus growled at his men, and as one, they trudged through the darkness to the farthest tent. They reached it in moments, their world now a shrieking cacophony as Vitulus and his men slaughtered anyone that came within reach. Victorinus could hear warriors from the other tents emerging now, shouts and cries over the wailing of the dying. The wind continued its ferocious barrage as they reached the tent, just in time to see a head pop out from an opening in the canvas, a bearded face with sleepy eyes taking in the carnage on the beach. Victorinus didn't give the man a chance to compose himself. He drew his sword and chopped down hard on the head, his blade crunching through bone, hot blood splashing across his face. The dead man dropped without a sound. Pulling back the canvas, Victorinus held it open and urged his three men inside.

There were already screams from within by the time Victorinus entered. The canvas swung shut behind him; the tent illuminated by the light of a brazier in the far corner. Immediately, he saw that he'd made a mistake. He thought there were just a few guards in there with the prisoners. There were ten at least. He sprang forward, catching a swinging sword on his blade before punching its bearer in the face with his left hand. He let out a cry as he felt his knuckle pop, shaking his hand as if the action would free him of the pain. In the act of scrunching his hand in to a ball he'd re-opened the cut from the night before, and already dark blood smeared the dirty bandage wrapped around it. His assailant sprang back at him, sword driving low to high. Victorinus side stepped the blow and swung his sword backhand, catching the man on the back of his head. He drove the blade through the man's back before he could rise.

Pastor was on his feet in the corner, hands and feet bound with rope. Victorinus lifted a knife from his belt and threw it in his direction, trusting him and Drost to figure the rest out for themselves. He moved forward, the sides of the tent giving way, the roof now touching his head. His three men were cornered. One had snatched up a shield and was desperately trying to cover the other two. As Victorinus moved through the tent to join them, he saw the shield bearer block a blow to his left, but wasn't quick enough to bring it back around and stop the next one. He went down howling in agony, a sword stuck in his right hip.

Victorinus launched himself at the backs of the barbarians. He thrust his sword through a torso, wrenched it free and smashed the blade in to the back of another's head. Quick as thought, he ducked an axe blow that would have decapitated him, and drove his sword up in to an exposed groin. Pastor was free, Drost too, and they snatched up fallen weapons and leaped upon their captors, venting the fury of the last few days on them.

The fight was over quickly. 'We have little time, we must move,' Victorinus said, running a hand over Pastor's bruised face before the youth could speak. 'Can you all fight?'

Drost's men, rolling aching shoulders and flexing under-used legs, were also armed. 'Aye, we can fight. How many men are with you?'

'Just nine,' Victorinus paused, turned to the corpse that was the auxiliary. 'Eight now.' The body was that of Demetrius, the cook who had made him the stew. He forced himself to turn away. There wasn't time for empathy. 'We have Vitulus and the rest of his men out there ready to help us cut through the last of the resistance, then we make legs inland and in to the woods. Ready?' Good, let's go.'

They burst from the tent and out into the darkness. The beach was chaos. The inferno that was the burning tent was still roaring, a beacon in the darkness. Squinting, Victorinus could make out a half circle of men fighting off twice their number to the right of the flames. 'On me!' he called and loped off, sword held out before him. They smashed into the unsuspecting backs of the Saxones. Ten men died in a heartbeat, their bodies falling from view. Victorinus picked his way through until he was hugging Vitulus tight, the centurion sporting a deep gash in his left cheek.

'Have you lost anyone?'

'Two. You?'

'Aye, Demetrius. No time to bring their bodies with us centurion, we need to move.'

Even in the darkness, he could see it hurt Vitulus. Felicius had instilled a great belief among his men that no man was to be left behind, whatever the circumstances. Felicius, though, was not there. They moved off, Victorinus lurking to make sure he was the last man. He realised he could see more easily now, the murky light of pre-dawn beginning to see off the night. A horn sounded out on the water, and

Victorinus fixed his tired eyes on three row boats making for the shore, each boat bristling with armed warriors. 'It's going to be a long day,' he said to himself.

Looking back to his men, taking comfort in seeing them halfway up the bank they'd clambered down seemingly just moments before, he jogged after them, muttering under his breath. 'Too old for this shit.'

X

Londinium teemed with people.

Felicius allowed the crowd to push him along the quayside, fully aware that he was in the middle of a pickpocket's dream. Marcelina seemed more relaxed, though. Her hood down for the first time since leaving the north, she stared in wonder at the ships lining the dock, and the vast warehouses built across the road from them. Not for the first time, Felicius regretted leaving his wife and daughter in Britannia when he had gone east to fight for Theodosius. Marcelina had seen so little of the world. Felicius had seen cities so grand they made Londinium look what it was: a small provincial capital with no real wealth.

But for his daughter, Londinium might as well have been Rome. 'Look father!' she exclaimed excitedly, pointing to a ship swaying in the dock. 'That ship is bigger than Vindolanda! And that building there, what is it? Some sort of palace?'

He chuckled. 'It's just another warehouse. Doesn't even have any windows! Not sure it's somewhere an emperor would want to set himself up in.' It had taken them just three days to get there. A ride to Eboracum followed by a brief stay on a transport ship heading south, Felicius had been grateful for the letter Maximus had given him, topped with the *Dux's* seal. There had been no charge for the journey, and the ship's captain had treated him like a lord.

'What ship is it we are looking for?' Marcelina asked.

'It's named Mars, I'm sure we'll see it soon enough.' Felicius had thought it a bad omen when he'd first heard. A ship named after the old Pagan God of war was surely no good thing, and once again he wondered what it could be Maximus was having shipped halfway around the world.

He felt a presence on his left shoulder, the slightest touch on his arm as someone pressed up close. He didn't move, didn't adjust his pace or stance, but felt a weight leave his hip as they cut his purse from his belt. *Oh no you don't.* He nudged Marcelina on her shoulder, easing her away from him. Just as he felt the presence at his shoulder move away, he spun on his heel, knife flashing out from his hip. A short frame hidden beneath a brown cloak was edging away from him, doing its best to fade in to the crowd. Felicius had their mark though. He reached out with his left hand, grabbed the figure by the top of the head, and heaved them in close. Knife held at their neck, he pulled the figure in close and backed off to the entrance of an alleyway, out of the way of the crowds.

'Father? What are you doing?' Marcelina said in shock.

'This little bastard thought he was going to steal my purse,' Felicius said with a grunt of satisfaction. Knife still held at the figure's throat, he yanked the hood free and was about to yell in triumph when a pair of quivering eyes stopped him in his tracks. A small boy, no more than ten. 'What's your name?' Felicius asked.

'Davos, sir,' the boy said, voice shaking. 'I'm sorry, sir, here,' the boy held out the purse. 'Please take it back, sir. I won't bother you again.'

Felicius sighed. Street urchins were a pest in any city across the empire. Wasn't their fault they lived in a world where no one cared about them, though. 'Davos, that Greek?' He took in the tanned complexion of the boy's skin, the dark hair and brown eyes. He wasn't a native, that was certain.

'Y-yes, sir. My father was a trader. We docked here last year.'

'What do you mean *was*?' Marcelina asked. Though Felicius reckoned he already knew the answer.

'He died, miss. Some sort of phlegm in his lungs. Couldn't shake it off.'

'Oh,' was all Marcelina could say in reply. Felicius had seen a few boys like this in his travels across the empire. A son off on an adventure with their father, all fun and games until the father dies and the son is left stranded in a foreign country.

'What of the other men on the ship? Could they not have returned you home?'

The boy shook his head, a single tear running down his cheek. 'The ship had left by the time my father died. They didn't leave us any coin. We were in an inn, but they kicked me out after...' he trailed off, sobbing.

'God above,' Felicius muttered. 'So you've been here alone this whole time?'

'Not alone, sir. I got some friends, they look after me. Got some new clothes and even a bed to sleep in-

'As long as you cut a few purses every day and bring them back to them, eh?'

Davos nodded. 'Ten a day, sir. Then I get to eat.'

'Ten? How have you managed to avoid getting caught?' Felicius gawped. 'You weren't exactly subtle with me!'

Davos shrugged. 'I'm quick when I have to be. And I'm hungry.'

Felicius took in the boy's threadbare cloak, a single tunic, riddled with holes, beneath. He wore open topped sandals a size too small, blue toes sticking out the end. 'Who is that you take the purses to?'

'Man named Cyclops. He runs the biggest gang on the docks.'

'Cyclops?' Felicius scoffed. 'Let me guess, big guy with one eye?'

Davos nodded. Felicius leant out of the alley and looked into the clouded sky. He could just make out the sun, still high. He had time. 'Take me to this Cyclops. Let me see if I can talk some sense in to him.'

***

'Are you sure this is wise?' Marcelina asked as they reached the end of another alley. It was so deep it seemed even sunlight didn't venture there.

'I am a prefect of Rome. This man is a gangster, a common criminal. If he has any sense, he won't lay a finger on me.'

'I'm more concerned about him laying a finger on me, I must admit,' Marcelina said, stepping carefully over a brown puddle. Davos knocked twice on a wooden door, it seemed to be some rear access to one of the many warehouses that lined the riverside. The door opened a crack, stopped short by a metal chain on the inside. A pair of eyes appeared in the crack of dim light, squinting down at Davos, then up to Felicius and Marcelina. 'No visitors,' the voice said, before the door slammed shut.

'Well, that was rude,' Marcelina said.

Felicius stepped up and rapped his knuckles on the door. 'Open up! I am a prefect of Rome!'

A pause, and then the door opened a crack again, the same set of eyes staring out. 'You have no authority in here, *prefect.*'

The door slammed shut once more. 'We'll see about that,' Felicius muttered. He took two steps back, bared his blade in his right hand and then leaped forward, left foot slamming in to the door level with where he thought the metal chain was. Safe to say it wasn't the best door Rome had ever built. It crumbled like kindling. Felicius stepped through without hesitating, revealing a face and body to go with the squinting eyes.

The man was on his back, blood leaking from a cut on his bald head. His hands were up to protect his face and before he could move, Felicius hacked down with his sword, carving a bloody hole through the man's fatty torso.

'That's my fucking authority,' he spat, stepping over the man.

'One way to make an entrance, I suppose,' Marcelina said, skipping over the dying man to stand beside her father. 'Davos, how many men are there here?' she asked.

Davos shrugged, snot pouring from his left nostril. 'This time of day, a hundred or so? The rest will be out earning their coin.'

'A hundred?' Felicius blanched, bloody sword still in hand.

'Perhaps you could have asked a few more questions before storming in and killing the door guard,' Marcelina said. Felicius thought he could detect a feint smile on his daughter's lips. It seemed no matter what danger they were in, witnessing her father make a mistake was entertaining, regardless.

'Yes, well,' he rolled his shoulders. 'The man was only a door guard. I'm sure this Cyclops won't make a big deal out of it. And besides, I am a prefect of-

'Who the *fuck* are you?!' a voice boomed from within. Out of the murky light stormed a barrel of a man. He wasn't muscular, just big, with a rounded belly and shoulders to match. He wore a stained blue tunic that fit him like a second skin, his rolls of fat seemingly set to burst free at any moment. His right eye was gone, a mass of scar tissue all that remained. Thinning hair clung to a sweat sheeted skull. His face was dirt marked and hadn't seen a razor's edge in a good long while, and two giant gold hoops hung from each ear.

'I am prefect Felicius, commander of the Fourth Cohort of Gauls. Who may I ask, are you?' Felicius kept a wary eye on the knives Cyclops held in each hand. Just eating knives by the look of them, but if he allowed the man to get close enough, they'd do the job well enough.

'Cyclops,' the man sniffed. 'And I'm in charge round here, not some damn *prefect*!' he all but spat the last word.

'No,' Felicius said patiently. 'Around this part of Londinium, the dock master is in command. He reports to the local council, who reports to the governor. Are you by any chance the dock master?'

'Do I look like fuckin' cream to you?' Cream was the term the masses used to describe the ruling class. 'Cream of the crop,' was where it originated, though Felicius was sure that wasn't quite what men like Cyclops were referring to when they used the term.

'So you hold no rank. You own this warehouse?'

'No one owns this place. Fuckin' thing is falling to the ground. Look around you prefect, this seem like the type of place that's worth any coin?'

He allowed himself a moment to inspect what he could see. Rotting beams above him, cracks of daylight piercing through the wall at his back. 'No, I'm sure it's seen better days. But *someone* owns this warehouse, whether that be an individual or the state. You are trespassing.'

'Ha!' Cyclops snorted a laugh. 'No one cared about me when I was left on a street at eight years old to fend for myself. No one cared when I snuck in that door behind you and slept on the floor. Fifteen years I've been in here, no one's cared. The fuck has it got to do with you, anyway?'

Felicius nudged Davos in the shoulder and eased him forwards. 'I caught this young man trying to cut my purse along the quayside. He said you make him do it. That true?'

'Little shit grassed me up, did he? You'll pay for that later boy,' he pointed one of his knives at Davos, who let out an involuntary squeal and shuffled back behind Felicius. 'And besides, what else is the lad supposed to do? Sell his body at the local brothel?' Cyclops spat on the floor. 'Fuck that. Just like me, no one cared about the kid when they turned him out of the inn. His father's body wheeled off to an unmarked grave. At least I gave him a roof over his head, food in his belly and a way of making his way in this world.'

'Crime is not the answer!' Marcelina cut in. 'Will you vouch for Davos when he's caught by the City Watch? Will you stop them cutting off his hands, or worse, hanging him?'

'Hang me?' Davos piped up, his voice a terrified squeak. 'No one said nothing about hanging me!'

'That's what they do to criminals, young Davos,' Felicius said, eyes still on Cyclops. 'And there are many honest ways to earn a living. Crime is not the answer you seek. As for you, Cyclops, or whatever your name really is, I'm going to the dock master now, and if I were you, I'd make sure you and your little gang are long gone from here when I return.'

Cyclops just smiled. 'Good luck with that. Guess I'll be seeing you soon, prefect.' He spat once more, before turning and walking back in to the darkness.

It seemed little brighter outside, or warmer. Felicius pulled his cloak tight about him and trudged out of the alley. 'I can't believe the impertinence of that man! I am a prefect of Rome! How could he look at me with such... disinterest, like I was just another foot soldier on the road! Davos, where are the dock master's quarters?'

Davos pointed back to where they had come. 'At the end of the dock, sir. But I don't think you're going to get anything more out of him.'

'And why's that?' Felicius snapped.

'I assume because Cyclops pays the man off,' Marcelina said.

Davos nodded. 'I take the coin to him myself some months.'

'God help us,' Felicius muttered. 'Davos, you will take us to the dock master immediately.'

'Do we not have other pressing concerns?' Marcelina asked.

'That can wait,' Felicius said firmly. 'I will not see Rome's laws broke so brazenly by one individual.'

They set off, Davos leading the way. Felicius simmered as he walked. His whole life had been given in service to the empire, and it grated him when others took such liberties with their positions. He knew the governor of the southern province, by name at least, if not well. He would call on him if he had time and express his concerns in person, by letter, if not. Glancing up at the grey sky once more, checking the position of the weakening sun. He still had time.

'In here sir,' Davos had reached a tavern, and was pointing at the door.

A swinging sign hung outside the building, 'The Dock and Duck', crudely painted on the wooden boards. 'Funny name for a tavern,' he said to himself. 'And why is the dock master living here? He will have quarters, on office and staff?'

Davos could only shrug. 'Only ever known him to be in here.'

Felicius stormed through the door, in to a smoky, warm chamber. Two braziers flickered on either side of the room, a long wooden bar at the far end. Tables and chairs littered the floor between the bar and door, mostly unoccupied. Davos tugged at Felicius' cloak and pointed to a man sat in the far corner. 'That's him?' Davos nodded.

He marched over, rage still simmering just beneath boiling point. 'You there, name and rank, now!'

The man started. He had been leaning on his left arm, eyes closed. When they snapped open, they revealed blood shot grey eyes, bags big enough to hide a body in beneath. 'W-what?' he slurred.

'I said name and rank,' Felicius slammed a hand down on the table, upturning a half empty jug of wine.

'Hey you! What you doing? I'll have no trouble in here!' a voice called from behind the bar.

Felicius turned and in one motion freed his still bloodied sword. He called out his name and title, a challenge to the tavern keeper.

'Just keep it down, will you? You'll put off my regulars,' the man said, backing away, hands raised.

'Name. Now,' Felicius said, turning back to the drunk.

'Sextus Amaurus, I'm a fucking tribune!' he uttered through a thick tongue.

'Under who's authority?'

'The governor's, of course! Governor Priscus is an old friend of my father's.'

'How convenient for you. On your feet, tribune.'

Amaurus rose unsteadily. He had waxy skin, a broken nose, and matted hair that looked as though it would be teeming with lice. He was thin around the chest and shoulders, but a bulging belly sagged beneath his grubby blue tunic. 'You call yourself a tribune of Rome?' Felicius snarled. 'Look at the state of you! Why are you not in your office?'

'It's my day off,' Amaurus said.

'And how many 'days off' do you take a week?'

Amaurus squinted, 'a couple?' he said without conviction.

'I've just learned of a gang operating here on the docks. Run by a man who pays boys to cut the purses of people as they walk along the quayside. I'm also told that not only are you fully aware of this gang and their exploits, but they pay you to do nothing about it! Now, if I were to take this information to the governor, do you think his friendship with your father would be enough for him to throw you out of office?'

Amaurus gulped. 'I-I,' he slumped forward, at a loss for words. 'I don't think so.'

'Me neither! So what are you going to do about it, tribune?'

'Get them to stop?'

Felicius grinned. 'And they'll do that will they?' How will it go, you'll swan along to their den, ask them nicely to stop robbing people, stop whatever else it is they have going on, and they'll just nod their heads and be on their way? Come on, tribune, think! What are you going to do?'

Amaurus squinted again, running a hand through his hair. 'I don't know.'

'You don't know, *sir*!'

'I don't know, sir!' he said louder, even managing a wonky salute.

'You ever served in the military?' Felicius asked.

'Gods no! All that armour and marching, not for me.'

'Ever killed a man? Used one of these?' Felicius gestured to his sword.

'No,' Amaurus said quietly, eyes suddenly fixed on the sword.

'Then I suggest you round up the local guard and bring them with you. Now, how soon can you get this racket closed down?'

'I'll go over the river today, see Darius and his people.'

Felicius' eyebrows creased together. He turned and frowned at Davos. 'Darius runs the other gang here at the docks. Owns a couple of brothels, a tavern and a gambling house. Him and Cyclops split it, Cyclops runs the streets, Darius his properties.'

Eyebrows raised, Felicius turned back to Amaurus. 'There are two gangs? You're being paid off by two gangs?'

'That's just at the docks, sir. There are more deeper in the city, they all pay off someone. You know how much stuff they move through the docks? Wine comes in and doesn't get taxed, fresh meat and other foods, spices especially. All of it comes through the docks here. This bloke takes a couple of coins to look away.'

It was the most Felicius had heard Davos speak since he'd met the boy. 'Is that all true, Amaurus?'

Amaurus' face moved from fear to anger. He stood straighter, trying and failing to make himself look more imposing. 'Just because I know the way of the world don't make me a wrong'un. This is how it's done in every city across the empire, from here to Palmyra! If I were you, I wouldn't ask too many questions!'

'Oh, and why's that?'

'Father,' Marcelina muttered quietly from his back.

'Because the gangs know they're better with me than without me, and there'll go to any length to make sure I'm still around to take their coin.'

'Father,' Marcelina muttered again, more urgently this time.

'You really think the gangs are going to protect you?' Felicius scoffed.

'Sure I do.' Amaurus' face split in to a sickly grin. 'Just look behind you.'

Felicius turned. Marcelina had hold of Davos and was edging away towards the bar. They were both pale faced, quivering eyes fixed on the men coming for them. There were six, big bastards with the looks of hardened killers. One had a military tattoo on his right arm, two others matted scars where the tattoo would have been. Deserters then.

'Gentlemen, there's no need for this to get violent,' Felicius said, feeling the adrenalin build within him. He looked back to the bar, noticed the tavern keeper had made himself scarce. No chance of him warning off this fight then. Not that Felicius blamed the man.

'Put down that little pig sticker then,' one of the men grunted. Felicius didn't feel so inclined.

'I am Prefect Gaius Felicius of the Fourth Cohort of Gauls. I command an army of five hundred men and serve the *Dux Britanniarum,* Flavius Maximus, commander of all Rome's forces in Britannia. By attacking me, you're condemning yourselves to death.'

Two of the thugs stopped moving, another took a small step back. Thieves and low lives these may be, but no man wanted to die swinging from a noose. 'Fuck you,' another snarled, one of the men who'd cut the military tattoo from his arm. He leaped forward, upturning a table and causing Marcelina to scream. Felicius stepped in to his assault, shouldering the man before he could bring his knife to bare. When he staggered back a step, Felicius swiped right to left with his sword, slashing the man's throat in a neat cut.

One down, and Felicius stood, panting. It had been a while since he'd been in a bar fight. Despite the peril he and his daughter were in, he grinned. 'Who's next then?'

Two came for him, one with a length of wood, the other a knife. Felicius kicked a chair at the knife wielder and blocked a blow from the wooden bat. He heaved the man away, ducked another swing from the bat, then lunged forward, striking the gangster high in the chest. He was done for. Felicius turned back to the knife wielder, who threw his weapon across the tavern. Felicius ducked and rolled, crashing in to a table and sending chairs flying. Marcelina screamed again. He staggered back to his feet and flung another chair at his attacker, who was rampaging toward him. As the man ducked away from the chair, Marcelina ran up behind him, punched his own knife she'd scooped from the floor through his back.

Four men left, but even at a glance Felicius could see they'd no stomach for the fight. 'If you want to live, leave now,' he said in a cold, low voice. They didn't hesitate, just ran for the door.

Amaurus hadn't moved through all the commotion, but as Felicius turned back to him he slumbered over his table, spewed the contents of his stomach on the floor. 'So tribune,' Felicius said, wrinkling his nose at the rotten scent of sour wine, 'exactly how many gangs in the area are paying you not to do your job?'

XI

Victorinus dripped blood as he ran. The bandage on his left hand had fallen off in the night, he didn't know when. His popped knuckle burned with pain, the two wounds on his left hand rendering it completely useless.

They'd reached the makeshift camp Vitulus and his men had made relatively quickly. What they hadn't accounted for was for their pursuers to be so vigorous. All night they'd had to run, no idea where they were going, or when it would end. They just knew they had to be away.

A weak sun broke the gloom of the winter's night. The air got no warmer for it. 'Got to stop soon,' Drost said beside him, echoing his own thoughts.

'We keep moving,' Vitulus called from ahead. 'Our friends back there aren't stopping. That means we can't either.'

There were forty or so men behind them, the same men that had been rowing to shore when Victorinus and his friends had made their escape up the grass bank. Whoever their leader was, he must have been furious at having his prisoners taken.

'The tribune's losing a lot of blood,' Pastor said through his swollen mouth. He'd been badly beaten, his face a mass of purple and green bruises. And those were just the wounds Victorinus could see. He'd not had the breath to ask Pastor or Drost any questions yet, figured that could wait until they were safe. Whenever that would be.

Vitulus stopped and turned, the first time he had all night. He met Victorinus' eye before looking him over, frowning as he did. Victorinus was pale, sweating and shivering. He was an old man, and he'd felt every one of the steps they'd run through the night. Just breathing hurt him, black spots flashing in his vision. 'Leave me,' he panted out through ragged breaths. 'I'll just slow you down the longer this goes on. The important thing was you got away,' he said this last to Pastor.

'You know it's you they're looking for,' Drost said. 'I don't know what you've done to piss them off, but their leader's got a hard on for you.'

Pastor went to speak, but Vitulus cut him off. 'We're not leaving anyone behind.' His eyes met Victorinus once more. 'Not anyone else, anyway.'

'So what do we do?' Drost asked.

Vitulus swivelled, eyes scanning the horizon. 'The high ground to the north. We head for there.'

'What do we do when we get there?' Pastor asked.

'We fight.'

***

It took them another hour to get there. Victorinus leaning on Drost, the tribal chief all but carrying him over the hilly terrain. The black spots in his vision became more persistent as he stumbled along, coupled with flashes of blinding light that had his head pounding like there was a smithy trapped in there beating on an anvil.

'Keep moving!' he heard Vitulus call from time to time, though most of the journey passed in a haze. He was conscious when the ground rose up to hit him in the face, though. He coughed, spitting mud, rolling on to his back. 'Are we there?' he croaked out.

'Aye, though what good it will do us I don't know,' Drost said, kneeling beside him. He opened a skin of water, tipped the contents in Victorinus' mouth. 'Drink. I'll see to that hand. Vitulus, can we get a fire going?'

'Fire?' Victorinus slurred, worried.

'The cut on your hand has become infected. We need to seal the wound. Trust your body to do the rest.'

'And if it doesn't?'

'We cut off your hand, or you die.' Victorinus slumped back, fatigue taking over. He didn't want to die. He wanted to be with his sons, to watch them become fathers, to see the men they would grow in to. Although thinking on it, he didn't much fancy losing his hand, either. He thought of the Saxones cast out to sea, their right hands taken from them. Wondered briefly if they made it home.

'We make our stand here!' Vitulus called out. Victorinus could just make the centurion out, dragging his foot along the half frozen mud to form a line. Breath clouded his face as he spoke, but to Victorinus, the man looked as formidable as ever. 'Who has a shield?'

The five men left from the tent party Vitulus had brought with him stepped forward, their oval shields in hand. 'You five will be the centre of our wall. Drost, whilst you help the tribune, could your men gather rocks and wood, anything we can pile up to cover our flanks?'

Drost didn't respond, just turned to one of his men and nodded, who said something to the others in their native tongue. They moved off to follow their orders. 'What about me?' Pastor asked. 'I've no shield, but I have a sword.'

'You're pretty good with it too, from what I remember,' Vitulus clapped the younger man on the shoulder. 'Fight on the right wing of the wall. Don't let any of the bastards get around you.'

Drost had a small fire going. There was no need to conceal where they were. The enemy were so close behind they'd be there within the hour. No chance of them going unnoticed. The Briton took a knife from Victorinus' belt and thrust it in to the flames. 'You going to kill me with my own knife?'

'Save you, hopefully,' Drost said without his usual good humour. 'Trust you to get yourself mixed up in something you don't even understand.'

'I'm sorry I have dragged you in to it.'

'Be sorry if I survive,' Drost said, this time with his wicked grin. 'If I make it through all this, my wife is *definitely* going to kill me!'

Without another word, Drost gripped Victorinus' left arm and scooped the dagger from the fire, wincing at the heat from the handgrip. Victorinus opened his palm, turned his head away. He thought he'd black out when Drost did it. He'd been on the verge for hours. But the gods were not merciful. Searing pain rippled through his body. He arched his back and roared, eyes bulging as the burning blade scorched his skin.

'It is done,' Drost said, after what felt an age. Vitulus had his men formed in a line, ready for the inevitable attack. Drost picked up one of their discarded packs and rummaged through, selecting a clean white tunic. 'You Romans, always prepared for everything.' He tore a strip from the tunic, wrapped it tight around Victorinus' hand and tied it off.

'They're coming!' a voice called from the line, and Drost stood, taking one last look at Victorinus. 'Stay here,' he said.

'No shit,' Victorinus muttered, turning his head so he could see the line of shields. Vitulus had picked his position well. The enemy would have to charge uphill in to the face of the waiting shields. The Romans had no spears or javelins to throw, but across a narrow front, their big shields would prove a mighty obstacle. Drost's men had built piles of wood and rubble the height of men to protect the flanks. It wasn't much, but it would have to be enough.

Shuffling up to a sitting position, biting down on his tongue at the agony it caused his hand, Victorinus dragged his sword free and held it ready in his right hand. Just because he couldn't stand in line didn't mean he couldn't fight. If anyone broke through, he would die fighting, not lying down.

'Brace!' Vitulus called, and Victorinus could feel the tremor in the earth as the enemy charged up the slope. He couldn't see them, not through the legs of his friends, but he heard their war cries and saw the flash of light as their blades caught the winter sun. They slammed in to the small Roman wall, the men of the Fourth Cohort of Gauls forced back three paces, four. Vitulus roared an order over the din of battle and Drost's men pushed in to the backs of the Roman soldiers, halting their retreat and forcing them on to their attackers.

Drost leaped in from the right, sword held in a two hand grip. Victorinus saw nothing but the spray of blood as the Briton fought to ease the pressure from the Roman shields. He heard his friend shout his battle cry, and his roars of triumph as he single-handedly turned the tide of the battle. 'Form around Drost!' Vitulus called, and his men responded at once. Together they took three paces forwards, hunched behind their shields, battering their foe with the linden boards, swords snaking out to snatch lives away.

Pastor ran around the back of the line, seeing a threat the others had not. The enemy were trying an overload on their right flank, overwhelming numbers surging forwards, hacking at Drost's four shield-less men who used their blades to defend for their lives. Pastor jumped upon the mound of dirt they'd built to cover their flank. He slashed down twice with his blade, an enemy falling from view. Then he leaped down, sword held above his head, hacking down as he landed. Drost's men followed, and for a worrying moment, all were lost to view as they slipped down the bank.

Victorinus panicked, heaved himself up using his sword, and staggered towards the fray. The stench of any battle, the iron tang of blood, the rot of open bowels, assaulted his nostrils as he looked frantically for Pastor. He stopped short when he saw the youth, flanked by Drost's warriors, driving a wedge in to the enemy formation. He gasped when he saw the numbers they were facing. Forty enemies, fighting against a fraction of that number. It had seemed shorter odds when their pursuers were still a mile or so behind them.

Who are these people? And why do they want me dead? He had no time to ponder it. Through a gap in Vitulus' wall a warrior wriggled through, long sweat sheeted hair plastered to his face. With a snarl, he locked eyes with Victorinus and charged him, a short-handled axe held before him. Exhausted, mentally and physically, it was all Victorinus could do to bring his blade up and block the strike. Gritting his teeth and blowing out hard, he turned the axe out wide and jabbed feebly at his attacker's exposed torso. The strike didn't even break the man's mail.

The warrior grinned, sensing an easy victory. He brought the axe up high and slammed it down with all his might. Victorinus didn't really dodge the blow, just allowed himself to fall to the left, where he landed with a cry and struck his head on a rock. The blow missed him though, and dizzy, eyes full of stars, he staggered back to his feet and swung his sword wildly, just wanting to keep his attacker back. 'Help!' he tried to cry, but all that came out was a gurgle.

Blinking rapidly to clear his vision, he more sensed than saw the flash of the axe as it cut the air a hand's width in front of his face. Replying with a swipe of his own sword, felt it bite at his attacker's hip but didn't lodge. He cleared his eyes just in time to see the axe coming for him again, the face of its bearer fixed in a snarl of frustration. He ducked another blow, tasted blood that trickled down his face from his fall, and was all but ready to drop his sword when his attacker went down with a crash. Pastor jumped back to his feet, his face and mail spattered in blood. With two short, sharp jabs he finished the man, and Victorinus slumped to the ground in relief. 'Stay down until it's over!' Pastor called, turning back to the battle.

'You don't give me orders. I give you orders,' Victorinus slurred, but no one was listening. Maybe he should just lie down, rest his head. It was a comforting thought. His eyelids grew heavy and he could even trick himself in to thinking he was warm and comfortable, tucked up in his cot above the stables at home.

An enormous crash snapped him back to the waking world. Vitulus had formed a small wedge with his men and they had charged the centre of the enemy formation. The ground was a tangle of limbs as men fought to get back to their feet before their foes. Vitulus was the first up, sword sinking in a stomach, left hand snapping a jaw. Then Drost was at his shoulder. Pastor too. The Caledonian warriors charged in, blades scything down in the drab light. And then it was over.

The enemy were hurtling back down the bank, their dead and wounded left behind. Drost gave a roar of triumph. Victorinus clawed himself back to his feet once more, vision blurred, head spinning. He staggered to the crest of the ridge, standing on the line Vitulus had marked out in the mud. It was churned up, wet, reduced to slush by the warm blood that carpeted it.

He had to focus his eyes to see, but at the bottom of the incline, the remnants of the Saxone warriors were regrouping, their commander trying to get them back in to a line. The mass of dead shocked Victorinus. Seemed the fighting had only been going on moments, though in his state time was hard to judge. There must have been twenty dead enemies strewn out across the slope. From what he could see, Vitulus and Drost had lost no one.

His eyes still on the enemy, he watched as the leader of the Saxones stepped out in front of his men. Seemed to Victorinus the man's eyes were locked on him. The hairs on the back of his neck stood on end, and he felt quite faint, eyes widening as he stared down. There was something familiar about the man. Something. He couldn't quite place it.

'Do you remember me, Tribune Victorinus?' The Saxone called up the slope. The man threw down his sword, and with his right hand, reached behind his shield. Victorinus was too far away to see what the man was doing, but after a moment's work, the man seemed to free his shield from some sort of strap, and threw it to the floor. He had no left hand.

'Good gods,' Victorinus muttered, staggering back a step. Drost was at his shoulder, ready to catch him if he fell.

'Sixtus, are you ok?' The chief muttered, looking down at the Saxones too. 'Do you... know this man?' he said with a pause.

'That's what I was going to say to you earlier, sir,' Pastor said at his other shoulder. 'The man who kidnapped us, it's the same man we killed-

'My name is Aldhard, chief of the Sturii. Your tribune here witnessed my death not four weeks ago, on some nameless land just down the coast. Yet here I stand! Strong and hale! I have come for you, tribune. Just as I said I would!'

'It cannot be,' Victorinus muttered. But the more he looked, the more certain he was. The long hair that billowed in the breeze looked to be the same colour. There was a mark on the man's left cheek. If he were closer, Victorinus was sure it would be a long curved scar that ran from eye to mouth. And of course, the man was missing his left hand. 'How is this possible? He had his head cut off.'

'Are either of you going to tell me what the fuck is going on?' Drost said.

'That man down there. I saw him die,' Victorinus said again.

'He don't look very dead to me.'

'With the gods as my witness, I vow my revenge on you, Tribune Sixtus Victorinus!' With that, he turned and stalked off, gesturing for his men to follow.

Victorinus' head swam. He stumbled back a step and fell to his arse before letting his head slump back to the mud. He had so many questions, but his knackered mind couldn't bring himself to think about them. How was Aldhard alive? And why did the man seem so intent on getting Victorinus? Maximus had been the one to order his death. Maximus had led the Roman army that defeated his raiders. What had Victorinus done to incur such wrath?

It was too much for him to process. He was dimly aware of the heads hovering over him. Pastor, Drost and Vitulus, all with anxious expressions. He went to say something to them, anything, but he had no words. In delirious silence, he slipped in to blackness.

***

It was dark when he awoke, and for a blissful moment, he remembered nothing of where he was or how he came to be there. Then it all came rushing back in a flood. He wretched, vomit splashing down the front of his mail. His head pounded.

'Feeling better then?' Drost said through a lopsided grin. 'You've been out for hours.'

'Water,' Victorinus croaked, throat as dry as old leather. Drost passed him a skin.

He drank greedily, wiping water from his beard when he finished. 'Where are we?' he squinted around. The night was dark, the moon hidden by thick black clouds. He could make out the silhouettes of trees bereft of leaves, but not much else.

'Same place we were when you passed out. We've moved off the hillside a bit, trying to get out the wind.'

Victorinus nodded at that. Made sense to move away from all the dead bodies, too. 'The enemy?'

'Retreated south for now. Vitulus reckons they'll be back on us come the dawn though. Wants everyone up before first light, ready to move.'

'Move where?'

'Now that's the question.' Drost shuffled in his cloak, hands reappearing with a small package wrapped in leather. 'There's some salted meat there, all we got. I made sure to save you some.'

Victorinus grunted. Last thing he wanted was food, but he took it all the same. 'We reckon we ran north for most of yesterday, though none of us saw the sun and we weren't exactly focusing on where we were going.'

'Just who we were running from,' Victorinus said.

'Exactly that. Plan is to move west for a few miles, then try to loop back south. We can't be more than half a day from the Wall.'

Victorinus chewed it over in his mind. He thought they might be further north than that, but kept it to himself. He hadn't been very alert the whole time they'd been moving yesterday, and he didn't want to say anything that might dampen morale further. 'I still refuse to believe that was Aldhard,' he said instead.

Drost sucked his teeth. 'Pastor told me about the battle on the coast. Seems an odd one. You are sure this Aldhard was killed?'

'He had his fucking head cut off,' Victorinus snapped. 'Yes Drost, I'm sure he was killed!'

'Aye, well,' Drost exhaled, leaned back on the damp ground and rubbed a hand through his beard. 'So it's not him,' he said with a shrug. 'You didn't see him up close. Could just be someone who looks like him. A relative with a grudge.'

'It's him,' a voice said from the shadows. Pastor emerged from the darkness, a cloak held tight around him. His eyes were sunken in his bruised face, black bags the size of shadows underneath. 'I saw him up close. We all did. Those of us they kept in that tent.'

'You are sure?' Victorinus asked.

Pastor nodded. 'Aye, certain. Same eyes, same scar on his cheek. Same... everything,' he finished.

Victorinus moved, so he sat next to Pastor. He opened his cloak and wrapped it around the young soldier, taking him in his arms. 'How bad are your wounds?' There had not been time for him to properly assess Pastor since the rescue, but looking at him now, Victorinus could see how battered and exhausted he was. He'd almost forgotten about the whipping he'd seen Pastor take. The youth had been through a lot.

'I'm fine,' Pastor said.

'No, you're not. I saw you get whipped on that beach the other day. The wounds on your face aren't the only ones you're carrying. Forget about Aldhard, or whoever he is, for the moment. Tell me how bad it is.'

Pastor sighed. 'It's my shoulders that are the worst. Pretty sure my tunic is stuck to the wound, don't really want to check.'

Victorinus and Drost shared a look. Both men were old soldiers, and they knew what could happen to a wound if it when untreated. He held up his left hand, still swollen from the broken knuckle and crusted with dried blood from where Drost had cauterised the wound. 'I got one minor cut on my left hand, did nothing with it, and look what's happened to me!'

'You are old,' Pastor said, much to the merriment of Drost.

'You think that's the worst wound I've ever taken? You've seen me get worse and you know it! I want you to let Drost take a look, get you cleaned up as best we can. I can't promise you're going to get any rest anytime soon, so we need to take every precaution we can.'

Pastor sighed, but nodded his agreement. He shivered as he took off his cloak. Drost had to help him shrug off his mail, and Victorinus bit back a comment when he saw the lad was only wearing a single tunic. 'Rookie error,' Vitulus' men would have undoubtedly said. He doubted the men of the Fourth were wearing less than two each.

The wounds were worse than Victorinus feared. Deep gashes sliced in to the flesh of his back, bits of tunic nestled in to the raw wounds. 'Shit,' Drost muttered, calling one of his men to heat some water. 'You're stronger than you look, I give you that.'

Victorinus couldn't take his eyes from the wound, tears of anger pricking his eyes. He'd given Pastor a home when he had nothing, and the lad had repaid him with nothing but love and loyalty since. Losing him would be much worse than losing a comrade. Pastor was family. Dawn was making its presence known above them, the sky a glow of orange.

'Time to move!' Vitulus could be heard snapping at his men.

'He can't go now,' Victorinus spoke to Drost in a low voice.

'I know,' Drost still poked at the wound, trying to work out the best way to go about patching it up.

'Holy shit!' Vitulus was at Victorinus' shoulder, bent over, looking at Pastor's back. 'You fought with this yesterday? God lad, you're a tough one.'

Victorinus grabbed Vitulus by the shoulder and steered him out of earshot. 'Listen, Pastor will not make it another day at the pace you're setting.'

'We move any slower, we get caught.'

Victorinus winced. 'I know that. So why don't we split up?'

'Absolutely not,' Vitulus shook his head. 'I'm not leaving you up here, sir. Those men yesterday, whoever they are, they're here for you. I don't know why, and I don't care. But I'm not letting them take you.'

Touched by the words, Victorinus smiled. 'You're a good man, Vitulus, and a great friend. But I think this is for the best. You get back south of the Wall, let Felicius know what is happening up here. He'll know what to do. Pastor and I will go with Drost's men north if we have to. Worse case we scout out this supposed army coming for us, best case we keep out the way for a few days and let Pastor heal a bit before coming south. If this Aldhard sees I am not with you, he might even let you pass without a fight.'

'My boys will get through those whoresons. You've no worry on that front.'

They both smiled. 'Just do me a favour when you get south. Check on my boys, will you? I worry for them, what with everything going on.'

Vitulus nodded. 'Of course I will, sir. Any message for Felicius?'

Victorinus thought. 'If we're not back ten days after you, start to worry. Send a messenger to Drost's people. If we can't go south for whatever reason, that's where we'll be. Oh, one other thing, do your men have any clothing Pastor could borrow? The only tunic he has is half buried in that mess on his back.'

'Aye, I'll sort that. Guess I'll see you in a few days, then?'
'You bet on it.'

The men of the Fourth moved out soon after, leaving two spare tunics for Pastor. Victorinus watched them move until he could see them no more, then scanned the southern horizon. Sure enough, a small band of men were just in sight, moving through a crop of trees in Vitulus' wake. 'Gods speed, my brother,' Victorinus whispered, then kissed his fingers and raised them to the rising sun. Vitulus and his men were going to need all the luck they could get.

XII

F elicius seethed at the latest delay. He stood on the deck of *The Mars,* the ship that had carried Maximus' secret cargo across the Mediterranean. 'So when will the cargo be unloaded?'

The ship's captain, a portly man named Calidus, scratched his bald head in his discomfort. 'Word is not until tomorrow at dusk, sir.'

'How can it take so long? There are a dozen or more empty carts sitting in the yard at the cartwright's workshop!'

'Aye sir, there's carts enough. Apparently, it's the mules they're lacking.'

'Where are all the mules? Horses? There's a stable not half a mile from here! Surely we can loan four horses for the job?'

'Yes sir, it's just that...' Calidus trailed off, quivering under the prefect's icy stare.

'One of the local gangs run the stables. Same with the cartwright, same with the-

'Yes thankyou!' Felicius held out a hand, his daughter smiling as he cut her off.

'You've pissed off quite a few people, it seems,' she smiled sweetly at her father.

Felicius sighed. All he'd had to do was come to Londinium, take possession of Maximus' cargo and get back north. Seemed he'd made a right mess of it. 'So what do we do?'

He had considered taken *The Mars* north, sailing up the east coast of Britannia and darting inland using one of the rivers. Calidus though, had claimed it was not possible. *The Mars* was a sea-going vessel, with a deep hull and low keel. The ship would not survive a journey that far inland. Felicius, knowing little about ships and seacraft, had appraised the size of the ship. It was twice the length of a bireme, the standard war ship Rome used at sea. A fair bit wider, too. Made sense it would be deeper. The ship was built for trade, to take on as much cargo as possible, and get it safely across the Mediterranean. No, she would not survive a voyage through Britannia's narrow rivers.

And then there was the cargo itself. Twenty-four circular lead pots, each the height of a man and three feet across, sealed with an iron lid and wax. They weighed so much it took four burly sailors to lift one, and Felicius estimated each cart could hold no more than four. 'Calidus, what do you suggest?'

The sailor shrugged. 'I don't know, sir,' he said in accented Latin. He was an easterner, Felicius couldn't be sure from where. But in the east Greek was the native tongue those days, Latin reserved for the western provinces. 'Only been here twice before. But as I said earlier, we won't make it further inland on this ship. We had to pole off mud banks twice just to get here. The keel is too deep, see.'

'Yes, yes you said that,' Felicius said with an exasperated sigh. 'Maybe I should try to speak to the governor.'

'You said that in the bar yesterday!' Marcelina waved her hands in frustration. 'And a whole day later we're still standing on this ship, pondering what to do.'

'Right,' Felicius nodded, mind made up. 'Come on then, let's go. Calidus, you stay here and guard the cargo, you two with me,' he said the last to Marcelina and Davos.

The young Greek perked up at that. They had fitted him in a new tunic, boots, and a thick winter cloak. Felicius had taken the lad to the local bathhouse the night before, watched as the boy was oiled and scrubbed; he'd even taken him to the barbers that morning. The results were startling. Gone was the grubby street urchin you'd cross a street to avoid. He now looked half respectable.

He and Marcelina had to half jog to keep up with Felicius as he forced a quick march through Londinium's streets. They passed bakers and potteries, barbers and tanners, all with young boys of their own lurking outside their doors, shouting special offers and doing their best to entice customers onto their premises. Felicius ignored them all. The governor's palace was an impressive sight, not that Felicius took the time to take it in. Cut stone piled so high it seemed to block out the sun, curved pillars, intricately carved statues – and that was just the outside.

'Hold there!' a voice boomed from behind a closed helmet. A soldier stepped towards them, face hidden behind a bronze ceremonial mask. 'State your name and business.'

'Prefect Gaius Felicius of the Fourth Cohort of Gauls here to see Governor Priscus,' Felicius said in a haughty tone. 'I'm on the business of the *Dux* Maximus and have little time.'

The bronze face mask stared at the prefect for a long moment, before the soldier inside handed his spear to a man behind him and removed the helm. 'Prefect, sir. I didn't recognise you. My name is Titus Focalis. I served under you for a short time in Pannonia.'

'Well met,' Felicius said with a thin smile. 'Apologies if I don't return the favour, I've served with a lot of men over the years.' Focalis showed no sign of his rank, but neither did Felicius, wearing just a plain mail shirt and cloak as he was. Felicius didn't think the man could outrank him though, no one higher than a centurion would be tasked with guarding the entrance to a palace in the middle of a subdued city.

'I was just a recruit when we served together, sir. My first two years in the army were under your command. I wouldn't expect you to remember me! I was there when you wounded your leg, though,' the man said, looking down at Felicius' wounded thigh.

Felicius shuffled, thin smile fading. The wound had been a persistent problem for him since receiving it. It had been deep, missing his artery by only a finger's breadth. He knew he'd been lucky to survive; he also knew he'd be much more than a prefect if he'd not insisted on leading from the front in battle and taking the wound in the first place. He thought briefly of the last letter he'd received from Theodosius, and the offer of advancement it contained. Then pushed it quickly from his mind. 'It healed well. God be thanked. Is the governor here?'

'He is, sir, but he'll be off to the forum shortly. There are a couple of big court cases closing today. He will want to be kept abreast of the news.'

'I just need a moment of his time,' Felicius insisted.

Focalis seemed to consider it a moment, before nodding his head. 'Come with me. Leave your weapons with my men please, none are allowed within.'

Felicius handed over his sword and dagger, standard practice when entering any imperial residence across the empire. He followed Focalis across the marble floors, stopping now and then to drag Marcelina and Davos away from the mosaics and paintings that fixed their gawping eyes. 'Not the time for sightseeing,' he muttered to them both.

Up two floors and across another lavish corridor, they reached a set of huge wooden doors big enough for an elephant to pass under, with two guards stationed outside. Focalis ordered them open, and the guards duly obeyed. Inside was a chamber that even stopped Felicius in his tracks.

The floor was African marble, distinctive with its yellow colouring streaked with blue veins. The air was filled with the potent scent of lavender. A small wooden throne sat on a raised dais at the far end. This then was the governor's receiving hall, where he would receive petitions and emissaries and pass the emperor's judgement. The governor himself, an elderly man draped in a white tunic streaked with purple, busied himself with three rolls of parchment, bundling them up and handing them to a waiting slave.

The slaves themselves were another evident sign of the opulence of the governor. *Puer delicatus* is how the high society would have regarded them. Each a young man, so handsome they were almost beautiful, with soft, perfumed skin and well-proportioned figures. Felicius noticed with a hint of disgust the short length of their tunics, and guessed if one was to look underneath, they would find the boys worked without a loincloth. Felicius had never considered the governor to be one to indulge. The man had governed the southern province of Britannia for years, throughout the tumultuous rebellion that had nearly been the end of them all. He had always come across as an astute, no nonsense, God fearing man. Perhaps, though, that was the impression he wanted the outside world to see.

'Governor,' Felicius said, snapping a salute. 'I am sorry to intrude on your time. I know you are a busy man.'

Governor Priscus appraised Felicius with watery eyes. He was an old man, older perhaps than a governor of such a big province should be. Britannia, though, was always an afterthought for the rest of the empire. Or so it seemed to those stationed there. 'Prefect, good to see you. Has the *Dux* run out of men already? How goes it in the north? I get such little news.'

Surprised, Felicius quickly outlined Maximus' position and his overall plan. The governor nodded, taking it in, all the while snapping his fingers at a waiting slave, taking another roll of parchment and scanning it, then the same with a wax tablet. Felicius just had time to ponder why it was he giving the governor an update and not Maximus himself when the man spoke. 'Sounds like he has everything under control, for now at least. So why are you here?'

'The *Dux* sent me to collect some cargo for him. Something he's had sent from the east.'

'What is it?'

'I don't actually know, *domine*. But whatever it is, it's being stored in twenty-four lead-lined pots as tall as me. How I'm expected to get them north with the roads as they are, I'll never know.'

'Say that again?' Priscus said, eyes suddenly alert, rolls of papyrus forgotten. Felicius repeated it. 'Lead-lined pots? From the east?' he threw the documents to a slave and paced, mouth muttering inaudible words. '*Didn't think he'd go through with it*,' Felicius thought he heard, but he couldn't be sure.

'Yes, *domine*,' Felicius said, curious about the sudden change in the governor. 'I have been trying to arrange passage north for them, but let's just say I'm encountering some difficulties.'

'How so?'

'The gangs, sir. We've had a bit of a run in.'

Priscus sighed, dismissing his beautiful slaves with a flick of this wrist. 'Tell me everything.'

Felicius spoke of meeting Davos, then Cyclops and Amaurus, and his fight in the bar.

'I'm not proud of this,' Priscus said in a low voice. 'But you are right, we have a problem. There are four gangs. Cyclops and his 'Dockers' as they're known, Clodius and his 'Street Rats', as they call themselves, are the most prominent. There are two others, but we suspect they pay tribute to those two. I'm afraid that since the great rebellion, I have been so busy putting right all kinds of wrongs up and down the country – not just my province – that it has been allowed to grow rather out of control. Londinium has always been a tough city to control. People come and go from across the sea in their thousands. It's too easy for people to slip off a ship unnoticed in the docks. Not everyone arrives on our shores with the best intentions, I fear.'

'But surely we could change that? More men on the docks? An honest tribune in charge?'

'Ahh yes, Amaurus. Rather a lost soul, I'm afraid. Prefect, if I had a dozen officers such as you, I've no doubt I could have the situation covered in a week. As it is... there are many pressing concerns on my time, and alas, I am but one man. I will send someone to the docks to assist you, though, as soon as I can. Make sure you stay at the docks with that ship, you hear me? Good. Now, if you'll excuse me, I really need to be getting on.'

With that, he was gone, his slaves streaming after him.

'So now what do we do?' Marcelina said, her eyes still roaming the extravagant room.

'We go back to our cargo, I suppose. How did the two of you find meeting the governor? Not every day you meet a man of his status.'

'He seemed familiar,' Davos said.

'How so?'

The young Greek shrugged. 'I don't know, just felt like I'd met him before.'

Felicius slapped the boy on the shoulder. 'With the life you've had, nothing would surprise me. Come, we're for the docks.'

***

Morning rolled to afternoon, the sun passing its zenith out of sight, hidden behind the winter clouds. The wind skimmed up off the waters of the Tamesis, forcing Felicius and his small retinue to curl up in their cloaks beside the ship's railing, bundled together for warmth. Calidus fretted the day away. He was due to pick up supplies at Rutupiae at dawn the following day, and from there to make immediate passage back east. He had not allowed for this delay in his planning.

'We could unload the cargo on to the dock for you?' he asked. Felicius thought more in hope than expectation.

'And leave me stranded with Maximus' precious cargo and no means of defending it? No chance, captain. I don't know what it is inside those pots, but they have great importance to my commander. He is not a man you want to disappoint.'

Calidus grunted in his exasperation. Felicius felt for the man. None of this was his fault. He was a simple trader, just doing his job. Unfortunately for him, it always seemed to be the little people that suffered when the higher ups clicked their fingers. Felicius was a soldier. He knew that more than anyone.

They had just eaten their midday meal. Fresh bread and cheese, olives and a jug of warm beer Calidus rustled up from his ship's bows when Felicius scanned the quayside, skin prickling in anticipation. 'Where are all the people?' he said to no one in particular.

Marcelina stood shakily, purple lips quivering. She moved next to her father and scanned the dry land. Felicius could hear her teeth chattering. 'Does seem quiet.'

The riverside had been a hub of activity ever since their arrival. Traders, sailors, merchants stalked the cobbles, whilst whores and peddlers, some claiming they could tell your fortune, others offering to perform feats of magic for a coin or two, moved amongst them. Now, though, it was empty.

'I've just remembered where I've seen that governor before,' Davos said into the silence.

Felicius turned to the boy, arched an eyebrow. 'And?'

Davos didn't reply at first, just turned to look towards the warehouse he'd called home, poking out a trembling finger in its direction. 'In there.'

Felicius followed his finger. The dilapidated warehouse stood out alongside the others. Not just because of its state. But because of the mass of armed men that streamed from it. It all clicked into place. Cyclops being so derisive when Felicius had said he was going to the governor, Amaurus and his drunken debauchery, so brazen, right under the governor's nose. And Priscus himself, ears pricking when Felicius mentioned the gangs causing him problems. His sudden interest in what Maximus was bringing to the north. And then this. Davos had seen the governor before. And he'd seen him in that warehouse.

'Calidus!' Felicius bellowed, the portly captain jogging across the deck to him, breath steaming in the air. 'How quickly can you get this ship pushed out into the river?'

Calidus puffed out his cheeks, his eyes fixed on the mass of men coming towards them. 'Don't know what you've got us involved in here, but I can't see it being any of my business.'

'Those men are coming for this cargo.' Felicius pointed to the pots. 'And this cargo is under your command, under direct command of the *Dux Britanniarum*. Do you want to have to tell Maximus you lost his cargo because you wouldn't fight for it?'

Felicius could see the scenario playing out in Calidus' mind. His lips moved like a fish out of water as he desperately tried to think of a way out of their situation. 'Half my men are still ashore!' he blurted out, eventually. 'I gave them a day's leave as we're stuck here!'

'If we stay, we die. Can you sail this ship without them?'

The captain looked around at his remaining men, some playing dice behind a windbreak, others busying themselves with tasks on deck. 'We need to get the cargo back into the hold.'

'We can do that once we're on the river. How do we push ourselves off?'

'Dock hands use their poles to get us going usually. Don't think there'll be any on hand today.'

'Neither do I. Where are the poles?' Calidus pointed to two long poles strapped to the side of the deck. 'Give me one of your men and we'll do it ourselves,' Felicius said, freeing a pole as he spoke and leaping over the side of the ship to the dock.

'Father!' Marcelina squirmed. 'You don't have much time!'

'Tell me something I don't know,' Felicius muttered, already thrusting his pole into the water. He'd seen men do a similar task at his time in Bononia. They'd push out, aiming the pole as far down the hull as they could. With a thump, one of Calidus' crew landed beside him on the dock, the man immediately bringing his pole to bear. Together, they pushed.

'Hurry!' Marcelina called. Felicius looked up to her, seeing her desperate gaze in the direction of the mob. He could hear them over the current, over the wind, hear their whoops of joy and blood hungry cries. They were coming for him. He heaved on that pole, every muscle tensed as he forced his weight into the push, willing the ship to move. Slowly, it did.

'Just a bit more, then we can turn her with the oars!' Calidus called from the rear deck. 'Come on now, push!'

Felicius' face bulged with the effort. He could hear the thud of wooden clubs reverberate off warehouse walls. The tang of smoke from flaming torches reached his nostrils as he sucked in air. One last time, he threw his weight behind the pole, willing the ship to part from the dock. Eventually, it did,

'Jump on!' Calidus called and Felicius leaped for the side, pole forgotten, and clung desperately to the rail. Two sets of hands grabbed his, and he was hauled bodily onboard, landing unceremoniously on the deck with a bang. The wind knocked out of him.

'Oars left side, ten more strokes!' Calidus called out, and one of the crew called out the strokes. Felicius clambered to his feet and looked over the rail. Cyclops and his men were at the water's edge, a seething mob of wood, bone, and iron. Two of them tried to make the jump, one man reaching the side of the ship before a swinging oar swiftly swept away his hands. The other man hit the water, screaming.

'Both sides oars, let's go!' Calidus called and once more, the strokes were called out. Felicius breathed a sigh of relief to see the ship straightening in the middle of the river. There were just ten oars to each side, Calidus still being without a lot of his crew, but crucially, *The Mars* was moving.

'We should be safe for now,' he said to Marcelina, folding her in to an embrace. She clung to him in a way she hadn't since she was a little girl, and for a moment, her hair in his face, Felicius remembered the joy of receiving the unconditional love of the young.

'We're far from safe,' Calidus said, his eyes still fixed on the mob. 'Look ahead, see how the river narrows? They'll be able to get to us then. We make it past there, I reckon we'll be alright.'

Felicius looked. Ahead, the river curved off to the right. To his dismay, he saw the captain was right. It narrowed, not by much, but enough that with the ship's wide deck, they would indeed be close enough to the shore for the mob to be able to jump up at them. 'What do we do?' he called across to the captain.

Calidus grinned, pointing down at the sword hanging at Felicius' waist. 'We fight, prefect.'

Felicius looked around the deck. There were twenty-two sailors he could see, plus Calidus, his daughter and Davos. They needed twenty men to row the ship, and taking any of them from their oars would lengthen the time they were exposed at the narrows. 'Can you fight?' he called to Calidus, the wind kicking up as they moved further from the dock.

'Ha! I've been a sailor for fifteen years, prefect! You ever experienced a pirate raid?'

'Funnily enough I have,' Felicius shuddered at the memory. The crashing of two ships colliding, the vicious water hissing up from the deep. The utter helplessness of it. At least, he reasoned, as bad as this day got, it would not be as terrifying as that.

'Then you know the danger we live with. I train every man that sails with me with sword and spear. Not to the levels you'd be used to, of course. But we know which end is the pointy one.' He flourished a wink, shouted an order for one of his men to go below deck and gather their weapons. 'We'll take a man off the oars on each side. Won't make a lot of difference to our speed, but should help us in the fight. Main thing is we need to protect the rowers to our right. The ones on the left shouldn't be in much danger.'

'How do we do that?' Felicius asked.

'Line the right deck with shields, will give the rowers some protection and use a barrier to fight behind. Could your lad and daughter help bring them up from below?' A nod to Marcelina and she was off, dragging Davos with her.

'When the fighting starts, they need to be below deck,' Felicius said.

'Agreed. We've got moments left. Let's get these shields up!' Felicius and Calidus fixed the shields to the ship's rail. They slotted in easy enough, Felicius pleased to see specially made forks sticking out of the rail he'd not noticed before, seemed they'd been put there just for that. He'd wished he'd had them on the ship he sailed on from Rutupiae, on the doomed trip to Bononia to prevent a rebellion. The shields in place, the rowers fixed with helmets and thick cloaks rolled up over their rowing arms. They were as prepared as they could be.

'Won't the oars bite on the bank?' Felicius asked Calidus as they neared the turn. They could see the mob easily enough, a raging torrent of men hardened by lives spent on Londinium's streets. They may not have been soldiers, but Felicius was not about to underestimate them.

'Aye, they will. We used them to propel us along on the way in, unconventional, but it worked well enough then, should do the same now.'

'And the cargo? Won't it get in the way?' The led pots were tied down to the deck, Calidus worried about losing them even as his ship had swayed peacefully at the dock. 'Can't move them now! And if we do our jobs properly, we won't get boarded, anyway!'

Felicius kept his thoughts on that to himself. He hadn't bothered trying to count the enemy, but there were a hundred at least. They were four men. 'How long will it take to get past them?'

'Count to a hundred once the fighting starts. We should be clear of them by then!'

'I'll be happy to still be speaking by the time we get to eighty,' he mumbled to himself. He allowed himself a moment to long for Vitulus and his men. To just have eight of his cohort with him on that deck, he would hold the ship to the count of a thousand. And then there was no time to think at all.

He blocked a slash of a wooden club on his shield, sword point licking out to take its bearer in the chest. 'One,' he called. It was a funny thing to be fighting an enemy whilst in motion. He exchanged two blows with a flame haired swordsman and then had to leave the man be as he drifted out of reach. His count got to ten as he plunged his blade into an armpit, yanked it free and heard the cursing of the rower next to him, who got covered in blood. 'Better his than yours!' Felicius called, swinging his sword backhanded and cutting deep in to an arm. The rowing platform was on the deck, the benches fixed in place so the rowers didn't move. But Felicius had to adjust his stance as the rowers pulled their oars in as the banks of the river narrowed. Looking left and right, he could see no sign they had boarded the ship, and it satisfied him that even at this close encounter, it would still present a daunting challenge for the men on the shore to make the jump.

A clash on his shield had his head spinning left, and Cyclops himself was there, axe in hand. The gang lord roared and spat, phlegm plastering Felicius' face as the axe came in again. 'Thirty,' Felicius muttered, waiting for the axe to move again. When it did, he watched the swing and adjusted the grip on his sword, swinging it low to high, aiming for Cyclops's wrist. The blade struck home with a satisfying crunch. The one eyed man gave an anguished cry before falling from view.

'Halfway!' a voice came from off to his left somewhere, and Felicius grinned, growing in to the fight. He took two lives in quick succession, first with a jab to the throat, the other a sweeping cut that opened a man's bowels. Then their worst nightmare happened. A cry to his right alerting him to the danger, he stepped back from the rail and the battle, and saw to his dismay three men had clambered onboard. One of Calidus' men was already down and the nearest rower was completely unprotected. Felicius charged without thinking. He slammed in to the first of the enemy, the weight of his mail and shield proving too much for his startled opponent. The next came at him with a club studded with nails. The man swung it high to low and Felicius used his shield to catch it, twisting the shield as he did so the nails bit into the wood. Stepping inside the man's reach, he punched a hole in his groin and left him in a bloodied heap on the deck.

One more left. He turned to where he thought the man was, only to find him standing over him, club raised high. No time to bring his shield around, sword hand not ready for an attack. He could do nothing but watch in dismay as the club cleaved down towards his head. It never made it. Its bearer, a young man with long blonde hair and a pox marked face, staggered a step, grunted a surprised 'urk' before blood bubbled at his lips and he slumped to the deck.

Marcelina still held the spear she'd driven into the man's back. 'Sounded like you needed help,' she said, wide eyes fixed on the man she'd killed.

'Good God, Marcelina,' Felicius uttered, too stunned to say or do anything else.

'We're clear!' Calidus called, and a raucous cheer went up from the sailors.

'I...I killed a man,' Marcelina muttered, her eyes still transfixed on the corpse.

'And I am most grateful that you did.' Felicius dropped his sword and shield, grabbing Marcelina by the shoulders and pulling her in tight. He thought it wise not to add that she had in fact stabbed a man in the bar fight he'd got himself in to, and that this was probably the second time she had saved his life. No father, though, wanted to put their children through that kind of pain. She sobbed, a soft cry after the cacophony of battle. 'Come now,' he said soothingly, looking back to the rest of the mob stranded on the river bank. 'We're going to be ok.'

XIII

The weather cleared on the third day. They'd hobbled through the endless landscape, up and down the mountainous terrain. Broken men. Ruined men. Malnutrition took its toll, the hunting as bleak as the winter weather. Mainly though, they were just tired. And tired men are complacent men.

'Down the track there, look! In that thicket of trees.'

'Can't see a thing,' Victorinus said, wincing at the pain in his hand as he lowered himself to the frozen grass.

'I don't want to point as then they'll know we've seen them,' Drost said, eyes scanning the southern horizon as he sat with his back to a tree. It had been half an hour since they'd stopped, possibly half of that since Drost had quietly alerted the group they were being followed.

'How many?' Victorinus asked.

'Can't say. I've seen two for certain, but I'd wager there's twenty odd more where they came from.'

'And just eight of us,' Victorinus grumbled miserably. His stomach rumbled as he spoke, so loud he'd be surprised if the men trailing them hadn't heard. 'Gods, I'm hungry.'

'Alec is out hunting.'

'Alec has been out hunting every damn day. At this point, I'd be happy if he came back with a fig for us to split eight ways.'

'Not sure they grow up here, to be fair. Ooh, movement!' he said, suddenly excited. 'I see four men, five! Fuck it!'

'Fuck it what?'

'That one handed bastard is down there.'

Victorinus shivered at the thought. He moved his head left to right, casually as he could. He made out nothing in the trees. Truth be told, the trees themselves were a bit of a blur. Wasn't much fun getting old.

'How do you think they found us?' Drost asked.

'We've been blundering around in the wilderness for two days since parting ways with Vitulus. I doubt it was particularly challenging for them. The bigger question is, what do we do about it?' Victorinus felt despondent. An old, wounded man at the end of his tether. He had half a mind to stumble down the slope and hand himself over, maybe make a show of it and earn himself a quick death in battle. He was contemplating doing just that when Pastor tapped him on the shoulder.

'Something you both need to see,' he hissed. Pastor had been out hunting with Alec. Drost's men had obviously told him about their hunters, for he spoke in a low voice, eyes pointedly not looking south.

Victorinus sighed. 'Not sure I can take more bad news right now, lad.'

'It's not bad! But you both need to see it.'

'See what?' Drost asked.

'Abandoned Roman fort. Tiny place, just four rotting wooden walls and a collapsed tower.'

Victorinus scoffed a laugh. Such places were common enough between the Wall of Hadrian and the long abandoned turf wall made in the reign of Antoninus. They hadn't held the latter for very long. 'Pastor, a few rotting walls and a dilapidated lookout tower will not do us much good.'

'No, sir. But what's in it will.'

Drost arched an eyebrow, a half smile dancing across his beard as he looked to Victorinus. 'Worth a look, no?'

'Alec is there now. We've trapped four hares. He's skinning them as we speak.'

'Why didn't you say that to start with?' Drost quickly ordered two of his men to sit where he and Victorinus had been. They wanted to give the illusion that two men were on watch, the others resting within the trees at the top of the incline. 'Those bastards make a move, you run like dogs to find us. No heroics,' he told them, before helping Victorinus off the floor and following Pastor.

The walk was worth the wait. 'Gods below,' Victorinus muttered, staring into the wooden chest. 'And it was just sitting here in the open?'

'No, sir. Looked like an animal had started digging a hole, must have stopped when it hit the wood. Was Alec that noticed it.'

The chest was enormous. The length of a man at least and three feet wide, its lock and hinges all but rusted away. The contents, however, were almost as good as new. *Plumbatae,* the lead weighted darts issued to infantrymen to carry clipped on to the inner rim of their shields, were piled high on top. Gleefully pulling them all out and leaving them on the grass, they found a haul of *martiobarbuli*, similar to the *plumbatae,* but shorter. Beneath them, two sacks filled with caltrops, wicked little inventions used to lay a trap on the ground. Made from two nails secured together, the spiked tips positioned in a way so that no matter how they landed, at least one tip was always pointing up. 'Reckon we can put this lot to good use,' Victorinus murmured. There was one more surprise at the bottom of the chest. Ten thick spears, four feet in length, tapered with an iron head, lay in the bottom. Victorinus thought them most likely originally made for cavalry, but used on foot, they could be just as deadly.

'What you thinking?' Drost asked, his eyes still fixed on the arsenal in front of him.

'I'm thinking that a century or more ago, when this little fort was abandoned, they had no carts to transport this lot, so they buried them with every intention of returning for them when they could. Guess they just got forgotten about. I'm also thinking that if we plan this right, we could cause our friends back there some real damage before they even get close to us.'

Victorinus reached into the chest and took the spears out. Beneath them, nestled into a corner, was a roll of horsehair, once a shining dark brown, now a rusted red. 'We can use this too,' he mused. 'Right, we pick our ground. Somewhere with a narrow front, lay as many of these traps as we can, then fight the bastards.'

It didn't take them long to find what they were looking for. The remains of a Roman road ran north to south, close to the small fort. Not a road in the sense of smoothed cobbles, rather a track laid down with wooden beams. Would have been used for transporting goods back in the days of Rome's occupation north of the Wall, rather than a highway for the army to manoeuvre on. To each side was a crop of trees, thick, impenetrable, even in the depths of winter. Victorinus had no doubt there would be ways of their hunters circling them, but if there were, it would not be quick, and with the small numbers each side had, they would spot it easily enough. Besides, they had very limited time.

'Dig here,' he said to two of Drost's men. They had limited Latin, as much as he had a small amount of their mother tongue from his days in the *miles areani*, and with some gesturing and demonstrating, he got his message across. To Pastor, he gave the task of stripping branches from the nearby trees and carving them into deadly stakes. 'Lily pits, lad,' he said when the boy questioned his task. 'First line of defence.' Drost's men got to work and soon they were sweating under the weak winter sun, the frozen ground unwilling to cede them its fruits.

Drost busied himself with the horsehair. He looped each end around a tree trunk; the hair spanning across the road. To the left side tree, he tied the end of the rope around a large fallen tree trunk and propped the trunk in the branches of two nearby trees. 'They'll trip the wire when they run for us. That will release the trunk, which will swing down and smash them in their faces. Reckon we'll trim them down by two or three before they get within thirty paces of us,' he said with a satisfied smirk.

Victorinus chuckled. He'd no idea if the little trick would work, from what he could see the trunk would swing so slowly it would be easily dodged. But if it cost the enemy a moment as they navigated the obstacle, it was another moment they had to set themselves. His hand still burned like hell, so leaving the others to their work, Victorinus walked back to the abandoned fort, checking the two men left on watch hadn't moved. They were still in place, one giving him a thumbs up as he cautiously approached, letting him know their enemy had not yet made their move. He pondered briefly what was taking them so long? Aldhard knew their numbers. Why did he not just charge up the hill and be done with?

Back at the fort, he scanned the interior of the building for any other hidden gems. He found nothing. Though in what was once a small yard, he did find a shield half buried in the undergrowth. It was round; the feint remains of red and gold paint on the front. He couldn't make out the symbol it once depicted. Not that it mattered overly. Most of the legions based in Britannia – or anywhere else in the empire for that matter – were long gone now, replaced by the field armies populated with mercenaries. *We were gods once;* he thought as he rubbed the front of the shield. Looking back to the ruined watchtower, trying to picture what it once was, he sighed, once more thinking of how far they had fallen. A soldier had held the shield that was in his hands now. A proud man, a fighting man. The shield still bore the faded scars of battle. He imagined a soldier holding it in a calloused grip, his own arms lined with matching scars.

No one remembers that soldier's name, was his lasting thought, a slight bitterness on his tongue. History remembers the generals, the Caesar's, but not the men that fought and died to bring their names to immortality. He walked back to the men. The jubilance and hope he'd felt when he had seen the contents of the chest had evaporated like morning dew. He was an old man, and war was a young man's game. He cast his eyes up to the weak winter sun, kissed his fingers, and raised them high. An old salute to Sol Invictus, one his father had performed every morning. Today he did it in his memory. Tomorrow, he thought, there might be no one left to remember him.

They came an hour or so later. Victorinus had the lily pits dug, the sharpened branches dug into the bottom, and as much detritus from the woodland covering the pits. It wasn't perfect, and he worried Aldhard and his men would spot them immediately, but it was better than nothing. Drost paced out a battle line, running a foot through the mud, same as Vitulus had when they'd fought before. Victorinus moved along the line, placing the darts and spears on the ground, ready for the men. That was when Drost's two scouts came running back. It was time to fight.

'Use the longer darts first,' Victorinus said to Pastor, as much to calm his own nerves as anything. 'They've a bit more range and I've seen them punch clean through a shield when thrown well. Once they're past the lily pits, we throw the shorter ones, then we heft the spears and try to pick a few off before they come in range to use their swords.'

'I've never used one of these before,' Pastor said, holding up one of the smaller darts.

'Throw it just like a javelin. You'll be fine.'

'Never used one of those, either. Not fought with a spear before, come to think of it,' Pastor said, reaching down and picking one up by the ash shaft.

'Gods, I've not given you much of an education, have I? How's your back?'

'Hurts like hell, but I'll get through it.'

Victorinus just grunted. He'd seen the wounds the lad had taken, and was pretty sure that if it had been him, he would have been good for nothing. His own wounds were problematic enough, and they were small fry compared to what Pastor was going through. 'We need shields,' he said to himself. They were to form a battle line, him, Pastor, Drost and the five men the chief had left. It wasn't much, and since none of them had shields, it felt even less. 'Drost, how many we facing?'

'Fifteen, according to Alec. So two each for you whoresons, five for me and we'll call it a job well done!' He grinned, and Victorinus couldn't help but responding in kind. If he was going to die, he was doing it with his friends. There were worse ways to go. They formed their line, darts in hands, ready. Victorinus felt naked without a shield, but knew he could not hold one in his injured hand. He checked the position of the darts on the ground, judged the reach to grab the spear. He was as ready as he could be.

'Here they come!' Drost called, and if on cue, the enemy stalked into view. They didn't come at a run, which worried Victorinus. He wanted them hurtling at their line. Not this careful approach. He was banking on their little traps thinning out their ranks, evening the numbers a little. What he needed was for them to be angry.

'Drost, maybe you could give them some encouragement?'

The chief smiled. 'I can do that.' Drost swaggered out of the line, dropping his dart and turning his back to the enemy. Grin still fixed to his face, he lifted his mail, pulled down his trousers and wiggled his arse at the Saxones faces. 'What do you think of that, hey?' he called, oblivious to whether or not they could hear him. 'Good stuff over here lads, form a queue and I'll get to you all in good time!'

His men laughed, even though they couldn't understand his Latin. The gesture spoke for itself. One of Drost's men stepped forward, brought out his cock and had a casual piss as the enemy stood on watching. Victorinus giggled at the sight. Then his own bladder twinged. *Always before a battle.* His throat was like leather, his bowels rebelling and suddenly the need to piss grew more and more urgent. Didn't matter how many battles you lived through, the sheer terror of it never went away.

Drost's provocation worked, and in an instant, the Saxones moved from careful consideration to outright charge. Fifteen men may be a small number, but group them together and arm them with swords and shields they can look a mighty force. Victorinus felt the inevitable urge to take a step back when they charged, Aldhard howling at their centre. They were forty paces off, each of them snarling a war cry as their boots thumped across the ground. Then Victorinus remembered the little surprises he and his men had set up for them, and his confidence grew a touch.

First was the trip wire. The horsehair was all but invisible to those not looking for it. One of Aldhard's men stepped through it, and almost instantaneously Victorinus saw the fallen trunk lodged in the trees to the Saxones left twinge. But twinge was all it did. He was about to curse Drost and his impotent schemes when another of the enemy pushed the horsehair with their boot. And then with a snapping of branches, the trunk was free and hurtling down at their unsuspecting heads.

Drost whooped with joy. Victorinus, however, did not. He saw the trunk fall, but saw also the speed at which the Saxones moved and he was certain they would outpace the booby trap. He had not quite realised the full extent of Drost's wicked scheme, though. The trunk swooped in an arc, but rather than swing directly across the broken road, it came at an angle, smashing in to the back of Aldhard's men, taking three out before they knew what had hit them. Two more fell as they heard the clatter of wood on iron, just to force their bodies from its path.

The others, however, didn't break from their stride. Pastor let his impatience get the better of him, and he hurled his first dart, it thumped blade first into the flat of a shield. 'Not yet!' Drost called, his own dart ready. 'After the pit!'

The ten remaining Saxones had lost their cohesion, and Victorinus thought a little of their courage after seeing five of their number taken out by the trunk. Three were looking behind them as those at the front found the lily pit. Aldhard himself jumped it, albeit unintentionally, his huge strides taking him clean over. The two men behind him were not so lucky. The first plunged left foot first into the pit, the *snap* of bone audible even over the shout and cries of imminent battle. The second warrior stumbled when he saw his comrade fall, but could not stop his momentum taking him into the pit. He impaled himself on a stake, falling face first to his death.

'Darts!' Drost yelled into the chaos, and as one, they unleashed their *plumbatae.* Victorinus grunted as he threw, watching the flat arc of the dart, seeing with pleasure it slam into Aldhard's shield, piercing the wood and bursting through the other side. He was just twenty paces from him, the dart not slowing him down. In a panic, Victorinus scooped up his *martiobarbulus* and hurled it at Aldhard. This one gave the one handed Saxone pause. He slowed his run, hunched behind his shield, and let the linden board take the blow. It was a mistake. The board splintered as the dart burst through, and when Aldhard lowered the shield, Victorinus let out a cheer to see a savage looking cut on the man's left cheek.

He bent down and scooped up his spear, buoyed by his success with the dart. He was about to charge forwards and engage with Aldhard when Pastor yelled 'caltrops!' and stopped him in his tracks. Cursing, he back stepped, so he was in line with his friends, and cast a glance behind Aldhard. The two men that had dived to dodge the trunk were back on their feet. Three men in total had succumbed to the lily pit. That was five men from their first two dirty tricks. A further three men were down, with darts sticking out of their heads. That left just seven. Suddenly, living to see another sunset seemed a real possibility.

'Come on you bastards!' Victorinus screamed, blood up, eager for the fight. Aldhard smiled and took a step forwards. He used his sword to cut the shield strap from his left arm, and let the dart weighted board fall to the ground. He roared a wordless battle cry and leaped forward, and found one last obstacle.

His left foot landed on a caltrop. They were two inches long, plenty enough to bite through boot and skin alike. He howled as the nail lodged in his foot, and Victorinus smiled to see another of his men doing the same. 'Three steps forwards!' Drost called from his left, and Victorinus took them gleefully. They'd planned for this, had even marked out a brief line by planting a rock on either side of the road. They could approach to the rocks and use the length of their spears, but any further and they were in danger of treading on the caltrops themselves. Victorinus launched a ranging blow at Aldhard with his spear, though the Saxone chief just had enough presence of mind to swerve his body out the way before it hit him. He was impotent, stuck there, unwilling to move forward for fear of injuring his other foot. But he couldn't reach Victorinus with just his sword. Pulling the spear back and thrusting it forwards again, Victorinus snarled in frustration as Aldhard hobbled back a step out of reach.

The battle – if it could be called that – ebbed, as Aldhard and his remaining men took stock of their situation. There were just four of them left, and suddenly the hunters were becoming the hunted. Victorinus stayed level with the rocks. They found themselves in an odd situation, where Aldhard could not advance and neither could the Romans, so they merely hurled insults over each other over six feet of caltrop ridden land. 'You will not win, tribune,' Aldhard hissed. 'I will see you to your end, mark my words.'

Victorinus did nothing but smile, though a chill ran down his back. The man looked like the Aldhard he had seen weeks before on the east coast, sounded like him. But how could it possibly be the same man? 'Why don't you come and say that to my face?' he called, knowing it for the childish retort that it was.

Aldhard grinned, a savage wolf's grin that revealed bloodied teeth. 'I do not need to beat you in battle, tribune Victorinus. I have this.' He sheathed his sword, useless as it was to him at that moment, and produced from his waist a bloodied bandage. He held it high. 'You left this behind in your desperation to be away from us. Do you know what my priests can do with the blood of an enemy? You will die an agonised death, sweating, shivering, with no control of your bowels. Men will tell you it is a fever, an infection your body cannot repel. But it will be me. I may not get to see you die, but I will know when you are gone. And when you are, I will come for your sons.'

With a gesture to his remaining men, he turned and hobbled away. 'Why are you doing this?' Victorinus called, suddenly desperate. 'What have I done to you?'

Aldhard paused, turned back to Victorinus, and fixed him with a glare. 'You took everything from me, so I will do the same to you.'

XIV

I t had taken them seven days to travel up the eastern
coast. Felicius spent the time with his eyes fixed to the
horizon, wondering briefly if they were going to encounter
a ship full of Saxones rowing in a circle. Of course, they
did not. The wind was their greatest foe, an endless barrage
to their senses, roaring southwards from the northeast,
forcing Calidus to keep his rowers at their benches, their
oars locked in a tussle with the brackish water.

Eventually, the wind battered ship found a river deep
enough to sustain her, and turned inland. 'Where are
we?' Marcelina asked, her blue tinged lips quivering as she
hugged tight her soaking wet cloak, as if her body heat
alone could dry it.

'Not a clue, but we're out of the wind, and I'll take
that as a win,' Felicius said, rubbing her shoulders with
numb hands. The journey had been tough on them all, but
for Marcelina, more than anyone. She had cried herself to
sleep every night, and even in her dreams, she was not safe.
He woke her from her nightmare the first night, snuggling
with her under the blankets, deep in the ship's hold. She
roused, though it brought her no comfort. The second
night Calidus told him to let her sleep, said nightmares

wore off quicker than tiredness. Felicius wasn't sure he agreed, but he heeded the advice none the less.

'We're not get much further!' Calidus called from the prow, his sun kissed skin fixed in a frown. 'River narrows too much up ahead. We'll have to bank her for the night.'

'And then what?' Felicius bit, irritated. He had been gone far longer than he thought he would. He itched to be back in the north. Had Maximus already made his move north? Had an army of Caledonians appeared on the horizon? And what had happened to Sixtus and Vitulus? He hated being out of the loop, out of control.

'Best bet is we find some wagons and mules that can take you the rest of the way. Honestly, sir, can't see what else I can do for you,' the captain said with a shrug. Felicius sighed. He knew none of this was Calidus's fought, though it did nothing to dampen the disappointment of the man and his sailors leaving him. They had been more than good to their word, even fighting to see Felicius and his cargo free from Londinium. He looked from the sailors to his daughter, and then to Davos, shivering in the corner. How was he to get this cargo north with just the two of them?

They banked the ship, Felicius walking unsteadily down the gangplank and on to the muddy shore. The weather seemed to turn for the worse. Thick black clouds rolled in from the north, snow seemed ominous. 'I'll send out three men, see what they can find. Why don't you and your children rest up for now, sir? We'll help you unload when we have a plan.'

Felicius, too tired to correct the man, and half amused that Calidus considered Davos to be his son, nodded, and walked back aboard, ushering Marcelina and Davos below deck. There they sat around a flickering candle, the only flame allowed aboard a ship, and ate a meal of stale bread and olives. He must have dozed off, for next thing he knew there was a firm hand on his shoulder and drool leaking from the corner of his mouth to his unshaven chin. 'Sir, we have news.' It was one of the sailors Calidus had sent out. Felicius, shaking his head clear and wiping his mouth, rose unsteadily to his feet. Marcelina and Davos still slept, huddled together under a thick blanket. He smiled to see them both so peaceful and left them to their rest.

Up on deck the clouds had burst, and he squinted as snow drops pelted him. A stranger stood on the deck, clad in thick trousers and a cloak that ran down to his boots. 'Salve,' Felicius hailed the man, walking towards him. 'I am Prefect Gaius Felicius of the Fourth Cohort of Gauls. May I know your name?'

The stranger was a big man, rounded shoulders and a haggard face, buried beneath a beard to match the falling snow. Felicius knew a veteran when he saw one, and this man was military through and through. He could tell by the way he stood, back straight, legs braced. It was the stance of a man who'd spent a lifetime on parade. 'I am Drax, once of the Fourth Cohort of Dalmatians.'

'Well met, Drax. You have some news for us, I hear?'

Drax smiled, revealing crooked teeth. 'I've got more than that. I've carts and mules to pull them. For a price, of course.'

'Of course,' Felicius grinned. They haggled for a moment, standard stuff. No one agreed on the asking price, after all.

'You haven't told him the rest,' Calidus said once the price was agreed.

'The rest?' Felicius arched an eyebrow.

'There's ten men up here looking for you,' Drax said. 'Well, not just ten men. Ten *scholae*.'

Felicius felt himself swallow despite himself. 'You are sure they are *scholae?*'

'Aye, met them myself. They came past my stables not two days ago, heading north up the eastern road. Said they were on the lookout for one Prefect Gaius Felicius.'

'What are *scholae?*' It was Marcelina that spoke, weary eyed, poking her head out from the hatch.

'The emperor's elite,' Felicius said. 'The divine Gratian has five units to call upon, officially they are his guard, though God knows even an emperor has no need of two and half thousand mounted men following him around everywhere he goes. Most of them serve with the field army, some indeed stay with the emperor at all times. The others, well, they see out whatever little missions they are given. Seems I've become one of their little missions.'

'Why?' Marcelina asked.

The snow fall thickened, braving the wind it assaulted them with its icy teeth. Felicius blew out a breath, steaming the air. 'Because whatever it is Maximus has in there,' he gestured to the lead pots. 'The emperor does not want him to possess.'

Calidus cleared his throat. 'Not sure what I've got myself into here. I'm just a simple merchant. Last thing I want is for any of this to come back on me or my men.'

'It won't,' Felicius held out a calming hand. 'None of this is on you, or me, for that matter. Each of us is just following orders. Drax, where even are we?' he asked, suddenly remembering he was completely lost.

'Dunum Sinus is the local town, just over the hills there to the south. It's where my stables are.'

Felicius racked his brain. He'd heard of Dunum Sinus even if he'd never been there. It couldn't be far from where Maximus and Victorinus had fought off the Saxone raiders a few weeks ago. 'How long will it take your mules and carts to make the Wall from here?'

Drax sucked air through his crooked teeth. 'Carrying that lot?' he gestured to the lead pots. 'Six days if the weather holds out. If this snow worsens...' he finished with a shrug. 'We are at the mercy of the roads.'

'We?' Felicius asked, a flicker of hope in the darkness.

Drax smiled. 'You've got yourself caught up in something here, sir,' he said, referencing Felicius' rank for the first time. 'But if twenty-five years in the army taught me one thing, it's that you stand by your comrades. I fought with the Gauls long before you were their commander. But in battle you form a bond stronger than iron, as well you know. I've another seven retired soldiers working for me at my stables. Together we'll see you to wherever you need to go.'

Felicius could have kissed the man, he was worried Marcelina might. The two men shook hands, and then they got to work.

***

Mercifully, the snow storm passed, leaving little evidence of its brief reign of terror. Felicius didn't think Calidus was sad to see the back of him, though Felicius made it all too clear how much he'd valued the captain and his services. The merchant was considering swinging back by Londinium to see if he could pick up the men he'd had to abandon. Felicius and Drax both implored him not to. Whatever it was they were all mixed up in, Calidus was not free of it just because he had offloaded his cargo.

Drax had been good to his word, and before Felicius knew it, they were on the road with six mule-drawn carts, each with four of the huge lead pots strapped to the back. Two mules pulled each cart, and the going was slow over the unmaintained eastern roads. 'We'll head north until we reach the Wall, then we can go west as far as you need,' Drax said, full of confidence.

Felicius had agreed, not knowing the local geography as well as he should. The weather seemed to warm a touch on their first day. Rain fell lazily from bursting clouds, the wind abated, and Felicius, Davos and Marcelina felt their spirits rise even as their clothes sagged under the weight of rainwater. Finally, they were leaving the troubles of Londinium behind them and going home. Well, two of them were.

'You're going to love your new home, Davos,' Felicius said, putting an arm around the lad and hugging him close. It was strange, and frightening, how quickly he had come to care for the lad. How he had immediately just accepted that he was now in charge of this young man's life. Some things just felt *right*, and this was certainly one of them. He had always wanted a son, not that he admitted it openly. He had been secretly envious of his friend Victorinus, as he and Sarai saw the birth of not just one, but three boys. Not that he didn't love Marcelina, and the events of the last few weeks had brought them closer together than ever before. But a son! A man to carry on his line, to bring glory to his name when he was only a memory. That was something to be cherished. Even if Davos was not of his blood, he could teach the boy the way of the army, sculpt him into a better man than he ever was. Had not the great Augustus himself adopted Tiberius as his sole heir? If Rome's first emperor could do it, he certainly could.

'What is your wife like?' Davos asked. Felicius felt the lad wilt slightly. He thought of the life the boy had lived so far. Taken from his home by his father, thrust to the world of a seafaring merchant. And then the horrors of that warehouse in Londinium, the things Cyclops had made him do, just so he could sleep on a louse ridden pallet come sun down.

'Ahhh Lucia. Boy, is she going to love you! Marcelina, tell Davos about your mother.' The two spoke as the cart rumbled on. Felicius driving the third cart in the line that trundled ever north. Drax had men driving the others, and he himself led on the first cart. There was the constant worry of the *scholae* finding them, though Felicius forced that from his mind. Wasn't like anything he was doing was illegal. All he was doing was following orders, and in the army, that's the only choice you had.

Drax leaped from the first cart, handing the reins to one of his men. He jogged back down the road to Felicius, squinting up at him through the rain. 'There's a *mansio* a mile or so up the road, thought it might be worth stopping the night. There's not another one until we hit the Wall, so we're going to have a couple of nights out in the open. At least there we can get a warm meal and a dry bed. They might even have the baths heated.'

'Are you not wet enough Drax?' Felicius asked, and both men laughed. 'It sounds like a plan to me. Do you think they'll have some tents we can pinch? We can always give them to the next *mansio* we find along the Wall.'

'Aye, they might. Do you have anything with the *Dux's* seal on it? In my experience, nothing opens door than an imperial decree.'

Felicius laughed again. 'Don't I just know it! I've a seal, and plenty of coin to boot. Don't worry friend, I'll see they put us up well enough.' In theory, any serving soldier was welcome at a *mansio*. It was, after all, what they were for. Used by the military and messengers alike, it was a safe space for those on imperial duty to rest, eat, bathe and change their mounts as and when required. An imperial courier could well pass three or four on a standard day, depending on which part of the empire you were in. You'd have to travel very far indeed to pass that many in Britannia.

Dusk approached as they entered a walled courtyard, each in the small convey shivering from the wind rippling through their wet clothes. Two stable lads appeared from the shadows, wordlessly taking their mules away to be fed. Felicius had to put his shoulder to a bowed wooden door to get in, but once he was he sighed as the warm air from a nearby brazier engulfed him in a welcome embrace. The chamber was small, ten tables that sat four in front of a rickety bar at the back. It was to there Felicius walked, ringing a bell to announce a waiting customer.

An elderly face popped around a door frame, a gap-toothed grin and a shuffle to the bar. 'Salve, friend,' the man said in a shaky voice. He was seventy if he was a day, back hunched, torso sagging, but the fading marks of a military tattoo were still prevalent on his right arm. 'Just you, or anyone else outside?'

'Greetings. There are eleven of us in all. I know it's short notice, but any chance you can take us in for the night?' He laid three gold coins on the bar, pushing them gently across.

'Eleven I can do. But military personnel always have priority. If another party turns up after sun down...' he left the comment hanging in the air between them.

'Then they shall be out of luck. I am Prefect Gaius Felicius of the Fourth Cohort of Gauls. I have eight retired soldiers plus two children with me. I am on a mission for the *Dux Britanniarum* Flavius Maximus, bringing important cargo north to aid us in the war.' Felicius reached into his cloak, pulling out a roll of papyrus, the seal of the *Dux* on the front.

'I apologise, sir,' the man said, head lolling above his bent neck. 'Of course, I shall have rooms and food prepared. We have a small bath house out back. The door to the building is unlocked. Unfortunately, there are no slaves employed in there, and I doubt all of you will fit in it together,' he said with a cackle.

'That sounds fine to me. Can you dry some clothes for us?'

'Of course, of course. Bring your fellows in and have a seat. I'll get you some beer whilst we ready your rooms.'

Sundown saw them all changed, bathed, with a plate of hot food and a cup of ale in front of them. Felicius smacked his lips in satisfaction as he drained his cup, reaching across the table to refill it from the jug. 'How many miles can we cover tomorrow, Drax?' he said to the old soldier who sat across from him.

'Twenty if the weather holds. The road gets better the further north we go, because the army uses it more. Shouldn't be much in the way of traffic this time of year, so we should make good time.'

'How many days to Segedunum at this pace?'

'Could make it by sundown the day after tomorrow if the gods are kind. If not, we'll be there the day after that.'

Felicius nodded. He wasn't actually sure what day it was, though in times of war, that rarely mattered. All he knew was he needed to be back in the north as soon as possible. Even sitting in the *mansio*, warm and full for the first time in days, he was itching to be back in the rain, on the road and back to his unit. He longed for news of Vitulus and Victorinus. As the days wore on, the fate of his friends frayed at his nerves. Surely Vitulus had found Sixtus by now? He imagined them both tucked up in Vindolanda, awaiting his return in the fort's warmth. It was a comforting thought, however unlikely.

Once the meal was done, Felicius took Marcelina and Davos up to their room and put them to bed. The three of them would share for the night, with Felicius sleeping on a small cot in the room's corner. He didn't mind. It was warm and dry, and after the last couple of weeks, he couldn't ask for more. He decided to pop out to the stables and check on the mules and cargo before he turned in, and he took a moment to wrap his cloak around him before heading outside. His sword belt was hung over his cloak, and it fell to the floorboards with a clang as he took his cloak. Cursing his clumsiness, he scooped it up and ducked under the doorway, back into the rain.

The wind battered him as he scuttled across the courtyard, not brave enough to lift his eyes from his boots. He paused when he reached the stable door, which sat on its hinges slightly ajar. Moving inside, throwing off his hood and rubbing rain from his face, he heard the rasp of hushed voices from within. Torches flared down the central walkway, horses and mules boxed in to either side. There were the normal noises of a stable, as the beasts huffed and snorted, some ate whilst others already slept.

Felicius moved past the animals, working his way towards a large open chamber at the rear. It was there that they had stored the carts and their cargo out of the rain for the night. And it was there he found a huddle of men, grouped around one of the lead pots. The lid prised off it.

He was suddenly very grateful he'd inadvertently picked up his sword. 'Hey!' he shouted, no pretence at stealth. 'Step away from that!' he stalked further into the chamber, sword free in his hand. Four men moved away from the cart. They wore helmets and mail under thick winter cloaks, dark blue trousers and fine looking boots keeping the rain from their feet. 'Who are you?' Felicius asked, eyeing their weapons, feeling a sense of doubt. How long before Drax came looking for him? The man was asleep in his bed, Felicius hadn't thought to tell anyone what he was doing. And why would he? They were in no danger.

'My name is Romulus,' a man with a thickset black beard spoke in heavily accented Latin. '*Domesticus* of the *scola scutariorum secunda*. You are Prefect Gaius Felicius. We met once before, I seem to remember. We have been looking for you.'

Felicius blinked as he took it in. Romulus would have been the rather unimaginative name given to this man when he enrolled in the Roman army. He was undisputedly German, his accent and appearance putting that beyond doubt. And then there was the man's rank. A *domesticus* ranked only one below a tribune in the scholae, so the fact that they had given this man leave from his unit to come and find Felicius meant the Emperor Gratian thought it a matter of urgency. And then there was the man himself. Romulus. The same man that had been sent to Africa all those years ago to assassinate the general Theodosius. Suddenly he was back at the bay of Carthage, the warm sun kissing his skin, the salt air blowing off the sea. He remembered the grin on Romulus's face, the glee as he drew his sword and prepared to swing the killing blow.

'You,' he breathed, taking another step forward, knuckles whitening on the grip of his sword.

'Do you know what you have here?' Romulus gestured to the open lead pot.

'Actually, no,' Felicius said. He was trembling with rage. How could this man be so casual? How could he not address what he had done?

Romulus scoffed. 'You are putting yourself in great danger, transporting this for your master. And you mean to tell me you do not even know why you do it? Ha!' he barked a laugh. 'You Romans, it is no wonder you are losing your grip on your empire.'

'Us Romans? Why then do you travel from your lands to serve in our army? If we are so doomed, why not stay at home? With your own people?'

'You know nothing of my people!' Romulus snapped. 'Or my reasons for being here. But right now, I am here to arrest you for treason.'

'Treason?' He imagined how Theodosius must have felt at that bay. The stoic calmness he had managed to maintain, right until the end.

'Yes. You seek to undermine our divine Augustus, to take from him which is his, behest on him by God.'

What is in those pots? Felicius thought, cursing Maximus to every god he could think of. 'I do no such thing. I am simply following an order given to me by my commander.

If you wish to question that order, then I suggest you head north and seek the *Dux Britanniarum*.'

'Oh I shall, have no fear on that. Nevertheless, I cannot allow you to continue down this path. These pots go no further than this *mansio*.'

Felicius was just weighing up what he could actually do to stop this Romulus taking possession of Maximus' cargo, when the stable door clattered open, and a dripping wet imperial messenger led a sodden mount out of the rain. 'Am I... interrupting something?' he said, coming to a stop as he took in Felicius with his sword drawn and four soldiers standing with hands on the hilts of their own.

'Not at all,' Felicius said. 'You are a fellow law-abiding citizen of Rome, on about your duty. Do carry on.' The messenger was a callow youth, pale skinned with arms like twigs. His wide eyes didn't leave the four soldiers as he walked his mount to a booth and put it in.

'Where are you headed?' Romulus asked the messenger.

'I... err,' the youth turned, lips quivering. 'Vindolanda, then up to the Wall.'

Felicius' ears pricked at that. 'Who do you seek at Vindolanda?'

The messenger dipped a hand in to the satchel at his waist, pulled out a roll of papyrus and read the name on the tag. 'Prefect Gaius Felicius, it is a letter from His Imperial Majesty Theodosius.' The messenger gawped, worried he might have said too much.

If ever there was proof that God was real. 'I am Prefect Gaius Felicius, commander of the Fourth Cohort of Gauls. You can deliver that to me now, if you'd like?'

The messenger looked from Felicius to Romulus and his men, then back to Felicius. 'How do I know you are who you say you are?'

Felicius laughed. 'You're new to this, aren't you?'

The youth nodded. 'Aye, this is my first solo run. Been training back in Gaul for the last three months. Didn't think they'd make me come all the way up here on my first job.'

'And how would you know it was me if you delivered me that scroll in Vindolanda?'

The youth thought about it a moment. 'You would be in your office. I would ask for you at the gates and someone would take me to you.'

'So you're saying you would know I am the prefect because a soldier in uniform would tell you I am?'

'I guess?' the messenger said in a squeaky voice, clearly feeling uncomfortable.

'Well, you see those four soldiers over there? They know who I am. The one with the beard is Romulus, a *domesticus* of the *scola scutariorum secunda,* no less. Why don't you ask them who I am?'

'It is him,' Romulus said with a sigh. 'Enough with the charade. Give him his letter.'

Felicius took the scroll, then looked to Romulus' men. 'Do you lads really think the divine Theodosius corresponds with a traitor to the empire?'

The three soldiers looked at each other, then at their still sighing commander. Slowly, their hands dropped from their sword belts. 'Alright prefect,' Romulus said. 'You win, this time. We shall leave you to your cargo and be on our way. But mark my words, you have not seen the last of me.'

The four soldiers left, Felicius noticed with a smirk that the messenger didn't dare draw breath as they walked past him. When they were gone, he moved over to the open pot, grabbed a torch off the wall and peered inside. 'What the... hey you, come here,' he called to the messenger. 'Look in here. Do they look like snails to you?'

XV

'What's he going to do with my blood anyway?' Victorinus asked as they walked.

'Forget about it,' Drost scoffed. 'The man's a fucking freak. He's trying to get in your head, put you off your game.'

'Off my game? What game am I playing here?'

'Staying alive,' Pastor said.

They'd been walking three days since the minor battle with Aldhard and his men. They'd seen no sign of the Saxones since. The first day they had walked north, the second west, and now they were moving south. Victorinus was eager to get back to the Wall and hook up with Vitulus and the others. He had a need for information, a hundred questions whirling through his mind at any one moment. Questions that needed answering.

He had been worried about his wounds, Aldhard's words playing on his mind. But his hand was fine, if still sore. Pastor was his biggest worry. The young man had been walking and fighting with huge chunks of flesh whipped out of his back. Despite the work Drost had done to clean and close the wounds, the daily exertions were taking a visible toll. Pastor was bone white, his breaths coming in shallow gasps. Victorinus had watched him closely as they broke their fast that morning. Again when they stopped for a midday meal, he'd barely eaten at all.

'Do you know where we are?' Victorinus asked Drost as they walked. Snow fell in a lazy arc from the dark sky, but if anything, it felt a little warmer than it had the previous days. The wind had dropped, a relief for them all, and he found himself thinking the first signs of spring couldn't be far off.

'No, but I would guess we're only two days from the Wall.'

'Why?' Victorinus chewed his lip in thought.

Drost shrugged. 'That abandoned fort we got the weapons from the other day, there aren't any of them over two or three days from the Wall. Plus, the land is different the further south you get, you know this. The hills are more sporadic, and the grass seems greener.'

Victorinus scoffed a laugh. 'The grass seems greener? You sure it's just water you've got in that skin?'

'There's less heather, no moss on the ground. You've spent half your life up here and you've never noticed?'

Victorinus looked around, seeing his friend was right. The further north you went, the more the green carpet was littered with a purple hue. Here, there was nothing, save the odd sprouting yellow of a gorse bush, which seemed to be everywhere the further north you went from Eboracum. 'Halfhand would have noticed that,' he said, more to himself than Drost.

'Halfhand noticed everything! That's why he was the best of us. I think even Severus would have spotted the heather though to be fair.' They both chuckled at that. Severus had been a veteran of the Rhine fleet, and had one day swapped the river for a saddle. He'd never told Victorinus the reason, and if he was being honest, the tribune had been weary of asking too many questions. Always desperate for men.

'What I wouldn't give to have them here with us now,' Victorinus said, his eyes glazed over, lost somewhere in the past.

'Aye. You seen Pastor? He doesn't look good.' The youth was trailing behind them, eyes locked on his boots as he trudged.

Victorinus shook his head, waking himself from his reverie. 'Aye, that's why I asked where we were in the first place. The lad hasn't got many more miles in him. If Aldhard catches up with us again, he won't be in any state to fight.'

'I don't think he will. Besides, I've got two men trailing us by a mile or so, keeping an eye on our backs. Plus Alec and two more out in front. We won't be caught unawares.'

Victorinus nodded, comforted by the reassurance. He squinted up at the sky. The snow seemed to get thicker, though the path they trod was still slushy mud. He didn't think it would lay. 'Sun's going down. Going to be an uncomfortable night.'

Drost grunted in agreement, and the two men slipped into an easy silence, walking until the last of the light was dying. Alec was waiting for them on the outskirts of a small crop of trees. They stood to the east of a large cliff face, which seemed to tower to the clouds. A large lake stretched to the horizon. 'Caught us some dinner,' Alec said, motioning to eight large fish that lay on a fallen trunk. 'And found a small cave, just in the trees, part of the giant rock face. Seems dry inside. I've got the other two out collecting firewood.'

'Alec, you really are sent from the gods,' Victorinus said with a smile, clasping the Caledonian on the shoulder. The cave was indeed dry, and they ate a heartening meal of roasted fish, washed down with the last of the water from their skins. Alec said he was confident he would find a stream come morning, and they could refill then. Victorinus allowed Drost to change the bandages on his hand. He winced as the old one was unravelled, but breathed a sigh of relief when the wound revealed no signs of infection. His knuckles were still swollen, but he was getting some movement back in the hand, and he allowed himself a smile as he thought once more of Aldhard's threat.

It still troubled him how Aldhard could be there at all. How can a man who had his head cut off be chasing him through the northern wilderness? It kept him up at night. The endless march during the days kept his mind focused on where they were going. But when he lay in the dark, physically exhausted from the day's exertions, his mind would not switch off. It couldn't be the same man, it just couldn't. In his time in the *miles areani* he had served with men from all over the empire, some sent to Britannia as a punishment, others running from a past they'd sooner forget. All had their own beliefs and superstitions, but none would have said it possible. It was only that Pastor believed it too that kept him sane. If he had been alone in thinking it, he might have thought himself delirious. But Pastor was a good egg, a young man with his head screwed on. No, he assured himself, it could not be the same man. There was a rational explanation for it.

Eventually, he fell asleep. He awoke in the half light of a false dawn. Eyes still closed, but ears open to the first sounds of a new day, he heard murmured voices, someone whimpering. Untangling himself from his cloak, rising and shaking some life into his freezing limbs, he saw Drost and two of his men huddled around Pastor. 'What's happened?' he asked, rubbing the last vestiges of sleep from his eyes.

'His wounds are giving him trouble. They're still clean, but they're rubbing on his tunic as he walks. Problem is everything is wet. We can dry them, but there's not much we can do to stop them getting wet again.'

Victorinus saw someone had built the fire back up. Pastor's two tunics were hanging over it, suspended on a makeshift washing line. He took in the dark blood stains that smeared the back of both of them, and his heart wrenched for his young friend. 'Pastor, you have the heart of a lion.'

'You've never seen a lion,' Pastor said through clenched teeth, and Drost laughed as he continued to clean the wounds.

'True. But I met a man who has, once, and he said it had the biggest heart he'd ever seen. Take it as a compliment.'

'Thanks,' Pastor groaned.

Victorinus took a moment to take in Pastor's wounds. He thought they looked better, less raw, scabs forming on his back. That was a good sign. Leaving Drost to it, he wrapped his cloak tight around him as he walked out into the half light. Snow had laid overnight, the ground a crisp white carpet. He walked off into the trees to relieve himself, but a slither of movement in his peripheral vision stopped him in his tracks.

Slowly, he lowered himself to a crouch, weary he wore no mail, left with his sword back in the cave. He was only ten paces from its mouth, and within shouting distance of his friends. He eased his head to the left, eyes scanning the bare trees as he did. He reached the point he thought he'd seen something and fixed his eyes on it.

Sure enough, there was someone there. A silhouette detached itself from a trunk, stepping into a pool of light. It was Aldhard. 'Knew I would catch up with you eventually, tribune,' he said, an evil grin fixed on his scarred face.

'Where are your men?' Victorinus asked, eyes scanning the trees.

'They are close. Though thanks to you, they are fewer than they were. I have come to talk.'

'Then speak.'

Aldhard's grin widened. 'I think you have some questions for me, no?'

Victorinus steeled himself. He could feel his heart thumping. *This man is not who he says he is.* 'You're his brother, aren't you.' He didn't frame it as a question.

'I don't know what you're talking about.'

'You are his brother,' Victorinus said again. 'You are here to exact revenge on the man you think killed him. On my honour, it was not me.'

'You lead the Roman army that day,' Aldhard said.

Victorinus shook his head. 'Not I. I commanded one unit in that army. It was the *Dux Britaniarum* Flavius Maximus that commanded. He who lead the cavalry charge that smashed the Saxone ranks. He who ordered the decapitation of their leader. You are not that man.'

'How can you be so sure?'

Victorinus gulped despite himself. He moved forwards, full bladder forgotten now, until he stood five paces from the man that called himself Aldhard. He forced himself to look the man in the eye. 'He was half a head taller, broader too,' he found himself saying, mind thinking back to that day on the east coast. 'His beard was thicker, and slightly darker. You've done a good job of it, making yourself into him. Had me going for a while. But I can see how fresh that scar on your cheek is. Aldhard's was old, faded. I *am* interested in your lack of a left hand though.' He looked at the missing hand, noting the heavily wrapped bandages around the stump. 'Can't fault your commitment, that's for sure.'

Aldhard – or at least the man pretending to be Aldhard, barked out a laugh. 'I had you going for a while though, didn't I?'

'Why are you doing this?' Victorinus pressed on.

'I have my reasons, revenge, of course, being one of them.'

'That is not what drove you here. You didn't need to go to all this trouble. You could have just sailed over with an army, flew your banner and met us in the field.'

'Just like my brother before me, huh?'

It was Victorinus's turn to grin. 'Ha! So he was your brother. You wait until I tell Pastor!'

'They made it back, you know.'

'Who did?' Victorinus asked, losing track of the conversation.

'The men whose hands you cut off. Don't ask me how they did it, but those bastards rowed back across the Narrow Sea and made it home. Four of them died once they got there, though.'

'Well, fuck,' Victorinus exclaimed. He was genuinely impressed. He didn't think he could row it with two hands.

'The survivors told the story of that fateful day, of the lives lost under the pretence of Roman *justice*,' he spat the last word in disgust.

Victorinus shook his head. 'That *was* Roman justice. What would have happened had our positions had been reversed? Would you have treated me and my men any better if we'd taken ships to your home? Threatened your families? You look at the world from your own perspective, but there are two sides to every coin.'

Aldhard – or whoever he was – considered that a moment, a sly smile tugging the corners of his mouth. 'You know I like you,' he said after a moment. A coin appeared in his right hand. He twirled it through his fingers a moment before flicking it to Victorinus. 'Maybe I shall not use your blood to put a curse on you after all.'

'Can we be real for a moment?' Victorinus asked. He'd caught the coin, hadn't wanted to allow it to distract him though, so refrained from looking at it. The man nodded.

'Why are you here? I get that a ship full of one handed men returned to your people. spreading tales of the horrors of Rome. But what you're doing here, hunting me, in lands that aren't even Roman! It is...' he sought the right word. 'Excessive. So tell me, why are you here? And how did you know I would be at that fort? You had men there, laying in wait.'

A crisp winter's silence spread between them, four breaths deep. Aldhard tilted his head, listening to the far off howl of the wind, somewhere over the naked canopy of the trees. 'I was invited,' he said after a while. 'Look at the coin, tribune. I saw it as an opportunity to revenge myself on my brother's killers, true. But there is so much more to this that you do not see.'

'Tell me something I don't know,' Victorinus muttered. He looked at the coin. Silver, unremarkable in every way. Except that it had the face of the divine Gratian on one side. It was new. He knew even the army was not paid in coins depicting their new ruler. He bent the coin between two fingers, it folded like parchment. Shaking his head, he wondered once more about how the might of Rome was waning. 'There are deeper reasons than simple revenge. Something else drives you. Something, or someone? Who gave you this coin?'

A shrug. 'I am not at liberty to say – that is how you Romans speak, no? But there were more coins where that one came from, a thousand more. I have been doing more than hunting you in my time here, tribune. But maybe, maybe if you walk west for half a day or so, you will see something you are not supposed to see.'

An army? 'Why would you tell me that?'

Another shrug. 'I have done what I was employed to do, just as my brother did before me. My part in this tale is done, tribune, and I plan on returning home to my lands, to mourn my brother, and plot the next stage of my life. My people always thought my brother was destined to do great things. It is important that his legacy lives on, in ways that I could never get you to understand.'

'You cut off your hand, scar your face. You go to all this trouble, and now you are just going to leave? Your employer must have deep pockets! How much have they promised you?' He had an inkling who the employer could be. Truth be told, he thought he'd known all along. He also knew he would never get a name from this man.

'I am paid in more than coin, tribune. And my sacrifice will be worth it, in time.' He looked back up to the lightening sky, for once clear of foreboding clouds. 'It is time for me to go. West tribune, to the west you will find your answers.' He turned away, walked three steps and paused. 'You and I tribune, we shall meet again. It is destiny. And when we do, I shall not leave you with your life.' With that, he was gone.

***

Pastor could barely move. Once his wounds had been cleaned and re-bandaged, the young warrior had barely risen to a standing position. They'd spent the morning trying to ease his suffering, Drost suggesting a series of stretches to ease the tension in his muscles, Alec rummaging the barren woodland floor for a herb he swore sprouted everywhere in the north, though apparently not in winter.

In the end, Drost and his men had built a makeshift litter using the strongest branches they could find, and Pastor was carried, lying on his front, as the small party moved east. 'So what's his real name?' Drost asked Victorinus, once the tribune had caught him up on his conversation.

'Didn't ask, actually. Not sure it matters.'

'So he's just upping and leaving, is he? After all the shit he's put us through. After what he's done to Pastor?'

'Seems so.'

'Fucked up if you ask me,' Drost spat.

Victorinus just shrugged. 'Sure the man has his reasons. And we did decapitate his brother, after all. I'm more interested in what he said about the going west.'

'You won't find a Caledonian army. I'd stake my life on it.'

'You might well be,' Victorinus mused.

'If the tribes were uniting to take on Rome, I'd know. I'm a bloody chief, after all!'

'Yes, but of a very small tribe, far to the north,' Victorinus said through a half smile. He was goading his friend, anything to help pass the time. They had Alec and two men out scouting ahead, two more of Drost's men bringing up the rear with a groaning Pastor between them.

'My people are mighty,' Drost muttered, and Victorinus almost spluttered out a laugh. He remembered the day well, when Drost had fought the previous chief for the right to lead the tribe. It had seemed an outlandish idea to Victorinus, but then different people had different customs. Who was he to judge?

He arched his back as he walked, body and legs stiff as a board. When he got back to the Wall, first thing he was going to do was take a long, hot bath. He flexed his injured hand. It tingled in the cold, worse than his right, but it satisfied him there was some movement coming back. His feet were his biggest problem. They were a ruin. The miles he had covered, bearing the weight of his mail and sodden cloak, had done his feet no good. His boots rubbed with every step, and his biggest concern was his feet blistering. His socks were punched through with holes and soaking wet, he had no spares with him. If the blisters came, he was finished. Still, not much longer now, he told himself.

It was then one of Drost's men came sprinting over the horizon, arms windmilling as he frantically sought his chief's attention. 'Think they might have found something,' Victorinus said, the sarcasm dripping off him like rain.

'Surely it's not-

'You know full well it is.'

'Gods above,' Drost muttered. His man was red faced and clouding them both in mist as he both tried to catch his breath and speak his news. Victorinus, too weary to interpret what the man was saying, waited patiently for Drost to translate. 'It would seem my men have stumbled across an army,' Drost said with a sigh.

'*They haven't!* Victorinus smacked his cheeks in mock horror. 'How many?'

'Alec thinks twenty thousand.'

Twenty thousand? Surely there weren't that many fighting men left in the north? In the last generation alone, the tribes had lost more than twice that number in the many battles and skirmishes they'd fought with the empire. 'They won't all be warriors though, right?' Victorinus said. chewing his bottom lip. 'They'll be cooks and healers. Some men would have brought their families along.' He knew the way of the tribes well enough, had spent enough time among them after all. When a tribe went to war, it wasn't just the men that set off from home. At heart, they were a nomadic people, life on the road the norm for many.

'Aye. That still means a sizeable fighting force. How many men does Maximus have?'

Victorinus considered that a moment. 'He'll have seven thousand, give or take. At Eboracum he was taking each unit's strength from paper. We both know from experience that won't reflect how many each unit can actually bring to the field.'

'Ahh, good old penny pinching officers. You know I almost miss it sometimes.'

'Bollocks! Still, seven thousand should see the job done.'

Drost smiled at his friend, refusing to take the bait. 'Leaves me in a predicament. They are my people, after all.'

'And Rome has been a great friend to you,' Victorinus cut in. 'I do not want to dump you in muddy water. Help me get Pastor back to the Wall and then get yourself home. That's all I ask.'

'Aye. Aye, I can do that. I suppose you want to have a little spy on the enemy first, though?'

'Don't you?'

'Course I do! Need to make sure none of my men are there! Feels an age since I've been home.'

They crept up on the army. And by all the gods, it was a sight to see. The Caledonians moved without the discipline and precision of a Roman force. Stretching from horizon to horizon, they walked in small groups, children and dogs running circles around them, wives and mothers atop carts filled to the brim with both food and weapons.

'Anything in particular you can tell me about this lot?' Victorinus asked as he squinted, trying to make out the banners flying in the wind.

'Looks like the Selgovae in the vanguard, if you call that mob a vanguard. See the red rabbit on the white banner? That's their mark. Behind them are the Novantae. I'm in a feud with their chief at the moment.'

'Over what?'

'He says my people stole sheep from his land. Bloke's full of shit.'

'Aren't the Novantae in the west?'

'Aye, and we're north east. Hell of a trek to herd a flock of sheep. Still, they tasted good when my lads got them home.'

Victorinus chuckled. He remembered all too well how easily disputes started north of the Wall. Nine out of ten of them were cattle related. 'Lean winter was it?'

'Would have been! Look, on their right, that's the Otadini. I'd wager their warriors make up the bulk of the army.'

'Aye, I remember them being a force. They still got the same chief? Forget his name, old guy, one leg.'

'Ha! No, Bellicus died years ago. His daughter rules now, and if you thought the old bastard was savage, he had nothing on her.'

'Any chance she could be leading this lot, then?'

Drost chewed on that a moment. 'If anyone could unite the people, I'd wager it would be her. Plus, she has the manpower to back it up. This would never work without the Otadini.'

'You have much of a relationship with her?'

'No,' Drost shook his head. 'Only met her the once, and that was enough.'

They stayed there a while longer, watching what felt like an immigration pass beneath them. Drost had sent his men on south with Pastor, and it was only when hunger gnawed at them both they forced their stiff limbs off the wet ground and moved off. One to ready for war, the other to prepare for another long journey home.

XVI

S nails. He'd come all this way, fighting gang lords and
confronting the emperor's personal guard. For snails.

Felicius slumped in a chair, half empty jug of wine
perched on his knee. He hadn't bothered with a cup. Maximus was there somewhere, busy with some general or
other, Felicius had been told to wait. And wait, he would.
He had words to say to the *Dux Britanniarum*, and he
didn't much care who else heard them.

Their progress north had been uneventful since the
confrontation at the *mansio*, mercifully there had been no
more signs of Romulus and his men from the *scola scutariorum secunda*. Felicius had pondered it all as trundled
along atop a cart, freezing his balls off, shivering himself
half to death. What on earth was Maximus up to? How
could it be so important to him he take possession of
these snails? And why would the Emperor Gratian be so
desperate to stop him? He thought too of his meeting
with Governor Priscus. Clearly, he was a man very much
in Gratian's camp. As soon as Felicius had spoken of the
cargo for Maximus from the east, Priscus has sent his min-
ions onto him.

And always, memories of Carthage came back to him. Theodosius' lifeless body slumping to the flagstones, hot tears on Felicius' cheeks. The twisted grin on Romulus' face as he wiped his blade clean. Could it be a coincidence that the same man that had been sent to Africa had now been sent to hunt him? Felicius hawked and spat. He didn't believe in coincidences.

It was a lot to chew over. He was but a simple soldier, and wanted nothing more than the monotonous routine of drilling his men and keeping his fort ticking over. Even fighting the occasional war didn't bother him overly. You soon forgot the bowel loosening terror one felt when engaging with an enemy, lost as you were in paperwork and settling petty disputes between soldiers. Sometimes it was even a welcome distraction.

He still had the letter from Theodosius tucked away in his satchel. He hadn't wanted to get the parchment wet. As soon as he saw Maximus and got dismissed, he planned to shut himself away in a quiet room and read the letter. Maybe Theo had some answers for him? He was just pondering the thought when a door opened, and a helmeted head peered around, nodding in his direction. 'He'll see you now,' the soldier said.

Felicius stood, swaying slightly. He'd not eaten a proper meal in two days, just whatever Drax's men could rustle up, which had been little. Maybe the wine had been a mistake? Bollocks to that. He had stuff to say. A bit of added fire in his belly wouldn't hurt. He followed the soldier through to a small room, where Maximus sat, face flickering in the light of a candelabra. 'Prefect! You are returned! And not a day too soon. I trust you have my cargo?'

How like the man to be all pleasantries and smiles. He knew all too well his cargo had been delivered. He also knew one of the lids on the lead pots had been prised open. 'Snails,' Felicius said as a way of reply. 'All of that, was for snails.'

Maximus grinned. His dangerous grin, the one he only gave you when you were in the deepest of deep shit. 'Yes, prefect. Snails. Why have you been looking? Why is one of my pots open? I gave explicit orders for them to remain untouched.'

Felicius told Maximus of the events in Londinium, plus his meeting with Romulus on the road. 'Whatever you had agreed to pay Calidus, I suggest you double it. Also, there is a carter named Drax who is owed a tidy sum of gold.' He'd paid Drax himself, but he was damned if he was going to tell Maximus that.

'Take whatever coin you need and dispense it to whomever you promised. Of that, we have no shortage. Food, weapons and armour, however, we are depressingly still light on.'

Felicius rubbed his eyes. Was he really moving the conversation on so casually? 'Why have I just risked both my life and that of my *daughter* to bring you pots full of snails?' He slammed a hand down on the table as he raged. A nice touch, he thought. The soldier that had shown him in poked his head around the door, hand on sword hilt. Maximus dismissed the man with a wave of his hand. 'Can I trust you, prefect?' he asked.

'To fight a war against the Caledonians? Yes. To involve myself in whatever game it is you are playing with Gratian and God knows who else? No. I want no part in it. I do my job. My job is to lead the Fourth Cohort of Gauls against the enemy.'

'So it is. But who is the enemy? That is the question,' Maximus mused. Felicius had put his half drunk jug of wine down on the table. Maximus used it to fill his cup. 'I need my commanders to be loyal,' he said in a light voice, but Felicius knew it was laced with menace.

'I am loyal to Rome,' he said, taking a swig of the wine from the jug. 'You will find no one more so.'

'And that prefect, is what troubles me.'

Felicius scoffed a laugh. 'You are troubled because I am loyal and you are not?'

'I am troubled because we see the world from different points of view. I need my officers to be aligned.'

'That is why you keep Victorinus and me at arm's length,' Felicius said.

'Perhaps. Though I needn't think I should have to worry about Victorinus any longer. He really is a resourceful fellow. You have to hand it to him. I mean, Valentinus would have succeeded all those years ago, would he not, if Victorinus had not simply refused to be beaten.'

'What do you mean, you do not have to worry about him anymore?' Since his meeting with Romulus, Felicius had put all thoughts of Victorinus from his mind. Fear gnawed at him now, bowels clenched, an icy tremor running down his spine.

'Silly bugger went and got himself lost north of the Wall, but you know that, don't you? Bumped into your man, Vitulus not two days ago, was shocked to learn that he was not in the hospital at Vindolanda, as you so told me. But had been in fact in the north, out looking for our dear Sixtus.'

'Where is Sixtus?' Felicius said, not caring one iota that Maximus had caught him out in his lie.

'Dead, supposedly. Seems there was a band of raiders on the eastern coast. They got hold of him somehow,' Maximus shrugged. 'That's really all I know. Wait, where are you going? We have supplies to discuss, an army to feed!'

Felicius was already leaving, quick marching back to the stables. Sixtus was in serious peril. He'd left him once, thinking it was his duty. Now he knew his only duty was to his friend.

***

'So how did he know where you were?' Felicius said. He was back in Vindolanda, his daughter and Davos already being fussed over by Lucia in the room next door, Felicius could hear her cooing over the boy, imagined her running a hand over his waist, tutting at the lack of meat on his bones. Normally, it would be a thought to cheer him. Today, he thought there was nothing that could.

He had ridden immediately for home after storming out of his meeting with Maximus. To hell with the man's war, to hell with the safety of the province. He wanted no part in whatever Maximus was scheming.

'I don't know, sir. All I can think is someone passed him a message once we crossed back south at Vindobala.'

Felicius sighed. His stomach ached through lack of food. His muscles protested their agony after weeks on the road, his bones creaked from the cold. He was in terrible shape, and as he seemed to be constantly reminded, he was no longer a young man. 'Tell me everything,' he said through a sigh, refilling his cup with heated wine.

Vitulus spoke of the raiders they'd discovered in the east, of how Victorinus and Drost had fought them off initially, only to then be caught at a farm. 'They were drugged?' Felicius cut in.

'Aye sir, the wine. Though thanks to the tribune's new-found love of sobriety, he was unaffected. Felicius considered his own wine for a moment, the way his vision blurred as he focused on it. All things considered, sobriety wasn't the worst idea. Vitulus carried on, covering Pastor's whipping and Victorinus' own wounds. 'Worst part of it is,' Vitulus said, lowering his voice and looking visibly uncomfortable.

'Spit it out, man!'

'The leader of the raiders, it was Aldhard. The man that lead the Saxones a few weeks ago.'

Felicius definitely needed to stop drinking. He could have sworn his centurion – a perfectly level-headed, sensible veteran of over twenty years – had just said a dead man was leading the men trying to kill Victorinus. 'Have you lost your mind?'

'No, sir. Pastor was the first one to mention it, Victori-nus thought it too!'

'The man had his fucking head cut off!'

'Yes, sir... I understand that.'

'So it isn't him, is it!' Felicius necked the last of his wine. Sobriety could go fuck. 'So Sixtus was alive and well when you left him?'

'Yes, sir. With Pastor and Drost and a few of Drost's lads. I'd wager they made it away from Aldha- whoever it was that was chasing them.'

'So where are they?' Felicius mused. He had a rudimen-tary map of the lands north of the Wall in front of him. Problem was both he and Vitulus were no experts when it came to the local geography. Vitulus couldn't even give a vague idea of where he had been when he'd left Victorinus. Sixtus and Drost would know, though, both having spent the majority of their lives up there. It gave him a minor comfort.

'It's late,' Felicius said eventually. 'Get some sleep. We wait here until we receive any further orders. I know Max-imus wanted us at the Wall ready to go, but far as I can see we're better off here. We wait, prepare, and when the order comes, we go. Understand?' Vitulus nodded, and left his commander to it.

Felicius lounged in his chair a moment, listening to his family talk through the wall. He should get up and join them, but this was the first time in weeks there wasn't someone or something clamouring for his attention. Was he not owed a small amount of peace? Remembering

Theo's letter, he ripped off the seal, settled a candle on the table next to him, and read.

***

To the prefect Gaius Felicius, commander of the Fourth Co-hort of Gauls, Vindolanda, Britannia. From the Divine Augustus Flavius Theodosius, lord and protector of Rome's eastern provinces. Greetings.

My dear friend, I dictate this letter to you from the sad-dle. These past weeks I have been hard at work, trying to rebuild the depleted forces of the eastern field army. Our war here stops for nothing. Through hale and snow, my men have been fighting. The heathen Fitigern remains at large, though I grow more confident by the day that we shall bring the cur to heel. My young family is thriving. I thank you for your concern for them, and I shall be sure to pass on your greetings when God next grants me the time to see them.

I have to say, even for a young man such as myself, that being an emperor is exhausting. Throughout my education, they teach us of the golden era, the glory days, where heroic generals lead immortal legions to victory after victory. Our strength was not just in our manpower, nor in the superior-ity of our weapons and armour. It was, I am increasingly certain, in our ability to delegate. Think on it, prefect. Did the divine Augustus drag himself out of his palace in the depths of winter every time some barbarian warlord or other stirred on his borders? Of course he didn't! A general would be ordered to see it dealt with, a legion or two allocated to him, and Augustus would lie in his bed sipping warmed wine, awaiting news of his latest victory.

Over the centuries, we have lost that ability, Gaius. Too many treacherous generals, too many incompetent emperors. My days are a blur of correspondence, simple questions from senior commanders in our army, asking for minute things they should be able to deal with themselves. But they can't, because over the years we have stripped away their power, their access to coin and armouries. We have become so paranoid about what could happen if they were to succeed – which, ironically, is what we expect them to do anyway – that they are impotent when is comes to facing certain challenges.

I find myself so frustrated! I need to be everywhere all at once! And this is just to deal with Fritigern. God only knows what I shall do if the Persians rear their head. They will have their spies, of that you can be certain, sniffing around our cities, perhaps even watching me. And what is it they report back to their overlords? That we are an empire on the brink? Our borders collapsing, our army in disarray, food shortages in every major city, disease rife, treasuries empty, taxation at an all-time high. It cannot last, Gaius, and I have no notion of how to fix it all. I am but a leaf on the breeze; the wind forcing us ever on to our end. God help me, but I fear for our future.

If I am granted the time, I shall see some of this put right. Our generals will once more have the freedom to act as they need, to make decisions in my name and bring glory to their standards. I will empower them, and they will see, as their forebears did, that only together are we strong, only together can we thrive. Our empire is a wounded beast, Gaius, tit-

tering on the edge. But I say that wound is not mortal! We bleed, yes, our energy is low, our enemies gathering. But we shall push through, come out the other end even stronger! Men like you and I Gaius, we shall set the world to rights.

As I have already said, my time is constrained, to say the least, but I have sent a man to the coast to enquire about this cargo Maximus is shipping all around the world. This man, I will not set his name to ink, due to his continued importance to me in his role, came back to me with nothing. Not only did this perplex me, for my man is 'most' resourceful, if you get my meaning, but it concerns me greatly that Maximus could organise this from Britannia, without leaving his mark on any of it. I don't know whether to write and congratulate my cousin or order his arrest. I would assume by now his cargo has arrived? Have you managed to discover what it is?

If you have genuine concerns for the safety of our beloved empire, and do believe Maximus to be acting against Rome's interests, I might encourage you to make contact with Governor Priscus in Londinium. He has his faults, even news of the unruly gangs he pays to keep quiet has reached my ears, but no one is perfect, I suppose. He is, though, fiercely loyal to the state, and would not hesitate to confiscate any cargo arriving at his docks should he be informed of its treacherous nature. I am too far away, my dear friend, to offer you more than moral support, and for that I can only apologise. But you have friends around you, reliable officers under your command that would follow you through anything, and I know that whatever comes of this, you shall meet it head on like a true Roman.

Finally, I would thank you for your kind words regarding my father. I live in a well of deep regret that I was not with him in Africa when the end came. And to think that cretin Romanus still serves at my cousin's court. My blood boils just at the thought. One day, Gaius, I shall be avenged on that man. Of that you can be certain. Still, I find my thoughts drifting often to my father. I judge my decisions based on what I think he would do. I do wonder if that is a rather unhealthy habit. I am an Emperor, for God's sake! If I am unable to back my own judgement, then what man is? Maybe it is just that which has brought our empire so low. Doubt, rather than greed. Have we become too meek, hiding behind our fine stone walls? Have we forgotten the lions we once were?

I have to go, old friend. There is a line of messengers waiting impatiently for my attention, seemingly stretching to the horizon. It would appear I am in for another long day. Stay strong, old friend, and stay alert.

Your friend always,
Theo

***

He read the letter, scoffed a laugh when Theo suggested he seek Governor Priscus. He suspected that bridge may already be burned. Snails. He couldn't stop thinking about snails. And weren't there snails everywhere? Certainly they lived here in Britannia, so why go to all the trouble of shipping them halfway across the world?

He yawned, pawed at his unshaven face. Lifting the wine jug, finding it empty, he sighed. He'd not expected much more from his old friend, if he was being honest with himself. Theo had an empire to run, an empire at war. He had seen but a small portion of the uphill battle facing his old friend in the time he had spent in the east. The terrain was mountainous, the enemy nomadic, popping up where you least expected them. Fritigern was a worthy adversary, that much he had deduced. And an adversary with a grudge. An eastern general – Felicius could not bring the man's name to mind – had tried to assassinate Fritigern and a fellow Gothic king at a dinner party of all places. The botched attempt had not gone to plan, the way botch jobs tended to go, and since then Fritigern had been running riot in the east, from Thrace down to Greece, causing havoc and leaving nothing but wanton destruction in his wake.

Theo had wanted to execute the general, Felicius remembered that much. But the man had powerful allies, and Theo had settled for sending the man into retirement, a black mark forever next to his name – whatever his name was. He'd remember it later. That was always the trick of it. Stop thinking about it, and it will appear in your mind unbidden, probably when you're trying to remember something else your wine sodden brain had forgotten.

His dark thoughts twirled and tumbled until his friend Victorinus was front and centre. Surely his old companion could not be dead. He would feel the loss the way he would if he lost Lucia or Marcelina, perhaps even Davos now. No, his friend was not dead. Outnumbered, wounded, stranded in a barbarian country. Sixtus had been there before.

Beaten the odds and come out swinging. He would do the same again.

Lupicinus. That was the general's name! He couldn't remember why it was important now. His head drooped, his breathing a repetitive rise and fall of his chest, arms slumped down by his side. He dozed for what he thought was moments, awoken by the brazen trill of the alert horn. Starting, arms flinging, sending the empty wine jug clattering to the floor, he rose unsteadily and made his way over the window, pulling back the shutter. Dawn was showing itself, strutting in front of the night, daring it to halt its advance. The night would not give battle.

There was a dull ache behind Felicius' eyes, an unpleasant tang on his tongue. His neck and shoulders protested after his mistreatment of them – a man of his age should not be sleeping slouched in a chair. He blinked twice, trying to shift the fog that clouded his mind. The horn sounded again, causing him to squint his eyes shut. He grunted at the lance of pain that shuddered through his head. Perhaps he should join Sixtus in sobriety. He bet his friend hadn't awoken feeling this rough in a good while. If his friend still woke up at all.

He grunted to himself, turning from the window, allowing the cold air to seep in and engulf him. Nothing like a bracing wind to shift a hangover. He picked up Theo's letter and stuffed it in the pouch at his belt. He would reply when he could. Not that he knew when that would be. The horn sounded again, and this time Felicius could hear his men stirring, officers ordering them out of their bunks, 'ready to march within the hour,.' he heard one call.

It seemed to Felicius that he and his hangover were off to war.

XVII

'What are they doing?' Victorinus barked. 'They're too narrow!' He growled in frustration, prowling left to right as the battle unfurled below.

He'd watched on for a night and a day as the Caledonian mob – he refused to call it an army, armies were organised – made its way inexorably south. Mid afternoon on the second day, a Roman force had appeared on the southern horizon, the Wall just visible at their backs. They hadn't waited, hadn't taken the time to appraise their enemy, they'd just attacked.

Victorinus could make out their dragoon banners, flapping on the wind as they galloped across the open ground. The First Asturians were leading the charge. He thought he could make out Felix at their head. His son would be there somewhere, spear held low, ready to pounce. He tried desperately to make him out, but from the distance it was impossible.

Behind them came their companion regiment, the Second Asturians. Victorinus could see Andragathius in a golden helmet leading the charge. 'Surely that general can see what's going to happen?' Drost said, mouth half full of a cooked chicken they'd bought at a farm earlier that day.

The cavalry charged in two narrow columns, three men wide with deep ranks behind. It was senseless. A formation perfect when travelling, but going into battle it meant less than a third of your force would actually engage with the enemy. Cavalry were shock troops, designed to engage hard and fast with the enemy and then gallop out of reach. Forming them up like this for a battle meant the rearmost ranks would still be fighting when the front ranks were a quarter of a mile past the enemy rearguard.

The inevitable happened. The Caledonians rocked under the first charge. A disorganised mass, they were like a wave retreating from the shore, spear wielding warriors giving in to their terror and turning their backs on the enemy. But someone rallied them. Sword held high above their head, a figure roared, voice just audible over the cacophony of battle. And the men responded. They regrouped, got themselves back into formation, and as gaps opened up in the ranks of the charging cavalry, they formed their battle lines and split the horsemen into smaller groups.

'Now we've got a battle,' Drost muttered, teeth still working hard on the chicken.

'Thought you were going home?'

'And miss all this?' he waved an arm. 'Pox on that. I've already been away weeks longer than I said I would, so I'm in the shit regardless. Another day or so makes no difference, way I see it.'

Victorinus grinned. The makings of a happy marriage there. He would know. He turned his attention back to the battle. His son was part of the first wing of the First, meaning he was always close to Felix. Meaning Felix could always keep an eye on him. Maurus had been told he was there because of his ability, and whilst that wasn't entirely untrue, Victorinus had made it quite clear to Felix what would happen to him if his son were to fall. In Victorinus' mind, Felix had made the sensible decision.

Those that had been the first to engage the Caledonians were wheeling to the east, their mounts sending spurts of fog into the freezing air. But the terrain was rougher there, lush green grass giving way to rocks and sprouting bushes. They slowed, and a group of Caledonians saw their opportunity and charged them.

Victorinus' heart stopped. He made a sort of squealing noise, impotent, helpless, desperate to be down there with his son. 'What fort is that over there? Fanum Cocidi?' Drost was pointing north, to the remains of a fort in the distance.

'Huh? Yeah, think so,' Victorinus said, distracted.

'The walls are almost intact most the way around. You reckon all those horses would fit inside?'

'What?'

'They need to regroup. This lot,' he thumbed down to the Caledonian army, 'is hardly going to give them the time to do that. They should ride for that fort and sort themselves out before attacking again. If they gallop there, they'll have time to get back in formation before the tribes catch them up.'

Victorinus jumped up and down on the spot, unable to keep still. 'Gods, you're right! They try it on open ground and the Caledonians won't let up. We need to tell them!'

'Tell who? And how? Don't forget we've still got Pastor in a litter just down the road.'

'I'm out the litter, and ready to help,' Pastor said from behind them.

He was slumped over, pale as winter, with a permanent grimace fixed to his face. But he'd shrugged his mail back on and had a sword in hand. Victorinus' heart hurt just looking at him. He loved the boy like one of his own. 'Maurus is my brother as much as he is your son,' Pastor said. 'And we can't just stand here and watch him die.'

Drost's men appeared behind Pastor. They were few in number, but each hefted a weapon and gave their chief a nod. Seemed Victorinus wasn't the only one with an attachment to Pastor. The lad gathered fans wherever he went. 'Right then. So we'll just run down the hill, into the middle of that bloody great battle, find someone in charge and tell them what to do – all the while expecting them not to just tell us to fuck off. Then, job done, we'll walk back past the blood thirsty tribes – most of which, by the way, hate my guts due to them thinking I'm a Roman bum boy, and sod off back home shall we?'

'Sounds like a plan to me,' Victorinus said, grinning from ear to ear. 'Let's be off then!'

They ran down the hill. It was too steep, and too long, and halfway down Victorinus remembered he was one old fattening man in mail that sat too snug. His ankles creaked, wounded hand jarring with each heavy step. And then he was face to face with the enemy. A tattooed tribesman swiped at him from high to low. He ducked under the swing, no room to bring his sword to bear, so he rammed it, hilt first, into the warrior's gut, driving the man to his knees. Swinging his sword up high, he swept it down with a blow to the back of the neck, warm blood spurting over him.

Pastor rushed past him in a blur, sword singing in the crisp winter air as he cut a half naked tribesman from shoulder to hip. Drost let fly a throwing axe, Alec and the others rushing after their chief, weapons held high. 'Keep moving!' Drost yelled to Victorinus as he passed him. The tribune nodded, more to himself than anything. They were amid the enemy. To stay still was to die.

They moved in a circle formation, each of them trading blows as they ran. Pastor pulled a man from a horse and Victorinus finished him. Then Drost threw another axe and whooped as it caved in a chest. He heaved it free; the blade coming loose, shards of bone flying. Alec threw a spear, then unsheathed his sword in one fluid motion, dancing between two tribesmen. He cut one in the leg and the other in the back, both dropped to the ground.

A cavalry squadron thundered past them, Victorinus catching the eye of a confused horseman as the man stopped fighting for a moment to frown at them, evidently wondering who the fuck they were. Victorinus gave the man a grin and kept on running. He hacked and slashed, heaving in air and cursing his aging body. Pastor was half bent over, back a ruin, but still trading blows with any who came his way.

All around them was chaos. The order of the battlefield, if there had even been one to start with, was in ruins. The Spanish horse was fighting in small units, some containing only two or three men, and the fight had become a desperate battle for survival. Even Victorinus, no famed general, could see what was going to happen. Cavalry were shock troops, best used in mass, wide formations to cause maximum damage. They had engaged on a narrow front, the rugged terrain not helping, and now they were being undone.

A huge painted warrior, naked, bearing a two headed axe bigger than most men, hacked at the neck of a felled horse, the head came free on the second blow. A clutch of unhorsed Romans fought in a square, but their small round cavalry shields offered little protection on foot, and in moments they were swallowed by a crowd of bloodthirsty Caledonians, their trampled bodies left full of holes.

Victorinus' helmet did nothing to muffle the awful noise of battle. The wounded screamed in agony, he leaped over a fallen Roman crying for his mum. The lad couldn't have been older than Pastor. Steeling himself, for there was nothing he could do, he forced his legs on, step after heavy step. The battle field stunk of rotting bowels and horse shit. The metallic tang of blood hung heavy in the air, assaulting his nostrils with every step.

He ducked under a flying spear and lost his footing. Staggering back to his feet, he didn't see the blow that cracked the back of his head. He bit his tongue as he slumped back to the ground, his world spinning, hearing muffled. Drost was shouting something, the blurred silhouette of Pastor in front of him. Was it Pastor? Or someone else? Good lad, Pastor. He spat blood, then threw up the meagre contents of his stomach.

Boots on the surrounding floor, the heavy rhythm of their tread reverberating through his body. And then something heavier. His vision cleared, the grass the greenest he'd ever seen – apart from the bits he'd bled and vomited on, anyway. He tried to pick his head up, but it seemed to weigh more than his mail. Giving up, he lay flat, head to the side, and watched in confusion as countless hooves thundered around him.

There was a clash of iron and bodies dropped to the ground, more blood splashing over him. He wanted nothing more than to sleep for a week or more if possible. Too old for this shit, was his last thought before the darkness took him.

***

He came back to the world of the living what felt like a moment later. He was, though, looking at different grass. He couldn't be sure how he knew that, he just knew it was. Maybe it was the lack of vomit?

Stirring, head pounding like the anvil under the hammer, he rose unsteadily to a sitting position, mouth as dry as the desert. 'Father!' a voice cried out from next to him, much too loud for his liking. 'We've been so worried about you!'

Arms encircled him, a crushing embrace he winced through, before slapping his dry tongue to the roof of his mouth. 'Water,' he croaked, a skin appearing in his hand.

He drank greedily. 'Where are we?' he said once his thirst was satisfied.

'Fanum Cocidi,' the voice said. 'Thanks to you, father.'

It only then that Victorinus' knackered brain registered the man talking to him was his own son. 'Maurus,' he said, raising his eyes for the first time. 'Gods be praised, you're alive!' This time it was him doing the hugging, his son laughing and squirming beneath him. 'Are you ok? You're not hurt?'

'I'm fine, father,' Maurus said through a laugh. 'You look like shit, though.'

Victorinus winced, tentatively touching a hand to the back of his head. It was sticky to the touch. 'I've no doubt had worse,' he said, not wanting his son to worry.

'Pastor has been telling me about what the two of you have been getting up to. Honestly, father, you find yourself in some troubling situations.'

'Aye. Your mother always said I needed to keep my head down. Anyway, what is going on with you? How goes it with the battle?'

'We've been penned in. Not sure exactly what happened, but our intel was the enemy was another ten or so miles further north. We weren't ready for battle when we met them.'

'But surely you had scouts out?'

Maurus shook his head. 'Andragathius had ordered them to stay with the rest of us until we were five miles north of the Wall.'

'What an idiot,' Victorinus muttered. 'That makes no sense at all. The terrain is all over the place. Any valley could be hiding an army up here.'

'Aye, Felix said much the same. Safe to say he isn't happy.'

'He's still alive, then?'

'Aye father. He was here just a moment ago. I'm sure he'll be back.'

'So what's the plan?'

'Originally, we were going to get our formation back together and then charge the bastards. But Andragathius spent too long dithering, Felix spent too long arguing with him, and now we're pretty much surrounded.'

'Marvellous,' Victorinus said. 'Sounds like a shit show from start to finish. Where's Maximus?'

'Coming up with the infantry tomorrow, or that was the plan last I heard.'

Victorinus grunted. 'Where is your brother?' he asked, suddenly remembering the last time he'd seen Silvius had been at his farmhouse, and the lad had been planning on signing up with the Heruli.

'Alaric signed him up under the Heruli's banner the day after you left for the north. I thought you knew?'

'Aye, I knew that was what he wanted. Thought your mother might have put a stop to it.'

'She tried,' Maurus grinned. 'But we both know what we want. We're stubborn. I wonder where we get that from.'

'More your mother than me, I can assure you,' Victorinus said through a laugh. 'Will the Heruli be coming north tomorrow?'

'Aye, I guess.' Silence a moment, the sounds of the Caledonian horde outside the walls filling the lapse in words. Both were thinking of Silvius and what he would be facing. 'Alaric will look after him,' Maurus said, though Victorinus thought it more for his own benefit than his father's.

'Course he will. Good man, Alaric. And Felicius will be with them. He will make sure Silvius is somewhere towards the back when it comes to the fighting.' Victorinus studied his son a moment. The same mop of floppy hair he'd had as a kid. Same button nose. His mouth was different though, a shadow of two-day stubble bristling his cheek. A funny thing, to think of the boy he used to be. He reached to the leather pouch at his waist, pulled out the wooden horse. 'Remember this,' he said, holding it out to Maurus.

'Amor,' Maurus whispered in reverence, taking it from his father. It was worn and faded, the wood receding from the rough edges of Victorinus' touch. 'I thought it had been lost.'

'Keep it with me always,' Victorinus said. 'A reminder of happier times.'

Maurus stroked the horse a moment longer, a childish grin fixed to his face. 'She still cares about you, you know.'

'Bah,' Victorinus waved a hand. 'I burned my bridges there, no mistake about that. She cares about me the way people care for their dogs. There's some love, for sure, but it ain't the same.' He felt a well of emotion build up within him, tears pricking the corner of his eyes. Must have been the knock to the head. 'It's fine, son. We have you boys, and seeing the both of you grow into fine young men has brought us joy. All I want is for you and Silvius to succeed in life, in whatever path you choose.'

'I wasn't under the impression we had a choice. You had swords in our hands the moment we could walk.'

Victorinus shrugged. 'Just because you know the pointy end of a sword from the handle doesn't mean you have to use it. The world's a shit place, Maurus, make no mistake. I just wanted you both to know how to take care of yourselves. You don't have to tread this path, you know. I know you've signed up for twenty years, but Felix would let you go. You can do anything you want to do. Maybe take a wife?' He let that hang in the air.

Maurus smiled. 'And let me guess, that wife would be Marcelina, would it?'

'Perhaps,' Victorinus said with a wink. 'She's a fine lass from a good family. I think the two of you could be happy.'

'Seems there's one thing you and mother agree on then.'

'Oh? She's spoken to you?'

'Aye, when you took us home, before you went north. Seems she and Lucia have been speaking.'

'And you know once your mother puts her mind to something...'

Maurus raised his hands in mock surrender. 'I know! I know! And for what it's worth, I agree. Marcelina would make a fine match. Now you just need to find someone for Silvius, and Pastor too!'

'Actually, I was thinking about Delphina?'

'Publius and Amata's daughter? Yes! She is a lovely girl. And I think she rather likes the look of Pastor.'

'Should I leave and let you talk more about me?' Pastor appeared through a clutch of men. Victorinus took a moment to fully take in his surroundings. He'd been so engrossed in talking to his son he realised he'd no real idea where he was. There were no buildings left standing with Fanum Cocidi, the stone long since repossessed by the local farmers for boundary walls and shelters. The walls, though, were four feet at least most of the way around, a few gaps that were being filed with men and beasts.

It seemed the Caledonians were content for the moment to leave their foe where they were. They couldn't get in, and the Romans couldn't get out, so an unhealthy stalemate was at play. 'Father was just talking about your marriage prospects,' Maurus said, rising to clasp arms with Pastor.

Pastor blanched. 'Marriage?' he said, puffing out his cheeks.

'Father thought Delphina might make a good match for you,' Maurus said, a wide grin fixed to his face as watched Pastor squirm in discomfort.

'Delphina?' he managed to croak out, his pale face suddenly redder than the sun.

'I've seen the way you look at her, lad,' Victorinus said, throwing Maurus a wink. 'Seen the way she looks at you, too.'

Pastor looked slowly from father to son, mouth blubbering like a fish out of water. 'We're surrounded in some long abandoned fort, seething tribesmen baying for our blood. And you two are talking about marriage? You were unconscious a moment ago!' he blurted out, pointing at Victorinus.

'That's settled then,' Victorinus said, clambering to his feet with a forced ease. His head swam, and for a moment he was seeing stars, but he fixed a grin on his face all the same and clapped his hands together. 'A double wedding it is! This spring.'

'Well, I'm glad that's settled,' Pastor said with an air of disbelief. 'Now just the small matter of making sure we're all alive come spring.'

'What's going on in here then?' Felix appeared at Pastor's back, his olive skin somehow still a picture of health in the midst of a northern winter.

'Felix! We were just discussing a double wedding this spring. Maurus and Pastor are to be married!'

'Not to each other, I assume?' he said with a laugh. 'Who are the two unlucky ladies?'

'Delphina for Pastor, she's our neighbour's daughter. And Marcelina, Felicius' daughter for Maurus.'

'Excellent! Well boys, if I had a skin of wine handy, I'd toast to you both.'

'Is anyone worried about beating the Caledonians?' Pastor all but shrieked, ripping free his helmet and rubbing his hair in his anxiety.

'Oh relax. We are Rome, we don't lose to barbarians.'

'I'll give you barbarians!' Drost roared, jabbing Felix with mock punches to his ribs. 'Sixtus! Back in the world of the living, I see.'

'And planning a double wedding for his boys,' Felix chimed in.

'A double wedding, hey? Count me in!'

'Seriously!' Pastor shouted. 'We are trapped on enemy ground, beset by enemies on all sides, and you lot are going on like we're at some summer garden party in Rome!'

'Ooh, I bet they're lovely,' Drost said.

'Too many flies. But apart from that, they can be quite pleasant,' Felix said.

Pastor had finally had enough. He stormed off, muttering under his breath. 'Idiots,' Victorinus thought he heard him say. It just made him grin wider. If you can't laugh when it seems as though the whole world is against you, then when could you? Seriously, the lad needed to learn to relax. Or maybe it was still the knock to the head muddling his brain. Either way, his head felt heavier than a bag of sand. But he'd had hangovers leaving him in worse states in his younger years. Just needed to bounce back.

'Right then. Now the important stuff is out the way. Let's go see if we can win this battle, shall we?'

VXIII

To the Divine Augustus Flavius Theodosius, lord and protector of Rome's eastern provinces, from Gaius Felicius, Prefect of the Fourth Cohort of Gauls, writing from Britannia. Greetings.

My dear friend, I write this letter from a campaign tent three miles or so north of the Wall of Hadrian. It seems Maximus was doing more than just scare mongering when he spoke of a threat to the north, but indeed had solid intelligence. We are to engage the enemy at first light. They are surrounding the long abandoned fort of Fanum Cocidi, two regiments of our own cavalry trapped inside. I know not how they came to be so, only that they are commanded by a general who has never fought a battle in the saddle. As you said yourself in your letter, we live in strange times.

It was to some amusement that I read your letter. Indeed, I read it upon returning home from an eventful trip to Londinium, picking up Maximus' cargo for him. I had a meeting with Governor Priscus, and found to my detriment that the gangs of Londinium are in his pay, when they attacked me and tried to prevent me leaving the city. I'll admit to finding the whole thing bizarre. It was on the road north, though, that I discovered what the cargo actually was.

Snails. Lead pots filled with what appear to be fermenting snails. Can you imagine if I'd have died for that? I'd have never have heard the end of it (that is, coincidentally, a joke I heard at a theatre in Greece when travelling back to Britannia after serving under you in Thrace)

Back to my point, I haven't the first clue what Maximus intends to do with all these snails, but safe to say Priscus was concerned enough about this special cargo. He was willing to kill me to get his hands on it. What does one do with a pot full of fermenting snails? The mind boggles. I shall make further enquiries here in Britannia as and when I can, though I fear our friends to the north are going to be keeping me busy for the foreseeable future. I can hear them now, their war horns and their cries lighting up the night. I shouldn't think there will be many among us who will get much rest, though that shall at least be the same for them.

I do have concerns about getting caught up in whatever scheme Maximus is weaving. Does Governor Priscus now think me a traitor? Am I to be tarnished with the same brush as Maximus? I fear Maximus has set himself on a path he cannot deviate from, no matter where it leads.

But enough of my troubles. How are you? How goes it in the east? We get no word of your exploits up here in the far north. Have you managed to rid the world of Fritigern yet? If not, then surely it is just a matter of time. Please write to me when you are able. You know I love to hear of the goings on in the world. It can be so isolating here, on the edge of our great empire.

I fear I must cut this letter short. Our own horns now muddy the night air. No rest for the wicked, as the old saying goes.

Stay well old friend. I sincerely hope I will have the chance to see you soon.
Gaius

***

'M ovement to the north west sir,' Vitulus said with a salute as Felicius emerged from his tent. It was the wolf hour, that half light where the night hadn't quite gone, but the dawn hadn't mustered the strength to announce itself. The ground was frozen mud turned to slush under the constant barrage of boots and hooves. Felicius sighed, breath fogging the air. He ran a hand through his hair before fitting on a cap and fastening his helmet over the top.

'You don't think they'd attack us, do you?' Maximus had ordered a full marching camp built, despite them being just three miles past the Wall. Felicius had considered asking the *Dux* to keep the men behind the Wall for the night, but had decided against it. Maximus' will was as unbending as iron. If he wanted the men three miles north, they would sleep three miles north. It seemed a lot of effort to go to, with two hours of the previous day lost to digging trenches and building earth walls. But Maximus got what he wanted.

'Not sure. There seems to be a good amount of them moving away from the Fanum Cocidi. They know we're here, couldn't have missed us. And they've come looking for a fight, right?'

'Aye, I suppose they have.' Felicius wiped mucus from the end of his nose, breathing in deep and resisting the urge to shiver. 'Muster the men, and sound the general alarm. We need every man ready to march in half an hour.' Vitulus saluted and walked away. Felicius clambered up the side of the earth wall. It wouldn't win any awards for its defensive prowess, but it would have served its purpose had the enemy come for them in the night. The sky above was a purple hue, the landscape blanketed in shadow. But he could make out the movement to the northwest, just as Vitulus said. A mob of people were moving south, the flames of their torches like stars in the darkness.

He squinted, trying to focus on the old fort of Fanum Cocidi. He wondered if the horsemen there had survived the night. Looking up at the night sky, he thought of his friend Sixtus. He'd had no news of his whereabouts, and for the first time he started to believe the words of Maximus. Maybe he was dead after all. He wondered also if Maximus had meant for him to die when he sent him south to Londinium. Surely the *Dux* knew there would be peril? He thought of his run in with the *scola scutariorum secunda*. Could it really have been Governor Priscus that set Romulus in motion, scouring the country for Felicius?

The more he thought on it, the more the time line didn't add up. Romulus and his men had come over from Gaul, specifically to hunt for Felicius. In order for Priscus to convey his concerns to Gratian, he would have needed a messenger. That messenger would have needed a ship, and then a good two-day ride once he landed in Gaul. Then troops would have been gathered, orders written and dispatches sent. How could Romulus have found him so quickly? Unless he was already in Britannia.

Could the *Dux* have set that in motion? What had he done? Had he himself sent word to the court of the emperor, laying his treason bare? No, Felicius shook his head. For all his faults, Maximus had more subtlety than that. He would have paid men to whisper it in the shadows of Gratian's court. Let the rumour spread, the fear take hold. Let Gratian send a man to Britannia. Worst that happens is he finds nothing.

And who was it that was sent? Another German officer, just like the ones Maximus surrounds himself with. Felicius went cold with shock, the realisation hitting him. Maximus had been planning this for months, whatever this was. He was exactly where he wanted to be, surrounded by an army, on the cusp of a great victory.

Heart pumping, ears burning with a surge of blood, he tried to calm himself. His whole life had been one of tolerance and embracing the different cultures that made up the peoples of the empire. He loved the fact he could be breakfasting with a German one morning, then dining with an eastern trader that evening. It was their diversity that made Rome what it was. He was not one to judge others on their past or their beliefs. Leave that to the bigots in the senate, the religious zealots that preached hate on over turned crates in the forums across the Roman world. The way he'd always seen it, the army was the great leveller. Didn't matter where you came from or what God brought you to your knees. When you locked shields in a battle line with the man next to you, you embraced him as a brother for life.

He stood there; the facts whirling around his mind. He could prove none of this, let alone do anything to stop it. Breathing in deep, he forced himself to focus on what he could control, and that was getting his men through this battle in one piece. Horns filled the air once more, the pre-dawn alive with the sound of mustering men. There was the grumbles and shouts, the trudge of boots on mud and the metallic clink of mail being shrugged on. Horses whinnied and stamped, men's breath streaming as they forced aching bodies out of the warmth of their leather tents.

'It's going to be a fine day, prefect!' a voice called from the darkness, and Felicius turned to see Maximus himself appear from the gloom. He was clad in shimmering mail, a gold trimmed helmet and a fine white cloak that looked at odds amongst the mud of the dreary north.

'I'm sure of it,' Felicius smiled, not wanting to show any doubt. 'What is your plan?'

'Follow me and you shall have it,' Maximus said with a gesture.

Soon after, Felicius found himself in an open-sided command tent, a cup of warmed wine in his hand. Maximus stood over a folding table, a rough map of the terrain in front of him. 'Gentlemen,' he said, quelling the murmurs of the gathered officers. 'Today we end the disruption of the Caledonians for a generation or more. Today we beat them so thoroughly they will have no men left to spill their seed in their womenfolk. No children to grow in to warriors and disturb our borders. Today we finally bring peace to Britannia.'

A ragged cheer met this, Felicius did not join in. Britannia had never really found peace. There had been good years and bad, but the good years comprised raids and skirmishes, Roman blood being spilt for little or no gain. The bad years were outright war, and God knew there had been enough of them.

'What is your plan, lord?' Ambrosius Castus asked. Felicius winced inwardly at the word 'lord'. Ambrosius was known as being one of the generals fiercely loyal to Maximus. He was, of course, another German. Once again, Felicius quelled his fears, though they lurked deep down in his gut. Innocent until proven guilty, wasn't that what the law men said? Well, if it was good enough for them...

'Felicius will hold the centre with his Gauls. They are by far the most experienced fighting unit we have. Prefect, your orders are to advance until you hear my horn, then you hold your line. I will have the right flank, and Ambrosius, you the left. Our men will push on, engulf the enemy, and box them in. Much depends on whether we can force their flanks quickly enough, and if Felicius' boys can hold the centre.'

'We'll hold, sir,' Felicius said, eyes staring at the map. He pictured the terrain to their north. A narrow patch of flat grassland that would be his to hold. To the right flank were steep hills, cliffs almost. That would be near on impossible for Maximus to advance over. To the left, the grassland gave way to uneven patches of rocks and heather, and beyond that, a river. Ambrosius, too, would find it tough going.

Once more, the cynical voice in Felicius' head told him he was being given a death order. He would have to hold back the brunt of the Caledonian assault, his five hundred men against the inexorable tide. He was in for a long day.

'Has there been any word from the cavalry?' someone asked.

'None,' Maximus said with a sorrowful shake of his head. 'But they are surrounded. Getting a man out to us would be impossible. But the tribes are still outside the walls. That tells me Andragathius and his men are still holding out.'

There was a commotion to the south side of the tent. Four men bearing a large wooden chest laboured to get under the canvas, before gently laying the chest to rest. 'My lord,' one of them said, before flicking open the clasp on the chest.

'No!' Maximus called, holding out a hand. 'Not now, after the battle.'

The gathered officers exchanged quizzical glances, Felicius included. Ambrosius Castus had a grin fixed on his face, one shared by Maximus when their eyes met. Felicius took in the two men, then looked back to the chest. He had a feeling that the answers to his nagging questions lay within.

'Any questions?' The *Dux* asked. No one replied. 'Then let us be to it.'

***

'First darts ready!' Vitulus bellowed, his voice carrying. The men of the Fourth Cohort unclipped their darts from the inner rim of their shields, not missing a step in their steady march towards the enemy.

Felicius felt as if he were being carried on a wave. In a way, he was. He was completely detached from the battle, oblivious to the danger he was about to put himself in. All he could think about was the chest.

'Fifty paces off, sir. When do we throw?' Vitulus said. He got no reply. Felicius felt a nudge on his left shoulder and he snapped out of his revery. 'Huh?'

'Fifty paces off. We need to start throwing darts!'

Felicius blinked, as if the act would clear his thoughts. It didn't work. 'Right, yes, of course.' He unhooked his own dart, the grip feeling unfamiliar in his hand. Looking left and right, he saw the full might of the Roman line, ready to be unleashed. His own men held the centre as planned, Maximus on the right with the Heruli, Castus the left with a mixture of auxiliaries pulled from their forts along the Wall. To their front, a charging enemy.

The Caledonians streamed down the slope from the fort of Fanum Cocidi, the cavalry they had been entrapping seemingly forgotten. Their painted bodies were bright blotches of colour in the grey morning light, their leaders bearing flaming torches like beacons for their warriors to follow. The ground shook with their charge, yet still Felicius felt none of the sensations that normally built up within him before battle. There was no urgent need to piss, no shivering and sweating, no boulder sitting at the base of his gut.

He just felt empty. That chest repeating itself in his mind's eye. 'Loose darts!' Vitulus cried to his left, and he went through the motions, planting his left foot on the frozen turf and hurling his dart at the snarling enemy. He might have hit someone, would have been an achievement if he'd missed to be fair. He didn't bother checking. He pulled free his second dart and threw.

What is the point? Was all he could think. If they won, then it would be a famous victory for Maximus, another gold mark against his rising name. And if they lost? Then it would be his fault. The officer's fault, whoever Maximus needed an excuse to be rid of. One despatch to the emperor would be all it would take, one line of ink on parchment, and his career would be in tatters. If he lived to see himself ruined.

A shield smashed into his, and he was rocked off his feet. Breath driven out of him, he crashed into the man behind him, who groaned with the effort of trying to keep his commander upright with his own shield. Felicius blinked. This time, it did clear his head. It appeared the enemy was not fifty paces away, but now right in front of him. With a rush of blood, he surged off the shield to his rear and launched himself at his foe. He jabbed forwards with his shield, lunged with his swo-

Fuck, he hadn't even drawn his sword. Snarling, he smashed his shield forwards again, ripped free his blade and hacked it into an exposed head. Blood spurted in his mouth, and something with more substance. He spat both at his next opponent, ducking under a whirling axe before punching his sword into an abdomen, one, two, three times and the man dropped screaming, hands going to his ruined intestines.

'FORWARD!' Felicius cried, his worries of before melting away. He wanted this, he *needed* this. Fuck Maximus and his scheming, fuck Rome and her high-born nobles and their politicking, Felicius was a soldier, the battlefield his office. And he was going to work.

His men leaned into their shields, one gruelling step after the other as they moved forward, their line unbroken. Tribesmen hurled themselves at the Roman line, spitting, cursing, shrieking in their blood lust. None made it through. Felicius stumbled on the corpse of his latest kill, his ankle twisting as his boot slipped off a bloody leg. He stumbled forwards, dropping his shield for just a moment, and then they were on him. Two men leaped over the fallen shield, the first grabbing his neck, the second pulling back a spear to jab at his face. Felicius snarled, a surge of anger pouring from him. He dropped both sword and shield and grabbed the man that had his neck. He leaned forward, lifting the man from his feet and hurling him to the ground. Bringing himself back to his full height, he saw the spear darting for him, and lunged to the left so the spear hit nothing but air. Grabbing the shaft before his enemy could pull it back, he heaved it towards him, the warrior on the other end staggering forwards, all but falling onto Vitulus's hastily grabbed sword.

'We're meant to be holding the line, not advancing!' Vitulus called over the cacophony of battle.

Felicius just snarled in reply. He scooped up his shield and bringing his sword to bear hacked at the nearest tribesmen, carving his chest into a bloody ruin. He took another step forward, the ground beneath him a mire of dead and dying warriors. He dodged a spear tip, an arrow pinged off his helmet, and then he was hacking away again. A horn sounded from somewhere to the right, the signal to stop the advance and hold. He paid it no heed. Stamping down on a wounded man, he stepped over him and rammed his shield forwards once more.

Fuck it all. He was paid to fight. And today he was earning his coin.

XIX

'You sure you're up to this?' Maurus asked, swinging himself into the saddle.

Victorinus blinked, squinting at the light of the rising sun. His wounded hand still hurt like hell, though the swelling seemed to have gone down when he changed the bandages during the night. His head was worse, swollen to the point he'd struggled to get his dented helmet back on. Vision still slightly blurred, it seemed to take longer than it should for his brain to tell his body to move where he wanted to go. Never the less he struggled onto his borrowed mount and rubbed the beast's mane. 'I do hope I get the chance to see Amor again,' he said, more to himself than anyone else.

'Where is she?'

Victorinus shrugged. 'Still at the farm I left her in when Pastor and the others got captured, I guess? Unless that scheming farmer has butchered her for meat.'

'Reckon you put the shits in him though!' Pastor said through a laugh as he clambered onto his own mount. 'She'll be there when this is done.'

'But I might not,' he muttered, closing his eyes a moment and feeling the blood pulse through him. Truth was, every part of him hurt. His blistered feet were in tatters from the long marches through the rugged north. His legs were so heavy he could have been forgiven for thinking someone had tied weights to them whilst he slept. Not that he'd done much of that. And that was probably his biggest issue. He was exhausted. He had no place in an army anymore. Already well past the age most soldiers retired at, having already seen out his twenty-five years and more. He was what a young Victorinus would have described as a 'Greybeard'. Some miserable old goat who'd fought the world and lost, and was now left with more scars than teeth.

His back twinged as he kicked the horse into motion, and he felt the familiar tremor as his body ached for wine. Didn't seem to matter how many years he put between himself and the flagon. The longing never went away. Like a lost first love that got away, your heart never quite let you forget. The trembling would start next, as inevitable as winter. He took a deep breath, forced himself to focus on the battle to come.

The Caledonians had given up trying to take Fanum Cocidi at some point in the night. In small groups they had retreated into the darkness, there to lick their wounds and prepare to try again come the dawn. But the weak winter sun's emergence had revealed the welcoming sight of a Roman army on the southern horizon, and the horsemen's spirits had lifted to see their companions come to their rescue.

Well, most peoples' spirits were lifted, anyway. 'We'd have beaten them ourselves this morning,' Andragathius said through his dark beard. 'And not a man here will say otherwise to the *Dux*.'

'Aye sir,' was the general reply from the officers that gathered around him. Victorinus grinned. There were too many 'yes men' in the army, he thought. Too many eager faces that would sell their own grandmother to see their star shine a little brighter. Had the great Caesar surrounded himself with such people? He wondered. Or had he men around him that would tell him the truth no matter the consequence? He'd like to think it was the latter, but he reasoned there had been leaches among men as long as there had been great men to clasp on to.

The First Asturians lead the way out of the fort. Bodies littered the ground, already being feasted on by the crows. Victorinus wondered how they always seemed to be the first on scene, so to speak. How did they know? Did they communicate with each other? He smiled again, registering the deflecting tactic his brain was employing. Anything to avoid thinking about what he was about to face.

The Caledonians were, it seemed, in a desperate race to the death with their comrades. He observed from the height of his mount one wave, followed by another and another smash onto Roman shields, only to be cut down moments later. 'Would have thought we'd have learnt by now, eh?' Drost said, steering his horse so he was alongside Victorinus.

'You still here?'

'Course I am. Reckon there's going to be a big change in the north after this blood bath. Need to be in the right place to capitalise, don't I?' He said with a wink.

'Sometimes I think you learnt too much from your time serving us,' Victorinus said. 'Fancy making yourself a king, then?'

'King Drost, lord of the north. Quite a ring to it, I think.'

'And will the mighty king Drost remember his friends in the south? Once he rules all the sheep these great hills have to offer?'

'Well, that's the million denarius question, isn't it? Certainly won't be one I answer to a mere fucking tribune once I've got my crown.'

'Oh of course not, mighty king,' Victorinus said with a mock bow, his tone laced with sarcasm. 'The Emperor Gratian will surely travel here in person, thus to make the proper tribute to his equal in the eyes of the Lord.'

The two men held each other's gaze a moment before bursting into laughter. It hurt Victorinus' head to laugh, and his chest, belly – pretty much all of him, if he was being honest. But by the gods it didn't half lift his spirits, and they had been low of late.

'When the two of you are quite finished,' Felix cut in. He held aloft the banner of his unit in his right hand, his other resting on the pommel of his sword. 'We have a battle to win.'

'Then lead the way, prefect!' Drost called. Felix nodded to the horseman to his right, and the air trilled with the sound of horns. As one, they moved from a standstill to a trot, each man slotting to his allotted place in the formation. Victorinus, who had never been much of a rider, found it impressive, and then disconcerting. No one seemed to be paying him any attention, not that they should, he supposed. But where was he supposed to go? What if another horn sounded, and they all moved? Where should he be?

'Father!' Maurus called over the thrum of the horses' hooves. 'Stay with me.'

Of course, he would stay with his son. Nerves settled, he squinted at the ongoing battle to the south. 'You've better eyes than me, lad. Where are the Heruli's banner?'

'Their right flank,' Maurus said, pointing with his spear. 'He'll be fine, father.'

Victorinus nodded, fear knotting his bowels as he thought of his son, right then fighting for his life. 'Where will we attack?'

'The centre. Andragathius believes the *Dux* plans to push high on both flanks. We are to crush their centre and force them wide. It will create two narrow killing grounds on both our flanks, and the enemy will be trapped between us and the infantry.'

'Then let us be at it,' Victorinus said with a shaky voice.

They advanced at a canter, easing the horses into the ride. Felix had his men form a wedge. To their right, Andragathius, in command of the Second Asturians, did the same. For a quarter of a mile or so, they kept that pace, officers keeping the men in line, ensuring no gaps opened between the horses. A horn sounded, and the speed increased, not quite a gallop, but not far off. Victorinus felt himself carried on the tide, powerless to stop it even if he wanted to. Pastor was to his left, his son his right, Drost and his remaining men behind him. Another horn, and it was time to charge.

He leaned forward, keeping low over his mount, mimicking the motions of his son. Drawing his sword and holding it out to his right flank, he tensed his thighs until the muscles roared in complaint. He was no great rider; he knew that better than anyone. He could ride his beloved old Amor around the countryside at a gentle canter from sunrise to sundown, but this was a whole different stamina.

His wedge eased to the left, so he leaned that way and nudged the horse with his right leg, hoping it was better trained than he was. Thankfully, it was. They crested a small ridge, a gentle slope beyond leading to the enemy. Once on the slope, they were in full charge, a mass of horseflesh and iron, powering towards the terrified faces of the enemy.

'They know they're fucked!' Drost called from behind him. 'They were hoping to break through the infantry before we could attack, and they've failed!'

Pastor bellowed a war cry, something close to excitement on his face. Victorinus took a moment to marvel at the young man's energy. He should still have been in a sickbed, nursing his ruined back. Oh, to be young again.

And then they were on them. Maurus claimed the first kill, leaning down with his blade and scything it straight through the top of a head. He reversed the blade without thought, hacking down at a warrior on his left. Victorinus leaned to his right and slashed the hamstrings of a tribesman facing the wrong way. A backswing took care of a bearded axe man, a quick jab to an open mouth ridding the world of another.

Open space before him and he tried to pull himself back upright, but couldn't. Heaving, left arm straining with all the strength his broken body had left, he could do nothing to right himself. A blur of motion to his front, and suddenly his horse was rearing, front legs kicking, and Victorinus fell with a cry, hitting the frozen ground with a bang. Wind driven from him, vision spotting, he rolled and got himself on all fours, aware if he didn't move fast he would certainly be killed. He staggered to his feet, somehow still had hold of his sword, and before he knew what was happening he was deflecting a probing spear, stepping inside the shaft and skewering its bearer. He roared, twisted his blade and pulled it free, ears full of the thunderous cavalry charge that still pressed on either side of him.

Where was his son? Where were Pastor and Drost? He'd no time to think as two more warriors came for him. One was a callow youth with a shaky grip on an ancient blade. He came in a crouch, sword held out before him, quivering like a leaf on the breeze. The other was old, grey streaks in his short beard. He held a single-headed axe in each hand and had the confidence to give Victorinus a grin as he danced in for the kill. Victorinus blocked the first axe with his sword and looked on through his blurred vision as the other appeared over the top of his blade. His left hand snaked out and somehow grabbed the haft of the axe before it could cleave his skull in. The two men were locked in a tussle, sword on axe, hand on hand. Victorinus leaned into both, heaving, spitting, cursing. Blood trickled into his mouth from under his helmet, the fall from the horse opening the head wound he'd taken the day before. But he was winning this test of strength, both axes moving further away from him with every renewed effort.

After what felt an age, the axe against his sword fell away, and doing nothing himself, his sword all but fell into his opponent's chest, lodging itself there. He grabbed at the other axe as its holder sank to his knees, and spinning, ran at the callow youth, who seemed to be begging for his life before Victorinus had covered two steps. He got no mercy. Two men down, an axe in hand, he spun around, blinking rapidly, still trying to clear his head. The Spanish horse was past him now, carnage up ahead. But four blurred figures were moving his way, the blue of their tattoos enough to tell him at a glance they weren't approaching for a chat.

His bloodshot eyes darted up to the pale blue sky, and for what he thought would be the last time he took in the sight of the sun. Kissing his fingers and holding them up, just as he did every morning, just as his father had done before him, he adjusted the grip on his axe and prepared to fight to the death.

'Duck!' a familiar voice called, somewhere off to his left. Took him a moment to register the voice was Latin, and therefore probably friendly. He followed the instruction and threw himself to the ground, looking up to see three spears carve a path through the air and bury themselves in his would be attackers. 'Can't take you anywhere!' Drost called, a wide grin splitting his face. 'Seriously, have you ever been in a fight you weren't a hair's breadth from losing?'

'Not my strong point. I'll be the first to admit.'

'Not your strong point? You're a fucking tribune!'

'You sure do know how to kick a man when he's down. You going to help me up or what?'

Drost swung down from his mount and pulled Victorinus to his feet. Might have been the repeated blows to the head clouding his hearing, but it seemed to Victorinus the battle was drawing to a close. 'What's happening?' he asked.

'We carved 'em up good and proper! Pushed them out to the flanks and the infantry are finishing the job.'

'So it's over?'

'Seems to be.'

Victorinus sunk back to his knees, ripping free his helmet and running a hand over his head. He could feel where the cut had been re-opened, blood oozing from the wound. 'Do you have water?' he asked Drost, who took a skin from one of his men. He poured some over his head, drinking deeply when he was done. 'My thanks.'

'Wondered where you'd got to!' Maurus said as he cantered up alongside him. 'One moment you were with me, the next you were gone!'

'You might have come looking for me,' Victorinus said, though he couldn't keep a smile spreading across his face. Maurus was alive. Now to find Silvius.

'I was a bit busy! Found little brother, though.'

'Silvius!' Victorinus barked out.

'Aye, he's well, he's with Felicius in the centre.' Maurus' face suddenly darkened. 'The prefect looks like he's been through hell, and he's saying he needs to see you urgently.'

Victorinus puffed out his cheeks. 'Then lead the way.'

***

'What you're saying makes no sense?' Victorinus hissed at Felicius as they jogged through the ranks of the Fourth Cohort of Gauls.

Around them the Roman army was already mopping up, wounded men being given the mercy of the sword, corpses heaped into piles to clear the field. It was bitterly cold. The snow of a few days previous had given the land a break from the freezing winds and icy rain, but winter had reared its head once more.

Felicius stalked ahead of Victorinus, who had Maurus and Silvius in tow. Silvius had stood in the rear ranks of the Heruli and had seen no fighting, much to Victorinus' relief. His account of the battle was one of frozen fingertips and numb feet, and if that's all his mother heard of the day's fighting, Victorinus would be very glad indeed.

'Can you not see?' Felicius hissed, spinning on his heels. 'He's planned it all. All *this*,' he waved his hands emphatically around. 'He wanted this war, may even have given the tribes a reason to rise up. He needed a victory, something to embolden him, help him stand out above his peers.'

Victorinus thought back to Aldhard – or his brother, or whoever he was. The man had said his job in the north was done. But how long had he been up there? And what had he been doing before he started chasing Victorinus through the wilderness? He thought of the coin the man had flicked him, Gratian's head imprinted on the side. 'How could he have done this?' Victorinus said, unsure whether to be repulsed or impressed.

'I don't know! I don't even know that he did. It's all I can think of, though. And there's something else.'

'Gods! There's more?'

'The cargo he sent me to collect from Londinium. That has something to do with this. He had it, I'm sure that's what it was, in a chest just before the battle.'

'You're not making any sense!' Victorinus cried, pulling Felicius back. 'Gods, brother! Just stop for a moment, take a breath. I've been north of the Wall for what feels like an age. I've no notion of what's going on. Just explain your troubles, properly this time.'

He watched as Felicius took two deep breaths and composed himself. 'You're right, I am sorry, Sixtus, and by God it's good to see you well. Maximus told me you were dead.'

'Something else you're going to need to explain,' Victorinus said, earning a laugh from Silvius. 'Whatever is going on here, I care nothing for myself. Whatever it is I'm mixed up in, I can handle it. But my boys are here Felicius, and I'll move heaven and earth to see them safe. So please, explain your troubles or suspicions in full, so we all understand what it is we're facing.'

Felicius was about to speak, but an uproar behind them silenced him before he could utter a word. 'There's more of the bastards!' someone shouted. 'Lines! Lines! Get back into lines!' another called.

'What the fuck is going on?' Victorinus muttered, more weary than he could remember being.

'It would appear that we haven't quite defeated the whole Caledonian army,' Felicius said.

Drost appeared out of the mass of Roman troops, Pastor with him. 'There must be five thousand more about to crest the horizon!' he called from atop his horse. 'You remember when we first saw their army?' this directed to Victorinus.

'Aye, they filled the landscape from north to south,' Victorinus said with a sigh. 'Gods, I can't believe I didn't notice. That couldn't have been all of them we've just fought. There just weren't enough of them.'

'In your defence, you've been quite preoccupied, you know, getting your arse kicked from one fight to the next.'

Maurus and Silvius tried and failed to stifle a laugh. Victorinus was about to bite back when Felicius cut him off. 'This is perfect!'

'It is?' Victorinus said.

'I feel like I've missed the start of this conversation,' Drost piped up.

'Don't you see? We can sneak off, the two of us. No one will notice. Then I can show you what I've been going on about! Wait here, I need to give Vitulus some orders.' And with that, he was off, back amongst his men.

'Father, what is going on?'

Victorinus didn't know what to say. He'd no answers for times like these. He reached into the pouch at his waist, pulled out the wooden horse, rubbing it absently as he saw the northern horizon fill with Caledonians. 'Boys, I'm going to need you to go back to your units,' he said in a quiet voice, still rubbing the horse.

'Back?'

'What?'

He swallowed. 'You know, the last thing I want is to put either of you in danger. But I've a horrible feeling you're going to be safer fighting that lot than coming with Felicius and me.'

'Now *you're* not making any sense,' Maurus said.

'I know lad,' he gave his sons a sad smile. 'But Felicius and I have a history of getting caught up in some weird shit. And I've a horrible feeling history is about to repeat itself. Besides, I'll be alright. I've got Pastor watching my back.'

Pastor rolled his eyes, swinging down from his mount. 'Not sure my back could take another battle anyway,' he said with a sardonic smile.

'I'll get these two back where they should be,' Drost said, gesturing to Maurus and Silvius. 'But we'd better be off now before anyone asks any questions.'

Victorinus hugged his boys, kissing them on their heads. He slipped Amor, the wooden horse, to Maurus, told him to tuck it under his mail. 'She's kept me safe all these years. May she do the same for you today.'

And then they were gone, Maurus swinging up on his horse and Silvius jogging beside him.

'Why not keep them with us?' Pastor asked.

Victorinus breathed deep, eyes still fixed on his sons. 'Because I've an inkling of what's going on here, and we're about to put ourselves smack bang in the middle of it.'

'Course we are.'

'Admit it lad. You wouldn't have it any other way, would you?'

XX

'It all started in Londinium,' Felicius said. They were moving away from the battle. Victorinus had worried they would look out of place, three soldiers walking away from the melee. So they'd stolen a stretcher being occupied by a dead soldier, thrown the corpse off and put Pastor in his place. 'I was sent there by Maximus to meet the ship carrying his special cargo. Thing is I got a bit caught up with one of the gangs at the dock-

'Course you did,' Victorinus said.

'But only because of Davos!'

'Who's Davos?'

'God! Another time Sixtus! Anyway, I couldn't get Maximus's cargo off the ship because of the gang, so I went to see Governor Priscus.'

'I can finish this one for you,' Victorinus said in a strained voice. He was sweating heavily, breathing laboured. 'But then you found out the gang was under the employ of the governor?'

'Yes! How did you know?'

'I was there a few weeks ago, remember? Didn't seem anyone was trying to keep it a secret.'

'Well, you could have bloody told me!' Felicius paused a moment. He was walking backwards, the strain on his calves so bad he worried they were going to cramp up. But there was this *energy* buzzing through him. Finally, he was going to get to the bottom of Maximus's schemes! He could feel it, sense it. 'Anyway, when talking to the Governor he asked me about the war and what Maximus was doing. Just an offhand question, but he also said he gets no news of the goings on in the north.'

Victorinus shrugged. At least Felicius thought he did. Shrugging was a hard thing to do when you were lugging a human body on a stretcher over uneven ground. 'Don't you see how strange that is? Why would the governor of Britannia's biggest province not know what's going on up here? And remember Eboracum? When Maximus said he hadn't communicated to Gratian about the planned war?'

'Maximus is the supreme military commander of all Britannia's armed forces. Think about it Gaius. It could just be that the man is doing his job, nothing more.'

That gave Felicius pause for thought. His mind raced over the correspondence he had shared with Theodosius in the east. Wasn't this exactly what Theo had been bemoaning a lack of? No leadership in the army, too much dependance on an emperor to oversee things in person. Could it be that Maximus was just actually one of the last competent officers left in the empire? And actually he was just discharging his duties as he saw fit?

No. No, he could not believe that. There was a line somewhere, an invisible barrier Maximus had crossed. What he was doing went beyond just discharging his duties. It was something else entirely. The inner conflict didn't leave him though as they trudged further away from the fighting. 'So where are we going?' Pastor asked from the stretcher.

'Hush your voice, you're dead, remember? We're going to the campaign tent, it's not much further. Sixtus, see where the hospital tent has been erected? It's just past that.'

Hospital tents were places no soldier wanted to think about. Open-sided, to let the clean air wash through, they were a maze of folding tables filled with surgeon's tools, pop up beds or mats thrown out on the floor once the beds were filled. You smelt them before you saw them sometimes, especially in summer. They waddled up to the hospital and carried Pastor under the canvas. 'Is he dead?' a doctor asked.

'Aye,' Felicius said.

'Take him straight through. They're stripping the bodies out back.'

Through the tent, past the cries and pleas of the wounded, the crisp winter air tasted joyous on Felicius' tongue once he was away from the rank stench of the dying. The dead, easily a hundred or more already, were being stripped of their armour and cloaks. *He died fighting for the glory of Rome*, the letters would say, read through the shaking hands of the deceased's family. A mother, a wife, maybe even a child. There was no glory in death. Never had been, never would be, and this was proof of that.

Three men picked up a naked body, a yawning hole where there should have been lungs, and threw it onto a pile. 'That one for us?' one of them called.

'No,' Victorinus said. Felicius suddenly felt too ill to speak. 'He's got a wound, but he's an officer. We're taking him back to his tent.'

'Too proud to die with the rest of 'em, is he?' the man called back.

Felicius debated whether he should stop and give the man a piece of his mind. But these men were no soldiers. They were locals some cleric had paid to come and perform a task for the day. He'd seen a thousand such men all over the empire performing the same task. Sometimes it was wounded soldiers not fit for battle. If there were none of them available, then the local populace would do. No doubt these men were pocketing anything they could, hoping everyone would be too preoccupied to search them on their way out. He sighed. There was nothing to be done about it, and he hadn't the time in any case.

They moved on without another word. The next tent they passed was the kitchen, slaves already hard at work to make sure there was warm food for everyone come day's end. The smell there was considerably better. But no one paid them any attention, and once they'd passed the tent, they lowered the stretcher and Pastor got to his feet.

'See there,' Felicius pointed up the gentle incline. 'Three guards posted outside. Look! See the wooden chest inside! That's what we've come for.'

'What do we do about the guards?' Victorinus asked. 'We're a prefect and a tribune, we can't very well walk up there and gut them in broad daylight, even with all that going on,' he thrust a thumb behind him, the cacophony of battle audible even at that distance, 'someone's going to notice.'

'We don't need to. You said it yourself, we're a tribune and a prefect! We just tell them we've been sent to collect it. Trust me, come on!'

They marched up the hill, Pastor lurking behind them. The three guards, burly Germans all, formed a small wall of shields at the tent's entrance. 'State your name and business,' the one in the centre said.

'Prefect Gaius Felicius of the Fourth Cohort of Gauls. We're here for the *Dux's* chest. He said it's time.' He gave the guard what he hoped was a knowing look.

'Don't look like time to me,' the guard said. 'Looks like it's still a bloodbath up there.'

From the top of the rise, they had a pretty good view of the fighting in the north. The Caledonians had not tried to hold the high ground around Fanum Cocidi, but had streamed down the slope and thrown themselves on the hastily reformed Roman shield wall once more. From where Felicius was standing, it didn't look like they were having any more success than when they tried it the first time. 'He says it is. They will be broken soon.'

Indecision flashed across the guard's face. 'You say you're a tribune?' he said with an arched eyebrow. 'Commander of the Gauls?'

'Yes. They're my men holding our centre. Now get out of my way before I have you digging latrines for a month! The *Dux* said it's time, so it's time.'

The guard wavered, his two friends taking a step back, the threat of digging latrines enough to convince them. Felicius thought the middle guard was going to follow suit, but the uncertainty on the man's face slipped into a cold smile. 'You are not one of us,' he said.

'Excuse me?' Felicius tried to keep up his facade, but he could feel his control of the situation slipping away.

'You say you are a tribune, and that might be true. But you ain't one of us. His imperial highness said this would happen.'

'His imperial what-

'Quiet Pastor,' Felicius said, holding out a restraining hand. He was surprised it stood firm, such was the rush of fear, energy and dread coursing through him. All his fears laid bare in that one sentence. 'Explain yourself,' he said to the guard.

'His eminence said this might happen. A traitor worming their way to the chest before he could get his hands on it. He said they walked among us, though he had done his best to thin 'em out. He said there would be people that didn't understand, would never walk the line. He said if we were to come across these traitorous curs, we were to kill 'em.'

Pastor reacted quickest. The guard to the left pulled free his blade with a rasp and swung it backhanded at Felicius' head. Felicius felt hands on his back and then he was stumbling forwards, the sword hissing over his head and he falling forwards onto the central guard. He lowered his head as he fell and felt his helmet smash the guard his the nose, whipping his head up he saw bright blood on the winter air and then he was scrambling for his sword. Before he could get it free, the guard had his hands on his, clamping them down on his sword hilt, stopping him from drawing it.

A clash of iron behind him, Victorinus and Pastor locked in their own deathly grapples, but he had no time to turn and see how they fared. His hands clamped on his sword hilt, he growled, snarled, spit and blood assaulting his face as the guard sought an advantage. He fought to free himself, kicked out with his right leg, and felt the satisfying *click* as the guard's knee jerked under the impact. In a moment, he had a hand free. Leaving the sword where it was, he pulled his dagger from his right hip and stabbed at the guard's face.

Wounded as he was, howling in agony and leaning heavily on his left leg, the guard still got a hand up and the knife plunged through his palm, the tip just tickling his face. Another agonised scream, more bright blood on the air, but still the guard wouldn't go down. Felicius took a step back and freed his sword with a flourish, grasping the hilt with both hands and ramming it through the guard's chest.

He left the sword there, quivering as much as he was, as the guard fell to the ground and slipped from the world. He turned to see Victorinus standing over a corpse, and Pastor nursing a bleeding shoulder. 'Gods lad, you get beat up more than I do, here let me take a look,' Victorinus said, sitting Pastor down on the cold ground. Felicius smiled despite himself. He pictured himself doing the same with Davos in a few years. Would he want the lad to go into the military? It was a nice dilemma to face, certainly more favourable than the one in front of him now.

'We need to get the bodies inside the tent before anyone notices,' he said. Victorinus rose with a sigh, telling Pastor he would live to see another day before helping Felicius with the three bodies. Once they were inside the tent, they quickly rolled down the sides, obscuring them from curious eyes. It was dark inside with the flaps down, the leather blocking out the weak winter sun, but he could still see well enough.

'That the chest?' Victorinus asked, nodding to the wooden chest Felicius had witnessed being brought in that morning.

'Aye.'

'Well, get on with it then,' Victorinus said. 'Pastor will need stitches. We need to get him down to the medics.'

'Right then,' Felicius said, icy shivers running down his spine as he moved across the tent. There was nothing remarkable about the tent, it was just a tent. He'd stood in hundreds like it before. There was nothing remarkable about the chest. Just a wooden chest. He had one just like it in his own tent, which was a tent just like this one. But it *felt* different, felt significant.

He knelt, trembling fingers fiddling with the lock. It opened with a *clunk* and gently, all so gently, he lifted the lid, and felt his world explode as he looked upon the contents. 'Good God in heaven,' he muttered, not hearing the sudden cacophony outside.

XXI

'What is it?' Victorinus asked for the third time. Felicius was frozen, wide eyes fixed on the contents of the chest. Pastor had gone deathly pale. Victorinus had thought the wound shallow, but there was blood everywhere.

'Cold,' Pastor mumbled through chattering teeth, and Victorinus tore off his cloak and wrapped it around the lad. 'Felicius, I need another cloak, or a strip of cloth, something to stop this bleeding! Gaius? Are you listening to me?'

With a flash of light, the tent flap was thrown open, and before them, Maximus stalked inside. 'What in God's name are you doing in here?' he boomed, taking in the scene before him. 'Where are the German guards?' his eyes flittered left to right, before resting on the three dead bodies. 'You two,' he said in a low voice, dripping with venom. 'You two cunts just won't die, will you.' Three soldiers rushed in behind Maximus, their bloodied swords already drawn. Victorinus felt a wave of emotions all at once. His life was about to end, of that there was no doubt. But there was a sense of knowing, too. In a moment he understood what Felicius had been trying to explain to him. He understood what Aldhard's brother had been saying outside that cave. He understood it all.

He rose, leaving Pastor to his slow death, stalked over to the chest, ripped the lid back and pulled from within a beautiful, shimmering, perfect, purple cloak. 'This is what it's all been about, isn't it? All of this! *All* of it! You seek to make yourself an emperor!'

Maximus smiled. His dangerous smile, the one that didn't reach his eyes. 'And what better way to do it, then to ride through my victorious army, and be acclaimed on the field of battle?'

Victorinus froze. He felt a fool. How could he have not seen this coming? There had been signs: the growing distance between Britannia and the imperial court in Gaul, Maximus suddenly desperate to have as many of the island's armed forces with him in the north. And, of course, the growing number of men he had promoted to high office around him. He had been building his inner circle, preparing himself for this very moment. But it went deeper than that. Maximus had been left there, right on the very edge of the world, and he had not spent his time skulking in the shadows. He had defended the people, and wherever he went, the populace cheered his name, calling him the defender of Britannia. He had even married one of them, his wife birthing three children on British soil. Right then Victorinus knew the people would be behind Maximus, not just he army, but the civilians too.

'Did you learn nothing from the last pretender who sought the purple in these lands? By God Maximus, you were part of the army that put him down!' Felicius blurted. 'Lupicinus Valentinus caused mayhem in these lands, thousand of innocent people died, Caledonians, Saxones, Franks running riot! Do you not see that all that will happen again? You cannot win!'

'I can, and I will. Valentinus was a fool. He overextended himself. He didn't have the numbers, didn't have the support in Rome or Ravenna. I do. And I will do what Valentinus did not. I shall not waste any more years on this rain swept wasteland! I'll take *my* army to Gaul and down to Italy from there! We shall seize the initiative! Don't you see? It will be spring in a month, six weeks at most! Perfect time to make the crossing and establish ourselves in northern Gaul. From there, we will push Gratian back until he has nowhere left to go.'

'Theo will support Gratian,' Felicius said.

'Pah! My precious cousin Theo! Son of a disgraced father! Exiled to his family estates, for what, two years? Then Valens goes and gets himself killed in the east, and who do they send as his replacement? My cursed cousin!'

'That's what this is all about, isn't it?' Felicius barked an incredulous laugh. 'Jealousy! Theo gets the opportunity to put the east to rights, and all you got was Britannia! So this is your solution? Your way of pushing back against those you think so cruelly overlooked you? Have you ever stopped to wonder why it is you were overlooked? Why you've never risen higher? You're a fucking child in a man's body! That has been clear to me since the day I met you, rolling around in the mud with the common soldiery!'

'You forget yourself, prefect,' Maximus spat.

'No. It is you that has forgotten! Forgotten the uncle that took you in and raised you up when you had nothing! Theodosius gave you opportunities you could have only dreamed of before! All you did was disappoint him.'

'Is that what he said? In his last days in Africa? I don't have many regrets in my life, but you know I would have liked to see that old bastard die.'

'Tell me you had nothing to do with that? It is not lost on me that the man sent there to murder your uncle was the same man that found me on the road north,' Felicius said. Victorinus could see the rage building in his friend. He'd never seen Gaius lose control before. A funny thing, that it might be one of the final things his eyes registered. He looked back to Pastor. The lad appeared to have lost consciousness. He figured that was for the best.

'Ha! No, I'm afraid I'm not guilty of that one. The old fool dug himself a hole he couldn't scarper out from. He was always so highly strung, so *decent*. He couldn't abide it when men around him sought to make themselves a bit extra on the side. He never saw that we all did it. Why, just look at this army we've raised. Fifteen thousand strong on paper, though barely ten thousand took the field with us. He saw the corruption and hated it. I see it too, though I plan to *act*, rather than write pointless reports to court, dropping names like they have no meaning and expecting nothing to come back on me.'

The soldiers behind Maximus were creeping forwards, blood dripping off the end of one of their swords. Victorinus was glad he'd sent his boys away. He hoped they could stay anonymous in Maximus' army, keep their heads down. Perhaps in time men would forget they were the son of a traitor, killed by the new emperor himself. He regretted not making it right with Sarai. No, making it right wasn't the right way of putting it. He regretted not making her happy. Though he couldn't change who he was, he supposed. He could give up the wine, give up the job, but once you stripped it all back, he was still the same man. And she did not want that man. Gods, wine. Just one last sip...

His strongest feeling, though, was one of acceptance. He'd never put much stock in gods or God. He prayed occasionally, saluted the sun, though the latter was more in memory of his father than anything else. But he accepted that this was the end, that his actions had led him to this place, and he had been in control of those actions. He thought of little Leo, his precious ever young boy. He would see him again soon.

One of the soldiers stepped forward and tore the purple cloak from his hands. It was only then his mind snapped back to the present, and he realised Maximus and Felicius had still been talking. 'I will never bow to you!' Felicius said.

Maximus seemed oddly calmer than he had been. Two of the soldiers had sheathed their weapons and were clasping the cloak around Maximus. He actually looked the part, Victorinus thought. With his tall, well-built frame, rugged good looks and a lion's mane of dark hair. He looked what he was, or what he would become. A conqueror. A leader men would follow into battle.

'Leave us,' Maximus said to the soldiers, who looked at one another before one opened his mouth to protest. 'I'll be fine. Take this young man here to the surgeons, see he gets seen to,' he said, pointing to Pastor. The men obeyed, gently lifting Pastor and carrying him from the tent. 'The two of you are by now aware, of course, that I tried to have you killed.' He didn't frame it as a question, nor did he wait for an answer. 'You were never loyal to me, not totally. Sure you'd follow a command, you'd actually both follow them well. You're capable of making your own decisions, acting independently and you have that all so rare quality of an officer in our army: you can actually get something done.'

He smiled again, though this time there was genuine warmth to it. 'But I knew when this day came, you would not bend the knee. You were here sixteen years ago, you saw what I saw. But I truly believe I can do this, truly believe when I win the inevitable war that is to come, I can make us strong again. For too long we have been weak, defensive. I would see that change.

And after all I have put the two of you through in the last months, you're still standing.'

'How did you do it?' Victorinus asked.

'Which part?' Maximus was once more wearing his dangerous grin.

'All of it,' Victorinus said, not knowing where to start.

'Most of my officers are German, I'm sure you've noticed. I needed a war, and to get one, I had to antagonise the Caledonians. No one else up here to fight, after all. So the plan was to get a couple of minor German chiefs to raid up the east coast, put the shits into the tribes a little. Then we started cutting some of the trade, subtly, just enough to hurt them. Trouble was our old friend Aldhard, some gods drunk maniac who thought himself destined to achieve great things, landed his ships south of the Wall when he should have been north. So we had to fight him.'

'He didn't know it was you that had paid him to come over to our shores,' Victorinus said, remembering that day on the eastern coast. Gods, it had only been a matter of weeks.

'No. My name never reached him, but he knew he was working for someone with connections. He was paid in Roman gold, after all. But his brother proved to be more effective. I knew you would go north and seek out your friend Drost. I knew the old fort you always met him at. It was easy to slip the brother the name and location of where he could find his brother's killer. Thought he'd finish you off, no bother.'

'He nearly did.'

Maximus gave a rueful chuckle. 'Aye, I bet he did. But he also stirred up the tribes, raided their settlements, killed their cattle. On every raid, he was ordered to leave a smattering of Roman coins on the ground, make it look like they'd fallen out a purse. The bigger tribes were paid in the coin, thousands of them, not that the silly bastards ever realised how poorly made they were. More tin than silver. I knew the smaller tribes would put two and two together and come up with five, eventually. The bigger tribes would encourage them, of course they would. They can't help themselves. Then it was just a matter of waiting.'

'And you had me provisioning an army and riding down to Londinium for what?' Felicius asked.

'Kept you busy, didn't it? Get you looking one way whilst I scheme in the other direction. Plus, I really did need that cargo. Look what I made from it,' he said, grabbing the hem of his purple cloak and giving it a flourish. 'Did you know the colour purple is made from fermented snails? They're not native to this island. Bet you didn't know that either! To get enough of them, you need a fisherman from the eastern Mediterranean. You wouldn't believe the expense. Guess that's why only emperors wear it!'

'You really did think of everything, didn't you? I take it Romulus is your man?'

'Naturally. Romulus is a friend of a friend, all too happy to help. He'll send word to Gratian about what has happened when I am ready.'

'And Governor Priscus? The gangs?'

'Ha! Not my doing. But I did enjoy hearing of it! Priscus, another problem I will have to face,' Maximus trailed off, facing twisting in a frown. 'But not today. Today I just have you two to deal with.'

'And what are you going to do with us?' Victorinus asked, just wanting it over one way or another.

Maximus looked from Victorinus and Felicius, an evil gleam in his wolf like eyes. 'Do you know I'm going to let you live.'

Victorinus blanched. 'What?'

Maximus threw his head back and boomed out a laugh. 'You know, I never disliked either of you. I just knew I couldn't trust you.'

'Didn't mean you had to try to have us killed!'

The would-be emperor offered a mere shrug. 'Seemed like the sensible thing to do. Anyway, like I said, it wasn't personal.'

'Well, I guess all is forgiven then!' Felicius spat. 'My daughter was with me in Londinium. It wasn't just my life you were putting in danger!'

'Like I said,' Maximus said in an icy tone, clearly getting irritated with the conversation. 'I have decided to let you live.'

'I will not fight for you,' Felicius said, and inwardly Victorinus winced. He tried to meet his friend's eye. *Why did he have to make it worse?*

'You, prefect,' Maximus pointed at Felicius. 'Are released from my service. Your unit, however, is not.'

'My men won't fight a civil war to see you crowned!'

Gods, just shut up Felicius! He willed his friend to stop. A sudden, overwhelming urge to live searing through his veins. He wanted to run out of that tent, find his boys and hug them close. He wanted to see Pastor, make sure the poor lad hadn't bled to death.

'Your men will cry 'Imperator!' with all the others when I ride through them. They will hail me as their lord and I will bask in their glory! You will run to my dear cousin, don't try to deny it!' Maximus held out a hand before Felicius could speak. 'It's fine. I want you to. Deliver him a message from me, would you? Tell him to stay out of the west. It is not his concern. He will sustain the east, I will claw back the west from the edge of the abyss. Together, we shall lead this great empire of ours into a new age! I expect you to be gone by spring. If you're not, I will have you killed.'

Felicius trembled with unbridled anger. Victorinus didn't know whether to put an arm around him in comfort or restrain him. Their eyes met, just for a moment, and he could tell Felicius was thinking the same thing he was. *We could end this, the two of us. Right now. One blow, and this rebellion is over before it started.* But neither of them did. Felicius stalked from the tent, bunched fists shaking beside him.

'And then there was one,' Maximus smirked. It irked Victorinus that the man seemed so at ease, so confident in himself, comfortable with his position. Was he not a mere mortal like everyone else? Surely he had fears? Doubts? If he did, he kept them well hidden behind that smirk he wore as a mask. 'What will you do?'

Victorinus took a moment to think before he spoke. A thousand different scenarios swam through his mind. He could go east with Felicius, see some of the world, just as he'd always wanted to. He could slunk off back to his farmhouse, to his cot above the stable. Maybe even build that house he'd been putting off. He scoffed to himself. Always had focused on the wrong things. In the end, he knew there was only one thing he could do.

'When you leave this tent, mount your horse, and parade yourself in that ridiculous cloak in front of the men, and they proclaim you the rightful emperor of the west. My boys will be among them. They will raise their swords, join in the merriment of the others. And when you march those men from these shores, when you land in Gaul and face another Roman army, another emperor at their head, my boys will be in your ranks, because they are sworn to serve you.'

A knowing grin split Maximus' face. 'And there lies your dilemma.'

'Aye,' Victorinus said. 'There it is. So here's what I'll do. I'll stick with you for as long as my boys are enlisted. I won't stay for you, piece of shit that you are. I'll stay for them. I owe them that much, and their mother so much more. But I warn you, Maximus. If either of my boys are hurt, carving you out this empire you so desire. I will kill you.'

Maximus sniffed, eyes never leaving Victorinus. The smirk came back, and he ruffled his purple cloak, moved over to the chest, and pulled out a purple crest for his helmet. He swapped it for the one already in place. 'I am not the monster you think I am,' he said after a while. 'All I ever wanted was to be respected, to be acknowledged as an equal among my peers. All I ever got in return was people looking down at me, thinking they were better men. My father used to tell me I would never amount to anything, that I was too unruly, that I did not see the world for what was. My uncle the same, though he at least threw me the odd bone. But I tell you tribune, I see the world for what it is, what it *really* is. I will grab it by the reins, shake it to its core, and reshape it in my image. Whatever is coming for me, whatever they try to do to me, I will face it head on, and *I will win!*'

Victorinus had nothing to say, he just gulped, unable to prevent himself from believing what Maximus was saying. Say what you want about the man, but when he put his mind to something, he got it done. 'I guess you'd better get on with it then, *domine*. The divine Flavius Maximus waits for no one.'

'Not Flavius, not anymore,' Maximus said. 'They will call me Magnus. Magnus Maximus.'

XXII

Felicius stood on the shoulder of the hill and watched the purple crest ride through the throng of men.

'Imperator! Imperator!' the Roman soldiers shouted, banging swords on shields and throwing helmets in the air. It seemed they had made quick work of disposing of the second Caledonian army, whose dead lay heaped in a line from east to west, presumably where they had thrown themselves on Roman shields and been found lacking.

His mind took him back to the history lessons he'd absorbed as a child. Constantine had been declared emperor in northern Britannia, Clodius Albinus, some hundred years and more before him. It had ended well for one of them, at least. He cursed himself for a fool once more. How could he not have seen this coming? His mind tumbled over the events of the last few weeks, but he didn't think there was anything else he could have done.

He could make out his own men, the Fourth Cohort, still in the Roman centre, cheering and clapping along with everyone else. Except, they weren't his men any more. He stood numb to the cold, to the howling wind that had the slaves and clerks scurrying around him shivering. All his life he had served the empire, thinking he served the greater good. Now, he failed to see the point in any of it.

No one learned from their mistakes. No one changed. He could see that now, clear as the pale blue sky. They were doomed to exist in a repetitive cycle, endless civil wars, countless deaths, an ever weakening empire. Until at last they would be overwhelmed. Unable to defend their borders, powerless to prevent the inevitable.

'Some day, eh?' Victorinus said, moving alongside him. 'I was certain that was going to be the end of the road for us.'

'Who said it wasn't?' Felicius said, eyes not moving from the spectacle in front of him. 'How's Pastor?'

'Going to live. Lad's the toughest person I know. He's lost a lot of blood, but the surgeon is patching him up.'

'Well, that's something, at least. What will happen now, do you think?'

'Maximus will march,' Victorinus said. 'He won't want to linger here. He'll be in Gaul before spring is done.'

'And that will just be the start of it,' Felicius spat.

Victorinus sighed, scratching the back of his head. 'I've told him I'm going to stay.'

Felicius took a moment to absorb that information, realisation then kicking in. 'Your boys.'

'Aye. Can't leave them. Sarai would kill me.'

Felicius smiled, a sad smile, but a smile none the less. 'You're a good man, Sixtus. What you've done for those boys, what you've put yourself through. You underestimate yourself.'

'I'm a drunk. I know I might have kicked the wine, but I've never lost the habit. Gods, even now I'm shaking, itching for that bitter taste. You don't need to humour me, Gaius. We both know what I am. I failed those boys for years, barely spent any time at all with poor little Leo. Least I can do now is have their backs. What will happen, do you think?'

'War. What else? Gratian will not, can not, allow someone to rise and challenge his authority. He will fight. Theo too, I think.'

'Isn't he a little busy? From what you've told me, sounds like he's already got his hands full.'

'Times are changing. Theo will have to change with them.'

'You will go to him? Out in the east?'

Felicius nodded. 'Aye, I will. Can't see I've any other choice.'

Victorinus sucked air through his teeth. 'We need to make a pact, you and I. A promise to never fight each other on the battlefield.'

'Scared you'll lose?' Felicius said under an arched eyebrow.

'Pah!' Victorinus barked a laugh. 'Just worried I'm going to have to tell my son I've killed his father-in-law.'

They both laughed. 'Guess we should get this wedding planned, then. If I'm to be gone by spring, it will need to be soon.' Felicius felt his mood lighten at the thought. The world could go to shit, as far as he was concerned. Wasn't like there was much he could do about it. But what he could control was how he dealt with it, and where he placed his energy. He'd always considered being sent to Britannia as a punishment. Now, he realised that the prospect of leaving it forever filled him with sadness. He resolved to make the most out of the next few weeks. He didn't know what the future would bring, but he could make the most out of the present.

'Come then, old friend. Let us leave this lot to their merriment. We've got a wedding to plan.'

Epilogue

Victorinus laid his head back on the grass and let out a sigh. The spring sun warmed his face, his belly was full, and he felt as rested as he'd been in an age. Crickets chirped away in the long grass around him, birdsong fell from the trees. Life was good–should have been, anyway.

With a grunt, he rose to a sitting position, shuffled backwards so he was within touching distance of the stone behind him. He stroked it, fingers running over the engravings on the tombstone. 'Oh Leo,' he murmured. 'Where to begin? So much has happened since we last spoke.'

He squinted up to the sun, sitting high and proud in the deep blue sky. 'For years now, I've been dining out on my heroics sixteen years ago. Stopping a traitor to the throne, putting an end to an uprising here on my own turf. And here I am, all those years later, and I've inadvertently helped a usurper drape himself in purple. Gods, the shame.' He looked once more to the sun, pictured his father kissing his fingers and raising them in greeting. Something he had done himself countless times. Somehow it felt wrong to do it now.

'I'm going to have to go away for a while. Civil war is coming. Gratian cannot allow a pretender to his throne to go unchallenged. For his part, Maximus will not content himself with being the ruler of Britannia. So he will empty our lands of soldiers, leave the people he has sworn to protect defenceless. That's irony for you. I've asked your mother to come with us, she of course, has refused. She'll stay here to keep you company. She can't bear the thought of you being alone, and I have to say a small part of me is happy about that. No one should be alone.'

Tears filled his eyes, and he pawed them away. 'Maurus and Pastor got married yesterday,' he said through a sniff. 'Was a grand day, full of happiness and laughter. Might be the last one of them we have for a while. Think we all felt the same, really made the best of it, you know. Maurus' new wife, Marcelina, she's going away with her mother and father. Felicius, my friend, has been given leave from Maximus to leave his unit and go over to Theodosius. Have to say I was worried he'd have Felicius killed. Me too, for that matter. But there is *some* good in Maximus, and I think for all his faults he knows he would not be where he is now without the two of us.

Felicius thinks Theo will ride from the east with an army. Said he doesn't think his old friend can stay out if it. Though he's already got his hands full, Goths loose in Thracia, the Persians rearing their head again. Gods, my whole life, this has all just been words to me. Goths, Persians, Thracia, the east in general. My whole life I've been here, stuck on the edge of empire, wishing I could see more of it, to be involved in some way. Seems now I'm finally going to get my wish.'

Tears ran freely, spilling into his beard. 'Truth is, Leo, all I want now is to be here. With your mother, your brothers, and you.' He rubbed the headstone again, fingers trembling. 'I'm too old, too scared, to be going off on some grand adventure. In my youth, I thought of war as some path to glory, a hero's road only the best got to travel. But I've seen my fair share of war, of blood and decay. Youth is wasted on the young, as people say, if only I could go back and tell that young man what I know now. What a different life he might have led.'

He thought back to his youth. To his own wedding day, the beaming grin fixed to his face, the certainty that it was just another step on his upward journey, that there was no chance of him ever falling down. What a fool he had been. A wasted career, a broken marriage, a dead child, and now complicit in a rebellion against the very empire he had longed to serve. He wished he'd taken steps to control his drinking in his younger years. Wished he'd been more present for his boys, for his wife.

'Can't turn back time,' he mumbled to himself. 'Guess I just got to look forward, make the best of it.'

'You talking to yourself again?' Sarai's voice breaking him from his reverie. 'First sign of madness, you know.'

Victorinus wiped the tears from his face and rose to his feet. 'Just talking to Leo,' he said. 'Reckon this could be the last chance I get, at least for a while.'

'Don't say things like that. You'll be back. You missed Drost. He left this morning, said that young wife of his will have his balls if he's away any longer.'

'He was saying that all winter! Good that he's gone, though. He's got his own battles to fight. Reckon there'll be a lot of change in the north now. He could carve himself out more land if he plays his cards right.'

'He said he's going to send someone to check on me every few weeks, make sure I'm not getting into any trouble.'

'That's good of him. I think you'll be fine here, for what it's worth. Maximus won't strip everyone from the Wall, he knows it needs to hold.' In truth, he wasn't certain what Maximus would do, but it made little sense to worry her.

'The boys are saying they'll be gone for years,' Sarai said, a slight quiver in her voice. 'They say Maximus won't stop until he sees Rome.'

'Aye. Might be there's some truth to that. But who knows? Maybe Gratian will decide against war, could be they come to an agreement of some kind.'

'You really think that?'

Victorinus sighed. 'No. But we can hope.'

She moved forward, alarming Victorinus slightly. Before he knew what was happening, she had engulfed him in a hug. 'Bring them back to me, Sixtus,' she whispered. 'I could not bear to bury another son.'

The tears came back. 'I will,' he said, praying to every god that would listen that he wasn't lying. 'I'll bring them back to you.'

He walked back to the stable, pausing in the shade to give Amor a rub. He'd gone and got her back a few days after the battle. He and Drost riding up to the farmhouse with a sense of trepidation. Darrow had kept his word though, and Amor and the other mounts they'd left behind were strong and hale. Out of habit, he pulled out the wooden horse from his pouch, fingers rubbing over the well-worn wood.

'Seems once more we're off to war, old girl.' She gave a snort in response. He couldn't help but notice the grey around her temples and down her flanks. 'Too old for this shit, you and I. But I couldn't bear to leave without you. As long as I have you, I know I'll be safe.' He continued to stroke her, and she nuzzled her head against his. 'So what do you say? Shall we see some of the world? See how far we can rise?' He got another snort in response.

In the courtyard outside Felicius was helping his family into a carriage. He'd had until spring to leave and he knew he was pushing his luck. His daughter and Maurus had been given just one night together, and Victorinus felt a pang of guilt. He hoped their marriage would not prove to just be a sham. He longed for the day he could reunite the two of them. Maurus appeared and gave his new bride one last hug, the bond the two shared clear in the way they clung together. Life was cruel. The quicker they both realised that, the easier they would find it.

He debated walking over and saying goodbye to Felicius, but the two old friends had said all they needed. With a wave to Lucia and Marcelina, a nod to young Davos, and one final knowing glance with Felicius, he turned his back on them and went back inside the stable.

He would see his old friend before too long. Despite their pact, he had a feeling that when he did, it would be from the opposite side of a battlefield.

HISTORICAL NOTE

'Magnus' Maximus, as he would come to be known, was born in Spain in around 335 AD. Rumoured to be related to Theodosius the Great (Theo, in this book). The most plausible suggestion is that the two were cousins. That is what I have stuck with in these books. Maximus served under Theodosius the elder, the revered Roman general who was one of Emperor Valentinian's right-hand men.

Theodosius the elder could fill a novel or two in his own right, and I must admit to being tempted to follow *Valentia* on with a story of his exploits in Africa, but in the end contented myself with having it as the opening sequence for this novel. He fought a campaign against Firmus and his Moors over a number of years. Sent there from the Danube frontier where he was fighting the Alamanni, he quickly uncovered the treachery of the Governor Romanus, who was allowing barbarians to sack his cities and being paid off with a portion of the profits. Arriving in Africa, he gave Romanus a wrap around the knuckles and sent the Governor off to take command of a force of men guarding a border. Once he got there, however, Romanus quickly realised he had been duped, and the men he had been sent to command were actually under orders to keep him prisoner. You can imagine he was not happy!

Romanus in custody, Theodosius took the war to Firmus, though his men were ill-equipped for a war in Africa, having been sent from Gaul, and he was vastly outnumbered. Theodosius, though, persevered, and the line I use in the prologue of this book: 'I am the *comes* of Valentinian, lord of the world, sent to destroy a murderous robber. Unless you give him to me at once as the invincible emperor has ordered, you will perish utterly with the race over which you rule' is a quote from Ammianus Marcellinus, and quite possibly one of the best quotes I've come across in my years of research. I had to get it in the book!

In the end Firmus hanged himself in custody of a tribal chief loyal to Rome, rather than face Theodosius's justice. Two further years, the general would stay in Africa, cementing the peace he had won with the sword. On the death of Valentinian, a long-time ally, and the rise of his son Gratian, an order for Theodosius's execution was sent to Africa. It was not uncommon for a new emperor to be fearful of the more powerful generals under the employ of their predecessors. These men, after all, commanded the loyalty of huge armies, and if you know enough about the history of Rome, right back to Marius and Sulla in the last years of the Republic, you will know how often inspiring generals sought to further themselves, using their armies as a springboard.

Another, less likely theory for this order has been mentioned, though. During the reign of Emperor Valens in the east, a soothsayer, using some form of Ouija board, revealed the name of the man that would succeed the emperor. The board got as far as THEO, before the whole thing was stopped. Could it be possible Gratian feared a usurpation from Theodosius because of this? I think it unlikely, but the Romans were very different people to us, with different religions and beliefs. It is possible he did. For the purpose of this novel, I chose to stick with the reason of Theodosius being too famous, too successful, to be left alive. It is also worth noting that Governor Romanus was not killed for his treachery, but sent back to court. Could the man have been whispering in Gratian's ear? Exacting his revenge?

As for Maximus, little enough is known for certain about his life. It is thought he followed the elder Theodosius back to the Rhine frontier after the great rebellion, there to fight against the Alamanni. He would also have probably gone to Africa and fought in that campaign, too. It is also possible he was on the field at the disastrous battle of Adrianople in 378 AD, which saw the end of the Emperor Valens. I have left these out of this book for two reasons. One: I wanted *my* Maximus to be a man fuelled by bitterness. I wanted him to burn with jealousy as his cousin was raised to the purple in the east, whilst he was left with just the defence of the poor diocese of Britain. Two: well, we don't actually know for certain he was there, and if I had covered every step of his military life, this trilogy would have turned into six or seven books!

We do know that Maximus had a wife, two daughters, and a son. We will be introduced to them in the next book. It is also not clear exactly when or why Maximus was raised to the purple in Britain. The general consensus seems to be that it was a spur-of-the-moment acclamation by the army after a victory against the Caledonian tribes. However, when you look at the timeline of how quickly things progressed once he had been acclaimed, it seemed obvious to me that some form of planning had been in the works. Maximus rushed over to Gaul in the spring of 383AD, and it seems impossible to me that he would have been able to organise it all so quickly if he had no prior knowledge of what was going to happen. So, I got to work. I had my scheming *Dux*, surrounded by generals loyal first to him before Rome, and I had his motive. All he needed then was a famous victory, and the rest, as they say, is history.

I read what felt like a thousand books researching this novel. For those of you interested in the history behind this story, may I point you in the direction of the following: *The Fall of the Roman Empire by Peter Heather; Roman Britain by Peter Salway; Magnus Maximus: The Neglected Roman Emperor and his British Legacy by Maxwell Craven; The Complete Roman Army by Adrian Goldsworthy; Roman Military Equipment by M.C. Bishop & J. C.N. Coulston; Handbook to Roman Legionary Forces by M.C. Bishop; Imperial Brothers by Ian Hughes; The Later Roman Empire by Ammianus Marcellinus* – I could go on and on! But these were the ones closest to me as I typed away. I'd also like to give an honourable shout out to the map of Roman Britain I found on Amazon that cost peanuts and has been an invaluable tool whilst writing both *Valentia* and this book.

As part of my research, I walked Hadrian's Wall from Newcastle to Carlisle in April 2023. It was a fantastic experience, seeing the landscape for myself, walking the paths and roads the Romans would have trod over two thousand years ago! It really stirred my imagination and this book would not haven been the same if I had not done it (there would also have been no mention of a Gorse bush, a plant that only seems to grow once you get to the north of England – thanks to my friend Harry for pointing them out to me!) I should at this point jot down my sincere thanks to my good friend Wayne, who walked (almost) all the way with me, and suffered terribly from blistered feet every step of it! I am sorry about your feet, mate (maybe buy better shoes next time!) If you ever get the chance to walk the Wall yourselves, I can't recommend it enough – though I would note you should do it from west to east, and not the way I did it, as you'll be walking into a head wind the whole way!

Puer delicatus was a term reserved for the most expensive of slaves. Young, pretty, the Romans dressed them in expensive, revealing outfits and paraded them in front of their friends. To own one was considered a sign of great wealth. African marble was sought after in the empire, distinctive with its yellow colour and blue streaks.

I use the terms 'left' and 'right' when describing Calidus and Felicius's escape from Londinium on ship, rather than 'starboard' and 'larboard'. We have no record of when these terms came into use, but I believe the words originate from Middle-English, and whilst I'm sure the Romans would have used their own words for it, they are lost to time.

Note that 'port' replaced 'larboard' in 1844, a direct from the Royal Navy, as sailors could not make out the difference between 'larboard' and 'starboard' over the hiss of the roaring seas! I wonder how many good men died from mis-hearing a word?

Trade between the Romans and the Caledonians was commonplace right across the Wall. Trade gates would be open in daylight hours for merchants to sell their products to the tribes, and the tribes would often trade for materials such as wool rather than pay in coin–in their world in the far north, they had very little use for coin.

As with all my novels, I wanted the history to be the backdrop for my character's story, rather than the driving force. Slipping a fictional character in to history is both challenging and enormous fun, and this story, as well as the one that is to follow, is primarily about dear old Sixtus Victorinus. I plan on writing one more book about his life, and in the next instalment, titled 'Imperator', we will see him leave Britannia's shores for the very first time. So Victorinus and Felicius will be back. Civil war is brooding, and our heroes will have to keep their weapons sharp. For this time, they won't be fighting on the same side.

Thanks so much for reading this book. It really would be a waste of time writing it if there were no readers to enjoy it! Writing books is so hard, seems to get even more so with everyone I do. If you've enjoyed this one, please consider leaving a little review on Amazon or Goodreads, I really can't exaggerate what a difference they make to the book's visibility. Want to reach out to me? Find me on Facebook/Instagram/Twitter under AdamPLofthouse. Or send me an email to adamlofthouse@adamloft house.com. I love getting emails from readers, and I always reply.

Also, if you want to be kept up to date with my new releases, you can sign up to my Newsletter over at adaml ofthouse.com, and bag yourself a free book in the process! No brainer, right?

Until the next time,

Adam Lofthouse

December, 2023

Printed in Great Britain
by Amazon